RAISING THE BAR

Distributed by
ArtScroll /Mesorah

RAISING THE BAR

The Collected Writings of the *Chosson Torah*,
M. Manuel Merzon

Edited by Gary Torgow

*Prepared for Publication
by Rabbi Hillel L. Yarmove*

© *Copyright 2001 by* Gary Torgow

First edition – First impression / December 2001

ALL RIGHTS RESERVED

No part of this book may be reproduced **in any form,** *photocopy, electronic media, or otherwise without* **written** *permission from the copyright holder, except by a reviewer who wishes to quote brief passages in connection with a review written for inclusion in magazines or newspapers.*
THE RIGHTS OF THE COPYRIGHT HOLDER WILL BE STRICTLY ENFORCED.

Distributed by ARTSCROLL / MESORAH PUBLICATIONS, LTD.
4401 Second Avenue / Brooklyn, N.Y 11232 / (718) 921-9000

ISBN: 1-57819-537-3 Hard Cover

Printed in the United States of America by Noble Book Press

TABLE OF CONTENTS

Approbations	IX
Foreword	XV
Preface	XVII
Acknowledgments	XXIII
General Introduction	XXV
Introduction	XXIX

Divrei Torah on the Parshiyos

  Sefer Bereishis

Bereishis	31
Noach	34
Lech Lecha	36
Vayeira	38
Chayei Sara	40
Toldos	43
Vayeitzei	45
Vayishlach	47
Vayeisheiv	50
Mikeitz	52
Vayigash	54
Vayechi	56

Sefer Shemos

Shemos	59
Va'eira	61
Bo	63
Beshalach	66
Yisro	68
Mishpatim	71
Terumah	74
Tetzaveh	76
Ki Sisa	79
Vayakhel	81
Pekudei	84

Sefer Vayikra

Vayikra	87
Tzav	89
Shemini	91
Tazria	93
Metzora	96
Acharei Mos	98
Kedoshim	100
Emor	102
Behar-Bechukosai	105

Sefer Bamidbar

Bamidbar	109
Torah Reading for Shavuos	112
Nasso	114
Beha'aloscha	117
Shelach	120
Korach	123

Chukas	125
Balak	128
Pinchas	131
Mattos-Masei	134

Sefer Devarim

Devarim	137
Va'eschanan	140
Eikev	143
Re'eh	145
Shoftim	148
Ki Seitzei	151
Ki Savo	154
Nitzavim	157
Vayeileich	160
Rosh Hashanah	162
Ha'azinu	165
Yom Kippur	167
Shemini Atzeres	170
Vezos Haberachah	171

Selected Writings

Shabbos	175
The Festivals	189
Miscellany	223

Appendix

The Keys of an Honest Lawyer	239
Biography	243
Eulogy for Bertha Merzon	263
Glossary	266

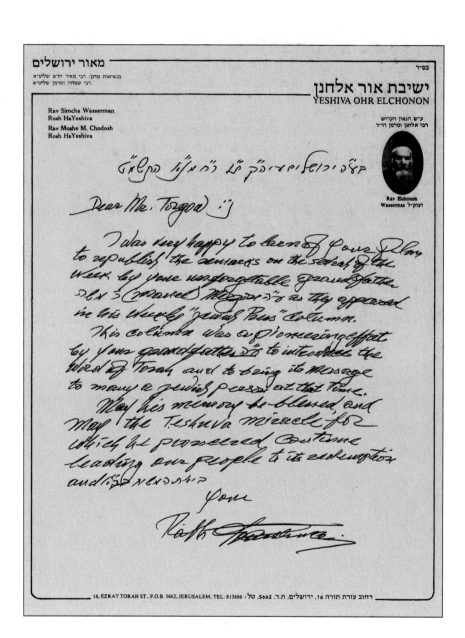

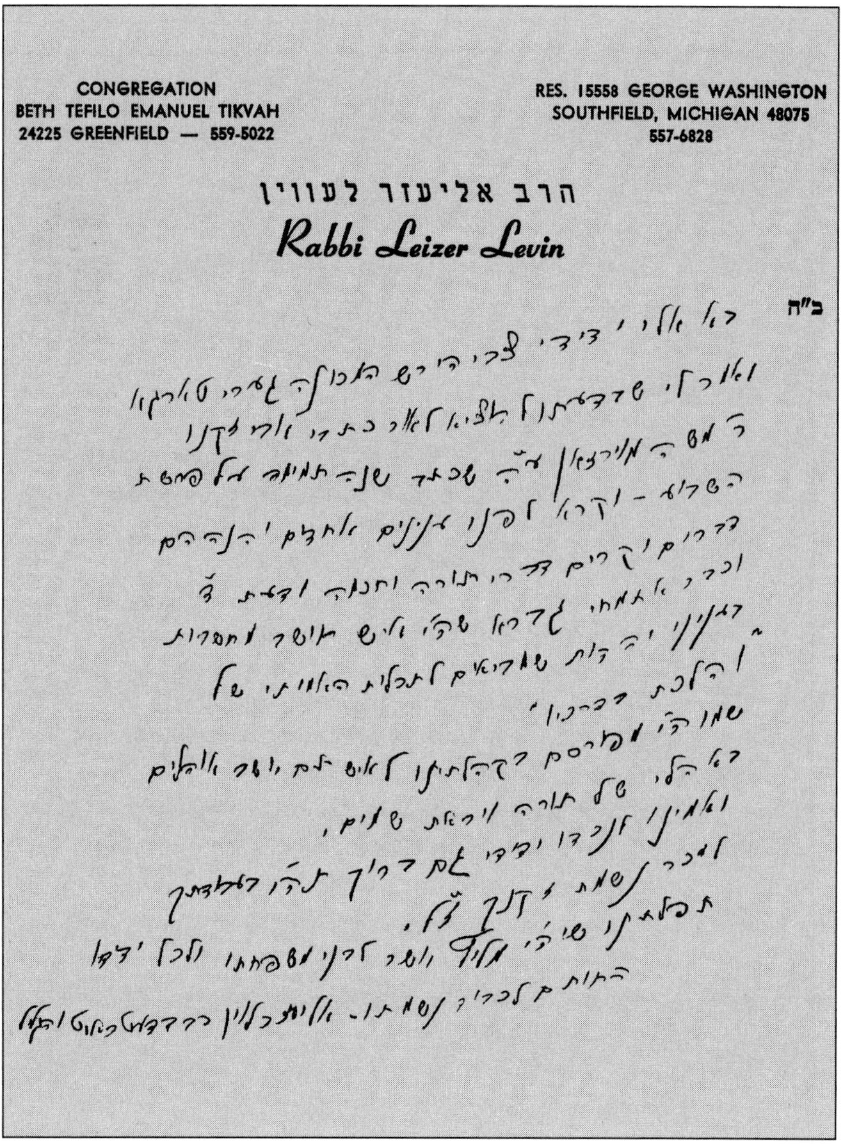

CONGREGATION
BETH TEFILO EMANUEL TIKVAH
24225 GREENFIELD — 559-5022

RES. 15558 GEORGE WASHINGTON
SOUTHFIELD, MICHIGAN 48075
557-6828

הרב אליעזר לעווין

Rabbi Leizer Levin

ב"ה

KOLLEL INSTITUTE OF GREATER DETROIT
כולל אברכים דעטראיט

The history of the Jewish people is largely the story of our ability to rise to the challenge of keeping the Torah's vision within the context of a general society whose moral and ethical sense has always been antithetical to that vision. Perhaps of all such societies, American society has proven to be the most difficult. Few were the Jews who came to these shores and kept their strong attachment to Torah. Fewer still were those who inspired their children and grandchildren to follow in their footsteps. To those heroes one can only well apply the words of the prophet Yechezkel:

וְהַכֹּהֲנִים הַלְוִיִּם בְּנֵי צָדוֹק אֲשֶׁר שָׁמְרוּ אֶת־מִשְׁמֶרֶת מִקְדָּשִׁי בִּתְעוֹת בְּנֵי־יִשְׂרָאֵל מֵעָלַי הֵמָּה יִקְרְבוּ אֵלַי לְשָׁרְתֵנִי. יחזקאל מ״ד:טו

But the priests the Levites, the sons of Tzadok, who kept the charge of My sanctuary when the people of Israel went astray from Me, they shall come near to Me to minister to Me. Yechezkel 44:15.

One of those notable exceptions was Mr. Manuel (משה 'ר) Merzon ז"ל, a person whom I was privileged to know and love. Despite the lack of Yeshivos and role models in Detroit in his formative years, Mr. Merzon went on to become a man who devoted his entire life to Jewish learning and practice and served as a shining role model for others. There was no distinction in his life between the synagogue and work place. A lawyer by profession, he always proudly wore his yarmulke while practicing law, even in the courtroom. His legal practice was imbued with the ethics and spirit of the Torah and filled with enormous compassion. Countless are the needy whom he served without recompense.

We are very privileged that his grandchild, Mr. Gary Torgow נ"י, a man whose whole life bears the imprint of his exceptional grandfather, has published his grandfather's Torah insights. May these words of wisdom inspire a new generation as they have inspired so many in the past.

Rabbi Shmuel Irons

Rabbi Moshe Schwab • Rabbi Shmuel Irons ROSHEI HAKOLLEL   Rabbi Reuven Green EXECUTIVE DIRECTOR

15230 Lincoln, Oak Park, Michigan 48237   Tel 248 968 1891   Fax 248 967 3233   email kollel@kolleldetroit.com

RABBI AVROHOM A. FREEDMAN
26135 HARDING ST.
OAK PARK, MI. 48237
248-968-5832

רב אברהם אבא פרידמן
15751 W. LINCOLN DRIVE
SOUTHFIELD, MI. 48076
248-557-9380

October 12, 1999 ב׳ חשון תש״ס

A Lamed Vovnik

Tradition has it that in every generation there are Lamed-Vov (thirty six) Tzadikim (most saintly persons). Mr. Merzon was one of them. He personified himself the edict that he prescribed to his grandson, Gary Torgow, when the latter was deciding on a career. "Gary become a lawyer to better serve G-d, His people, and mankind." Mr. Merzon was a lawyer who probably helped more clients gratuitously than those whom he charged. His office and home were the address where you could send holocaust survivors and others needy for legal help of all kinds, mostly at no charge. He handled in his lifetime literally thousands of legal cases for free - no charge - a Lamed-Vovnik.

It took a Lamed-Vovnik to come to America at age 16 to become quite the scholar that he was, as evidenced by this book. Let the generations know of a self-made person who resisted the American melting pot. He was very wise. He searched, discovered, adopted, and adapted to a life where prayer, study, piety, mitzvos, and chesed dominated. There was no Yeshiva in Detroit or almost anywhere in America in those times. He was self-made.

He was a Lamed-Vovnik in his dedication and pioneering to spread Yiddishkeit, as we see from this book. He was a Lamed-Vovnik in his piety. The Shul was his second, maybe first, home. He hardly missed a minyan. It was a life mission for him to provide for the decorous and physical needs of Synagogues.

He was a Lamed-Vovnik in his integrity and honesty. All this never protruded outside; it was all inside. His outward appearance was "every day-normal," completely modern American (except, maybe, for the Kipah which somehow didn't detract anything).

Mrs. Merzon, Gary's grandmother, the dedicated partner to this Lamed Vovnik, is well described, too. We salute Gary Torgow, his grandson, for arranging and printing this valuable book and for providing much of the priceless anecdotage. We also salute Mr. Torgow for emulating his grandfather so well and for following in his footsteps and his instructions on how to live.

This book is and will be an inspiration, not only for the descendants of Mr. Merzon, but for all readers. I am sure there will be many.

Avrohom Freedman

Rabbi Avrohom Freedman

בס"ד

Agudas Yisroel Mogen Avraham
Irwin I. Cohn & Sadie Cohn
Bais Hamedrash of
Yeshiva Beth Yehudah

THE AGUDAH
ק"ק אגודת ישראל מגן אברהם

Rabbi Dov Loketch
Rabbi Asher Eisenberger
(248) 552-1971

י"ח כסליו תשס"ס

תנן באבות סוף פ"ו "כל מה שברא הקב"ה בעולמו לא בראו אלא לכבודו שנאמר כל הנקרא בשמי ולכבודי בראתיו" פירוש שתכלית בריאת האדם הוא להרבות כבוד שמים בעולם. ר' משה בן מנחם מנדל מערזאן ע"ה היה מרבה כבוד שמים באהבת הבריות באופן נפלא, בעת שרק יחידי עולם חסו על כבוד שמים. כמו ששנינו באבות פ"ב מ"ה "במקום שאין אנשים השתדל להיות איש". ר' משה מערזאן היה עומד בפרץ במקום שאחרים לא ניסו לעמוד. בימי חורפו, כשמירת שבת באהבת הבריות היתה רפויה, הוא הדפיס ירחון עם מאמרים המזרזים ההמון על שמירת שבת. וגם לענין הימים טובים היה כותב דברים נעימים ונחמדים. שוב, לעת זקנתו, הריס קולמסו שנית לכתוב מאמרים על פרשיות השבוע והימים טובים כדי להרביץ תורה בעיתון שבוע שהגיע לאלפי יהודים על פני רוחב המדינה.

בכל דבריו היה בגגון שווה, אהבת הקב"ה, אהבת ישראל, ואהבת התורה הקדושה. זה היה תמידתו של ר' משה מערזאן, אוהב השם, אוהב ישראל, ואוהב התורה. אוהב השם, בדקדוק שמירת המצות בין אדם למקום, ובפרט לענין תפלתו, שהיה תופס מקום יקר בחייו. אוהב ישראל, איך שעור לאלפי יהודים נכסריים ונדלדלים אחר חורבן אירופה שבאו להאהבת הבריות לנטוע שרשים חדשים בארץ נכריה, בלי קבלת שכר פעולתו. ואהבת התורה, בין לענין השיעורים קבועים שהיה לו עם רביו, בין לענין השיעורים שקבע לעצמו בכל עת פנוי. ר' משה היה הולך לעבודתו עם ספר תחת ידו, ובכל פעולה היה משפתתו היה מתחיל הסעודה עם דברי תורה. בכל עת חופש היה נוסע עם ספריו למלאות זמנו על לימוד התורה. התורה היה חסקים שעפליו נננה ביתו, ובמשך ימי חייו השתדל בעבור כל מוסד תורני שהיה יכול לסייע בפעולותיו הבלתי נגמרות.

לא זכיתי להכיר את ר' משה מערזאן, אבל היה לי הזכות המיוחדת לעבור על כתביו המרובות, ועזרתי בסידורס לדפוס, למסור דבריו לדורות הבאות אחריו. בדרך זה זכינו להגיע לפני הקורא הנעים את הדברים הנדפסים בחייו וגם דברים שמעולם לא נדפסו, שהיו בין כתביו שהשאיר אחריו. ואני תפילה שדבריו ימלאו חן בעיני אלקים ואדם, וימשיך השפעתו לקרב את הבריות לתורה.

תשואות נשואות לנכדו היקר ר' צבי הירש טורנו נ"י איש רב פעלים שממשיך לעלות במסילות שכבר זקנו, שהקיס עולו של הדפסת הכתבים של זקנו ר' משה מערזאן ע"ה זכותו יגן עלינו. יה"ר שיראה בנים ובני בנים עוסקים בתורה ובמצוות מתוך בריאות הגוף והנפש יחד עם עקרת ביתו מרת מלכה (מבית גוטסמן) שתחיה, ויקוים בו דברי הפסוק "בכל אשר יפנה ישכיל" בעבודתו הקדושה להרבות כבוד שמים בעולם.

אשר ח. אייזנברגר

15751 W. Lincoln Dr.
Southfield, Michigan 48076

November 24, 1999   ט״ו כסלו תש״ס

Humility and strength of character are the two essential ingredients found in all Jewish leaders throughout the ages. Humility, in fact, is the conduit of all wisdom, as our sages teach us, "איזהו חכם הלומד מכל אדם" "Who is wise? He who learns from every person." Only one who sets no preconditions of ego in the way of acquiring wisdom is ready to be a receiving vessel of G-d's brilliance. Strength of character is indicative of one's conviction in an ultimate truth and the impeccable integrity required in true service of the Almighty. In addition, there is one more character trait of a true leader- a boundless desire and enthusiasm to give selflessly to others.

Reb Moshe Merzon, of blessed memory, was a shining example of humility, strength of character, and boundless giving.

With few learning opportunities in his childhood, Reb Moshe toiled to understand our Torah, and as time went on he developed a unique ability to delve into its depth. The results of his tireless efforts could be partially appreciated by enjoying the magnificent harvest of thoughts that were produced by the seeds of Torah which Reb Moshe planted day after day, week after week, throughout his years, to benefit the many interested readers of his weekly column in the *Jewish Press*. I have had the privilege to know and benefit personally from his remarkable personality, for which I am forever grateful.

Owing to the efforts of his beloved grandson and protégé, my very dear friend, Reb Tzvi Hirsch (Gary) Torgow, and the artful authorship of our revered Rabbi Asher Eisenberger, Rav of Congregation Agudath Israel Mogen Avraham, Southfield, Michigan, those precious jewels of wisdom are now easily accessible to Jews the world over. I can only imagine the נחת רוח of Reb Moshe ז״ל in the עולם האמת from this most appropriate project to eternalize his memory and his important messages for generations to come.

Rabbi Avraham Jacobovitz

Nathan and Esther Korman Building 15221 West Ten Mile Road, Oak Park, Michigan 48237 (248) 967-0888 / Fax (248) 967-0412/E-mail: machon@speedlink.net
Jewish Resource Center of Ann Arbor at the University of Michigan, 1335 Hill St., Ann Arbor 48104 (734) 332-8777
Rabbi Avraham Jacobovitz-Director, Gary Torgow- Honorary Chairman, Dr. Neil Blavin, Steven Ettinger, Stuart J. Snider-Presidium
Activities held at: Michigan State University, University of Michigan, Central Michigan University, Wayne State University, Western Michigan University, Oakland University, Oakland Community College, Eastern Michigan University, Thomas M. Cooley Law School, University of Windsor, Ontario, Canada

FOREWORD

ONE OF THE GREATEST HONORS THAT CAN BEFALL AN INDIVIDUAL JEW IN Jewish synagogue life occurs on Simchas Torah — the great day of the festival of rejoicing in the Torah — which completes the series of the holy days of the month of Tishrei. That honor of Simchat Torah is called "Choson Torah — the bridegroom of the Torah." A bridegroom has many qualities to him on the day of his wedding and every individual bridegroom is a unique and special individual unlike any others. However, there are certain qualities that are common to all bridegrooms. Some of those qualities are a spirit of adventure, the unbounded love extended to another human being, the feeling of hope and optimism, the realization of the seriousness of life and especially Jewish living, the soaring optimism of building one's future and the sense of family and communal continuity that being a bridegroom brings. These are the necessary qualities and character traits that a Jew must bring to its relationship with the Torah. Only the enthusiasm, devotion, loyalty and love of a bridegroom allow a Jew to develop and later deepen a connection with the Torah. All Jews who develop such a relationship are worthy of the title *"Choson Torah."*

My cousin Manuel Merzon, was an exemplary Jew and human being. He was a true *"Choson Torah."* Small in physical stature, quiet in demeanor, seemingly retiring in manner, he was a giant of a person of iron will and divine purpose who persevered and won the ultimate battle of life, being blessed with outstandingly Jewish children and grandchildren and great-grandchildren. His beloved grandson, Gary Torgow, an outstanding Jewish leader and person in his own right, has collected his grandfather's thoughts and organized them in this book form. Read Gary's introduction to the book and you will feel the greatness of Manuel Merzon and perhaps, even more importantly, the flow of Jewish love that passes between generations through the conduit of Torah life.

The greatness of Torah is that it is a never-ending study. There is no end to the insights and lessons to be derived from Torah. The chain of Torah is eternal. Every Jew has his contribution to make to the eternal lesson of Torah. In the pages of this book you will find the ideas and insights of a loyal and pious son of Israel on the weekly portions of the Torah. By reading his words, I am certain that you will find inspiration and intelligence. But you will also find room for your own thoughts and interpretations. Thus you will further Manuel Merzon's ultimate purpose, the purpose of all Jews — to enhance the Torah and make it even more glorious.

Rabbi Berel Wein

Jerusalem
Kislev 5762, November 2001

PREFACE

As I write this introduction, although nearly thirteen years since my grandfather's passing, I cannot help but feel both great sadness and immense gratitude. Sadness because my years with him ended before my thirtieth birthday, leaving unfulfilled my desire to learn more and more from his wise counsel. Yet my unlimited gratitude to the Almighty for granting me years of closeness to such an outstanding human being. He was a true *Oveid Hashem* (servant of God), never deviating from his purpose in this world, to become closer to the Almighty through prayer, good deeds, Torah study, and cleanliness of spirit and body.

It is my hope and prayer that through the words of this book, others will be similarly inspired, allowing Mr. Merzon's wonderful influence to continue for generations.

It is rare indeed that an individual is able to affect our world both during life and after. Yet, when it does occur, it is generally through some form of creativity. In the case of my grandfather, Moshe Manuel Merzon, it was a cadre of written words spanning nearly five decades.

It began with his participation in an essay contest less than three years after he arrived upon our great American shores as a refugee from Russian tyranny. The topic he chose "What Is a Jew," written in impeccable English, was awarded first prize. That entry began a career as a legal-brief writer, a commentator, part-time journalist, and codifier of the words of

Jewish thinkers. He was a man who claimed no particular expertise but was versed in an unusual fashion with a wide array of subjects.

One common thread is reflected in the thousands of written words; an undeniable and passionate dedication to his people, to *Toras Moshe* and the Almighty. From his first effort in 1918 to his last words authored in a private form to his children, his words (exclusive of American legal jurisprudence) were of a Torah orientation. Every letter-to-the-editor, every *Jewish Press* column, every public pronouncement was reflective of a man with a desire to promote *Yiddishkeit* and its perpetuation.

This book *Raising the Bar* is primarily a sampling of articles written by Mr. Merzon under the title *"Choson Torah"* in Rabbi Shalom Klass' *Jewish Press,* as well as a sampling of articles of different Torah topics which we believe reflect his general thoughts and beliefs.

My uncle, Melvin Merzon, described my relationship with my grandfather as "closer than a son." He was in fact my *Rebbi,* my loving friend, my mentor who directed and designed for me that path of my journey from childhood to adulthood. I was privileged to be his companion, the regular recipient of his thoughts and directives, and to be the archivist of his documents and creative writings. I was witness to many unusual events, uncommon in their selflessness and human compassion, which he in his wisdom made a part of his daily routine.

Although a man with two college degrees, his chief occupation was the service of the Almighty; every act, in concert with his role as a Torah Jew.

His synagogue attendance was impeccable. After prayers which lasted longer than anyone in the congregation there was the *Psalms* that beckoned. He felt that the words of King David had immense power and spirituality.

He had a remarkable quality to conserve and utilize every moment. There was never a second wasted on frivolity; always a pen in hand, a book clutched under his arm with a magnifying glass ready to capture every nuance, every word.

He had an intuitive feeling for what was right and a compulsion to stand up for it. He was a man of wisdom. Frequently, when a member of the family or a friend was faced with a problem, a difficulty, a perplexity, they went to Zaidy for guidance. He was uniquely equipped to give advice, he was constantly immersed in Torah and was true to the words of our Sages. He would consider the question laid before him calmly and express his views succinctly. His advice was always concluded with an admonition to have faith in and reliance on G-d.

He was a prolific writer, at one time publishing his own newspaper, *The Detroit Jewish Review,* which he created primarily to keep the community's focus on the plight of European Jewry. It was his opportunity to promote *Yiddishkeit* in a secular community.

He reserved his fondest feelings for his wife, our dear grandmother of blessed memory, Bertha. He sang her praises; his respect and love for her were immeasurable. She was truly his loyal helpmate, standing by his side in every phase of his life.

As a child I have vivid and indelible memories of his care and selfless actions, some so obviously painful in his compassion for a sick relative.

I have memories of a man who could never leave the synagogue without straightening the holy books upside down or out of place, of gathering a torn prayer book and patching it, protecting it from abuse or destruction.

A supplicant who corralled a court of his peers to recite special prayers because of a dream he had about the fate of his people, not once or twice, but hundreds of times.

Admonishing his clients that a last will and testament should not be made without a charitable device inserted or of the need to provide for a Jewish education for their children. His crying over the fate of a Jewish client who insisted on cremation over a Jewish burial, or over a client whose loan application was denied, and so instead of a fee, a reaction to lend his own money, rarely to be returned.

Of his tenacious and concerted efforts to better our world by reminding everyone always of man's chief occupation, to serve the Almighty with a full heart.

I remember his deep concern and intense desire to appear and speak at the local city hall at 85 years old on behalf of the new *Yeshiva Gedola* in town. After all, he said, "What more important landmark for a town than a Yeshiva and *Beis Medrash*."

I remember the phone conversation with a fellow Jew who had to be dissuaded from purchasing land from another Jew without a proper *Heter Iska*.

The appearance in court without payment or fee because of an unrepentant heir who refused to give the charitable devices demanded by the relative's last will and testament.

A man who would allow his food to go cold rather than embarrass his wife by reminding her that she had forgotten to give him a fork and knife.

His urging to promote *shalom bayis* both in our family and in our community. To be tough when necessary, yet never to achieve success or gain at the expense of your fellow man. To appreciate America, to protect Israel, to speak out against injustice, to never ever veer from absolute allegiance and service to the Almighty.

A remarkable 25-year management by Manuel and his wife and apparent ownership of a local Jewish cemetery when they extracted not one penny for themselves in profit or salary. It belonged to the community and it demanded their service.

Of his uncompromising dedication to his people; an intuitive feeling for what was right and a compulsion to stand up for it. Of his thoughts entitled "vital" in his last will, where he pronounced so many fundamentals of life.

He wrote that "learning Torah is a matter of pushing oneself, for failure to do so will cause inordinate delay and ultimate neglect."

That "kindness is the oil that tames friction in human relations. That goodwill is the cheapest investment which yields the greatest profit."

He seldom asked favors of anyone. When he did ask of me, it was invariably a mitzvah that needed to be done. To take him to Oakland County Probate Court to intervene without retainer on behalf of a local institution that was fearful of losing their charitable gift. To mail his charity solicitations at the Oak Park Post Office at a particular time to ensure that no letter would arrive on Shabbos lest it be opened by the recipient in violation of Jewish law. To have his *mezuzahs* checked because Bobi was ailing, and to find that all throughout the house needed replacing. To lend him a *Mishnayos,* or to drive him to his beloved *shiur* with the *Rosh Yeshiva,* Rav Leib Bakst.

To go to Florida for Pesach and to never venture out to the ocean, the pool, but to sit all day in the hotel synagogue pouring over the suitcase of holy books brought from home. To serve every charitable community cause with the same fervor and devotion he lent to his family and business. To don a *yarmulke* in a courtroom not to gain advantage or attention because for a Jew there was simply no other way. To commit to send out hundreds of charitable requests and his elation when a response was received (his elation for the giver more than for the recipient). To witness tears of joy over the successes of his family and tears of tragic sadness when he conjured up thoughts of people who were suffering.

To lament to excess the need for retribution against the Nazi "beasts" whom he insisted could never be forgiven; to constantly remind of the need to rescue our brothers behind the Iron Curtain, to devote all of our resources to help fellow Jews in need.

His idea of a successful lawyer was one who helped his client not measured by their ability to pay but by the lawyer's ability to help.

His unshakable faith, his incurable optimism, his devoted prayers, his aversion to gossip, his kindness, his compassion, his love, his demeanor, his selflessness, his firm beliefs, his love of Torah and Torah learning were all the sum of the parts that made up this remarkable man.

These articles provided herein are a mirror image of how my Zaidy conducted his life. The form they take is always the same; a quotation from the opening verse of each *Sedrah* followed by a repetition of an important Rashi or other relevant comment. Then and only then did he venture out into his own personal comment. If space was short, then just the Biblical quote and Rashi were

Rashi were sufficient. For after all (he would say), "the *ikar* (principal concept) is the *Divrei Hashem* (Words of G-d) and His scholars, not my comments." His life was much the same: no family gathering or public speech ever began with anything other than the first verse of the *Sedrah,* the relevant Rashi, and a message of faith.

May the Almighty grant Reb Moshe ben Menachem Mendel an elevation of soul in the merit of this printing, and may our family and all *Klal Yisrael* receive the spiritual benefits gained from helping to bring this work to publication.

Gary Torgow

Editor
Kislev 5762

ACKNOWLEDGMENTS

Without the guidance, encouragement, and fortitude of my dear friend Rabbi Asher Eisenberger, this book would not have been published.

Reb Asher, a brilliant and learned scholar, provided the structure, form and insightful concluding *divrei Torah* to each *Sedrah*. These thoughts underscore and enhance each of my grandfather's beautiful articles. Reb Asher pored over hundreds of pages of my grandfather's writings and selected the material for this book, bringing together a project I have labored over and thought of since my grandfather's passing on the 18th of Teves, January 8, 1988. May Rabbi Eisenberger and his wonderful family be granted years of good health and *Yiddishe nachas* in the merit of bringing this work to fruition.

My thanks to R' Hillel Yarmove, for moving this project to its fruition and for believing in and advocating the dissemination of my grandfather's words. Hillel is not only a wordsmith but also a Jew with a warm and caring heart.

To Rabbis Scherman and Zlotowitz my heartfelt thanks for their encouragement and friendship. It is an honor to be associated with such exceptional and wise men. Only future generations will be able to calculate how remarkably impactful their efforts are for the growth and scholarship of Klal Yisrael.

To Rabbi Raphael Butler for his devoted friendship and important help in seeing this and so many other projects to fruition.

Special thanks to my uncle, Mel Merzon, an outstanding attorney in Chicago who helped in the early stages of this process by reviewing and editing the original "*Choson Torah*" articles.

To my dear parents Robert and Bonnie Torgow, my deepest thanks for encouraging and facilitating the special bond I developed with my grandfather. May they enjoy continued *nachas*, good health and great blessings from the Almighty.

My gratitude to my dear cousin, Rabbi Berel Wein, world famous rav and lecturer in Jerusalem, Israel, for his special words offered in the foreword to this book. The closeness we have developed and the projects we undertake together are one of the great blessings G-d has granted my family and me.

I am very gratified that the publication of this book coincides with the Bar Mitzvah of our dear son Moshe Manuel. Moshe was the first child in our extended family to be named after our grandfather. It is our hope and prayer that he will emulate the wonderful qualities of his great-grandfather.

To my best friend and devoted wife, Malke. No words could express properly my appreciation to my life's companion. Her wonderful parents, Rabbi and Mrs. Menachem Gottesman, were and continue to be role models par excellence for building a Jewish home and community. May Malke and our wonderful children, Yoni, Elie, Racheli, Moshe, and Yacov, continue to be sources of *nachas* to each other, our family, and *Klal Yisrael*.

Finally, it is my hope and prayer that through publishing this book, in the merit of allowing my grandfather's words to inspire and educate, the Almighty will bring good health and blessings to my entire family and to all our people.

Gary Torgow

Detroit, Michigan
Kislev 5762

GENERAL INTRODUCTION

OUR SAGES HAVE TOLD US THAT OVER THE COURSE OF CENTURIES THERE has been a continual, inexorable diminution of the generations (*niskatnu hadoros*). Nevertheless, it seems that Hashem in His great, abundant mercy has allowed us to glimpse — true, only at rare moments — what it must have been like to live among veritable giants of the spirit, people whose entire lives bespoke truth and thorough commitment to the principle of our Holy Torah. In our generation, there lived such a man in the city of Detroit, Michigan. An attorney by profession, an immigrant from Eastern Europe by background, he was able to set a shining example for both Jew and non-Jew alike of exactly what it means to be a prince among men: in other words, a true son of Israel in every respect. His name was M. Manuel Merzon, of blessed memory.

We have begun with some of Mr. Merzon's *divrei Torah al haparashah* (exegetical pieces on the weekly Torah portion) — as well as his thoughts about our sacred Sabbath and the Holy Festivals — for inclusion into this volume. After all, in addition to his continual performance of acts of lovingkindness, he proved to be an unusually deep thinker; consequently, his substantial contributions to sacred Jewish scholarship also need representation in an opus of this sort.

Moreover, we have included a selection of his general writings — either articles from his column (entitled "*Choson Torah*") in

The Jewish Press (primarily in the years 1982-3) or other, earlier writings that appeared in Mr. Merzon's own paper, *The Detroit Jewish Review,* between the years 1943 and 1945. These articles are valuable not only as windows into the soul of a *tzaddik* (a saintly man), but also as a guide to the turbulent times of World War II Jewry — undoubtedly, one of the most troubled periods in history for the Children of Israel.

There are several reasons why this book has been entitled *Raising the Bar.* Even the casual reader will note that Mr. Merzon's sterling character traits worked in consonance with each other to present the world with an accurate picture of how a Torah-imbued attorney *ought to act.* (Here, the term *bar* is a metonymy for the legal profession.) That other people, both Jew and non-Jew alike, were deeply moved by his actions is, of course, axiomatic. Furthermore, M. Manuel Merzon raised the expectations of those around him, since after witnessing his many deeds of limitless lovingkindness, how could anyone else expect any less of himself! And as the chief advocate for so many poor, inarticulate souls — whether new immigrants or itinerant old-timers — Mr. Merzon removed, through sheer force of his powerfully devout personality, the various bars, restrictions, and obstacles which these people encountered at seemingly every turn. Indeed, it is hard to read this book and not come away believing that mankind really can achieve saintliness — if only they would emulate this great person.

One last word: We have endeavored to be as faithful to Mr. Merzon's inimitable style as possible, while updating some of the terms that he used which might have been more readily comprehensible to members of his generation — but somewhat less to our more "technological" generation! Although not a native-born American, Mr. Merzon eagerly — better, zealously — adopted the English language as his *mama lashon* (mother tongue), and his knowledge of it superseded that of many so-called literate people of our own day. No one should be surprised, then, at his occasional use of a French or Latin word if he felt that the term would suitably embellish his style and, more importantly, strengthen the force of his argument. Accordingly, we have been as unobtrusive as possible in our redaction of his material.

We hope that readers everywhere will feel that same sense of being uplifted and strengthened in their *emunas Hashem* (faith in G-d) as we did when we first perused this text.

Hillel L. Yarmove

Kislev 5762

INTRODUCTION

MANUEL MERZON WAS A LAWYER WHO CONSIDERED HIS PROFESSION A vehicle to aid his fellow man. Whether helping a European refugee, lending a voice to the voiceless, or arguing on behalf of the deceased in probate court, he represented those who could not represent themselves. His articles and letters reflect this commitment. He was bent on representing Hashem, His Torah, and His people. A prolific writer, his articles and letters span the wide gamut of his interests. We have selected only a sampling of his writings which deliver a pertinent message to their readers.

Some of the articles presented here were first printed in the Detroit Jewish Review, a publication created by Manuel Merzon to present a viewpoint which the other Jewish periodicals of the period would not. These appeared between the years 1943 and 1945 and reflect his reaction to that difficult time for Jewry.

Other articles were composed during the mid-70's to mid-80's. Most of the letters were penned to *The Detroit Jewish News*, but there are letters to the local daily newspapers, to congressmen, and to other national leaders. Ever faithful to the Torah, he would quickly respond to any article in print misrepresenting Scripture or corrupting the Torah's message, with the hope that his efforts would preserve the truth of Hashem's word. A staunch advocate for the plight of Soviet Jewry and an ardent supporter of Israel, he wrote many letters on behalf of world Jewry to advance the causes of His people. And again, as the representative of the voiceless, he employed prose as cudgels to castigate the Nazis and their cohorts, lest others forget the atrocities inflicted upon His nation.

A careful study of the sampling of articles and letters presented here will provide an insight into a thoughtful, caring man, who was not satisfied, like many others, to merely nod their heads and mutter "tsk, tsk" under their breath. He responded eloquently and forcefully, even if the message was lost on deaf ears, because he knew that one fateful day all of us will be asked, "And what did you do about . . . ?" No one could accuse him of not trying.

Rabbi Asher Eisenberger

Detroit Michigan
Kislev 5762, November 2001

DIVREI TORAH ON THE PARSHIOS

- **BEREISHIS**
- **SHEMOS**
- **VAYIKRA**
- **BAMIDBAR**
- **DEVARIM**

Sefer Bereishis

Parashas Bereishis

THE *SEDRAH* BEGINS:

"In the beginning of G-d's creating the heavens and the earth, when the earth was bewilderment and void, with darkness over the surface of the deep, and the breath of G-d was hovering upon the surface of the waters, G-d said, 'Let there be light,' and there was light."

Rashi comments: **"In the beginning of:** Rabbi Yitzchak said: Hashem need not have begun the Torah but from (Exodus 12:2) 'This month shall be for you [the beginning of the months],' because it is the first commandment which Israel was commanded. What is the reason that it began with the Book of Genesis? It began thus because it wished to convey the message of the verse (Psalms 111:6) 'The power of His acts He told to His people in order to give them the estate of nations.' So that if the nations of the world will say to Israel, 'You are bandits, for you conquered the lands of the seven nations who inhabited the Land of Canaan,' Israel will say to them, 'The whole earth belongs to the Holy One, Blessed is He. He created it *and He gave it to the one found proper in His eyes. By His wish He gave it to them, and by His wish He took it from them and gave it to us.'"*

RAMBAN ASKS: WHY DO WE NOT START THE TORAH WITH THE STORY OF Creation? After all, Creation is the root of our faith! Ramban answers that Rabbi Yitzchak's conclusion is predicated on the idea that it was not necessary for the Torah to give a detailed account of the works of Creation, Adam and Chava and their descendants, Noach and his descendants. And then the dispersion of mankind to various places in consequence of the sin of the building of the Tower of Babel. To believers, the summary of the Creation of the world is one passage. The fourth commandment would suffice: "For in six days G-d made heaven and earth, and the sea and all that is in them, and He rested on the seventh day." The significance of Rabbi Yitzchak's view, according to Ramban, relates to this idea: The Torah traces the process of Creation, and details various dispersions in order to teach us that when people begin to sin, they lose their place of permanence under the sun, and another people will come to inherit the land (of Israel), for such is the rule of G-d in the world. The choicest places of the civilized world, Ramban concludes, should be inherited by the seed of His beloved one, Avraham, cited as a proof of the text (*Isaiah* 41:8), "But you, Israel, are My servant — Jacob whom I have chosen, the seed of Abraham, My beloved," and (*Psalms* 105:45), "That they might observe His statutes and keep His laws."

It may be proper to conclude that the story of Creation emphasizes three basic essentials of our faith: First, Hashem created the world and all that is in it; second, *Toras Moshe* is primarily *Toras Yisrael,* and what flows from this is the obligation to follow the mitzvos of the Torah; and third, *Eretz Yisroel* is *L'am Yisrael:* The Land of Israel is for the Nation of Israel.

> *A proof that Hashem created the world is recorded by Rabbeinu Bachya ibn Paquda (eleventh century). He*

wrote in Chovos HaLevavos [Duties of the Heart] (Gate of Unity, Chapter 6): There are men who say that the world came into existence by chance. I wonder how any rational person can entertain such a notion. Do they not realize that if ink were poured accidentally on a blank sheet of paper, it would be impossible that legible lines such as are written with a pen should result? If a person brought us a copy of a script that could have been written only with a pen and said that ink had spilt on paper and that these written characters had come into existence by themselves, we would charge him with lying, for we are certain that this could not have happened without an intelligent person's guidance. Since this is so, how can one assert that something far finer in its art and which manifests in its fashioning a subtlety infinite beyond our comprehension could have happened without the purpose, power, and wisdom of a wise and mighty Designer? What we have selected from His works to demonstrate the existence of a Creator will certainly suffice to convince anyone who is intelligent and candid enough to admit the truth, and will serve both to refute those who maintain that the universe is eternal (and thus without a Creator), and to disprove their other contentions as well.

With the recognition that there is a Creator, we understand that we are expected to do His will. Those who deny Hashem's Creation of the world do so to avoid the requirements that this recognition entails. Therefore, the Torah's description of Creation is essential to understand our obligation to fulfill His mitzvos.

Parashas Noach

The *Sedrah* begins:

> "These are the generations of Noach. Noah was a righteous man, perfect in his generations; Noah walked with G-d. Noah fathered three sons: Shem, Ham, and Japheth. And the earth had become corrupt before G-d, and the earth had become filled with robbery. And G-d saw the earth and, behold, it was corrupted, for all flesh had corrupted its way upon the earth."

> Rashi comments: **"These are the generations of Noah. Noah was a righteous man:** Since Scripture mentioned him, it told of his praise, as it says (Proverbs 10:7), 'The mention of a righteous person is for a blessing.' Alternatively, the verse mentions Noah's righteousness at this point to teach you that the main offspring of the righteous is their good deeds."

Rashi continues: "In his generations: There are those among our Rabbis who expound this word as praise (of Noach) as follows: All the more so if he had been in a generation of righteous people: he would have been even more righteous. And there are those who expound it as deprecation of Noach, as follows: According to the standards of his generation he was righteous, but if he had been in the generation of Abraham he would not have been considered anyone of significance."

The commentaries differ as to the meaning of the term *toldos*, literally translated "generations." Here, as is evident from Rashi, depending upon the connection in which it is used, the word denotes good deeds. However, Ramban does not subscribe to this view. Ramban learns that *toldos* refers to posterity. Therefore, the very next verse states that Noach had three sons — Shem, Cham, and Yaphes.

Perhaps a homiletic explanation may be given to Rashi's position. The generation of humankind can live righteously when they are in consonance with the purpose of Creation. As it says (*Genesis* 5:1), "This is the account of the descendants of Adam. On the day of G-d's creating of Man, He made him in the likeness of G-d." It may be said to follow the rule: Man lives up to the purposes of Creation, when instead of descending to the level of the lower animal with whom man shares physical characteristics, he reaches upwards to emulate his Maker. Noach achieved that purpose; hence his generations are his righteous deeds.

> *As mentioned above, there is a disagreement whether the words "Noach was a righteous man in his generation" are complimentary or not. Rabbi Yaakov Kamenetsky (1890-1986) comments on the dispute as to whether Noach was only righteous relative to his time and place. Everyone agrees that Noach would have been even greater had he lived in a generation of righteous men. Everyone also agrees that in a degenerate generation, if only he and Avraham were righteous, Noach would have been overshadowed by Avraham's greatness. The disagreement is only as to the intention of the Torah. Why does it write "Noach was a righteous man, perfect in his generation"? Is the point to describe his praise or his flaw? However, according to the view that this was a flaw, it is difficult to understand why the Torah would choose to describe a flaw precisely when it outlines Noach's praises. Rabbi Kamenetsky answers that the Torah describes a flaw to explain why this righteous man could not save his generation from mass destruction. Even though Noach emulated his Creator and performed righteous deeds, he could not save his generation.*

Parashas Lech Lecha

The Sedrah begins:

"Hashem said to Abram, 'Go for yourself from your land, from your birthplace, and from your father's house to the land that I will show you. And I will make of you a great nation; I will bless you, and I will make your name great; and you will be a blessing. I will bless those who bless you, and the one who curses you I will curse; and all the families of the earth will be blessed through you.'"

Rashi comments: **"Go for yourself:** *for your pleasure, and for your benefit. There,* **'I will make of you a great nation,'** *whereas here you do not merit having children. And furthermore, you will benefit by going, for thereby I will make your name known in the world.* **And I will make of you a great nation:** *Because the journey causes three negative things to happen to the traveler — it diminishes reproduction, it diminishes money, and it diminishes the name (one's good reputation must be earned again in the new place) — therefore, Abraham needed these three blessings which Hashem promised him regarding sons, money, and reputation."*

Although Avraham already left his father, Hashem commanded him to go even farther. This was intended to have him avoid the deleterious situation of his native land. Rabbi Meir Leibush ben Yechiel Michel (the *Malbim*, 1809-1879) explains that the purpose of the command to set forth on the journey was so that Avraham should break away from the traits, conduct, and the doings of the people where he was raised. The character of the person is molded, in Malbim's incisive view, by three main factors: the atmosphere and the environment where he is; the city where he sojourns, from whose inhabitants he is apt to learn certain behaviors; and from his own parents' home. In all these areas, the origins of our father Avraham were not conducive toward making him the great and magnificent personality which he had become as the discoverer of the existence of the Creator of the World, through Whom we live and have our being. In order to have that new light remain untarnished, it was necessary for him to blaze a new trail in a new land.

It is generally accepted that a person's character is fashioned by inheritance and environment; as to which of these predominate there is no agreement. Nor is there any assurance that children born from the same parents and raised in the same household will be more or less equal in their conduct and achievements. However, Judaism has demonstrated that a G-d-fearing child will be more apt to lead a satisfactory life than one not so characterized.

> *The significance of the environment on the person is similarly stressed later in the Sedrah. "So Abram went as Hashem had spoken to him, and Lot went with him; Abram was seventy-five years old when he left Haran" (Genesis 12:4). Why does the pasuk relate Avraham Avinu's age when he left his homeland? The pasuk should read, "Abram was seventy-five years old when he came to Canaan." Would it not have been more appropriate to emphasize his age at the time of his arrival in the Land of Canaan? Rabbi Yaakov Weinberg (1923-1999), Rosh Yeshiva of Yeshivas Ner Israel, explained that there is an important message here. The Torah is teaching us that his arrival was not nearly as significant as his departure. If Avraham would have left Haran only in the physical sense, simply relocating to a new home, he would not have developed into Avraham Avinu, the father of the Jewish people. He had transplanted the attitude, culture, and weltanschauung of Haran to Canaan. His sojourn would have thus been merely*

symbolic. Therefore, the Torah emphasizes Avraham's age when he left Haran. His departure was a complete separation from his homeland and from his past. Only by severing his ties with Haran could he be certain that arrival in Canaan would mark a new beginning, the start of a remarkable relationship with Hashem.

Parashas Vayeira

The *Sedrah* begins:

"Hashem appeared to him (Abraham) in the plains of Mamre while he was sitting at the entrance of the tent in the heat of the day. He lifted his eyes and saw: And behold! three men were standing before him. He saw, and he ran toward them from the entrance of the tent and bowed toward the ground. And he said, 'My lords, if it please you that I find favor in your eyes, please pass not from before your servant.'"

Rashi comments: **"Hashem appeared to him:** *To visit the sick person. The Amora Rabbi Chama the son of Chanina said: It was the third day since his circumcision, and the Holy One, Blessed is He, came and inquired about Abraham's welfare.* **In the plains of Mamre:** *He is the one who gave Abraham advice about the circumcision. This is why Hashem was revealed to Abraham in his portion."*

THAT HASHEM VISITED AVRAHAM TO PERFORM THE MITZVAH OF *BIKUR Cholim* (Visiting the Sick) is an interesting reflection of the comradeship that existed between Him and His beloved. Also, from this passage the Sages of the Talmud deduce that every Jew has the duty to visit their fellows who are ill.

Mamre's part in counseling Avraham concerning circumcision evokes some speculation as to the person of Mamre and his aptitudes. It is apparent that if Avraham consulted him, Mamre must have been a man of consequence, perhaps one of the righteous gentiles of his day. That the problem of the operation Avraham was to undergo found expert advice in Mamre might be indicative that he was possessed of some medical knowledge.

In addition to the foregoing, however, consideration should be given to the authoritative comment of *Sifsei Chachamim* (Rabbi Shabse Shtrim, d. 1719), where the following question is propounded: Why did Avraham seek counsel about circumcision more than other commandments? Because on the latter he needed no advice. Avraham was endowed with prophetic knowledge of the mitzvos to be given to his descendants later, and he performed them. If for any reason Hashem reiterated such commandments to him, they could be performed again at a later date. But circumcision was obviously unique in that respect. It needed to be done with perfection. So the advice which Avraham sought from Mamre was whether to anticipate this mitzvah or wait until specifically commanded by Hashem. And this Avraham had done.

The *Midrash* (*Bereishis Rabbah* 11:6) describes an exchange between Rabbi Hoshaya and a philosopher. The gentile thinker asked: If circumcision is so dear to G-d, why wasn't man created circumcised? Rebbi Hoshaya replied that G-d made everything with room for man to perfect His creations. Wheat must be ground, mustard must be sweetened, and vegetables cooked. Similarly, man must be perfected and this task is accomplished through circumcision.

> *Rabbi Levi Yitzchak of Berditchev (1740-1809) explains with this Midrash why Avraham Avinu did not undertake this mitzvah before Hashem explicitly ordered him. The concept of circumcision is to understand that Hashem created everything in this*

world in the "raw" state, and it is up to mankind to bring everything in the world to perfection, including man himself. If Hashem tells man that he has the power to perfect His creation, there is no offense in taking such action. But without prior instruction, for man to take the initiative would be disrespectful, since doing so would imply that man can improve upon Hashem's handiwork. Therefore, if Avraham performed his circumcision without being told to do so, he would have been implying that Hashem did not create a perfect world. Only after Avraham Avinu was commanded to perform the circumcision could he fulfill the mitzvah without casting any aspersions against Hashem.

Parashas Chayei Sarah

The Sedrah Begins:

"Sarah's lifetime was one hundred years, and twenty years, and seven years; the years of Sarah's life. Sarah died in Kiriath-arba, which is Hebron, in the land of Canaan; and Abraham came to eulogize Sarah and to bewail her. Abraham rose up from the presence of his dead and spoke to the children of Heth, saying: 'I am an alien and a resident among you; grant me possession of a grave with you, that I may bury my dead from before me.'" Rashi comments: **"Sarah's lifetime was one hundred years, and twenty years, and seven years:** *This is why the word 'years' was written at each category, to tell you that each one is expounded on its own: to teach you that when*

she was a hundred years old, she was like twenty years old with respect to sin: Just as one who is twenty years old is considered as if she had not sinned, for she is not liable to punishment, so too, when she was a hundred years old she was free of sin. And when she was twenty years old, she was like seven years old with regard to beauty. The years of Sarah's life: They were all equal in goodness."

Ramban differs from Rashi in his interpretation of the meaning ascribed to the verse's repetition of "years." He feels that the text is not making reference to Sarah's extraordinary qualities. If this were so, Ramban argues, then why does the Torah use an almost identical characterization in detailing the end of Ishmael (*Genesis* 25:17), for there we would certainly not ascribe rectitude to the forefather of the Arab nations? According to Ramban, therefore, the Rabbis' accolades about our mother Sarah really stem from the redundant expression "the years of the life of Sarah," which includes and equates them all.

A statement by a rabbi in Bava Basra (15a) that Iyov was a fictitious figure, whose purpose was to teach men resignation, includes lengthy quotations from Iyov, and even an accolade by Satan about Avraham. "Sovereign of the Universe," the Gemara quotes Satan in Iyov, "I have not found one like Your servant Avraham. For You did say to him, 'To you I will give it [Canaan],' and when he wanted to bury Sarah, he could not find a [burial] place, yet he did not complain against Your ways." Satan was thus casting aspersions on Iyov, who was being portrayed as unequal to Avraham. An interesting comparison may be made between this testimony and that of Balaam the wicked, both of which attest to the greatness of Israel.

> The Mishnah in Pirkei Avos (5:3) teaches that Avraham Avinu endured ten trials in good stead. According to the commentaries on Avos, the last trial was the burial of Sarah. Even though Avraham Avinu met the monumental challenge of Akeidas

Yitzchak, where he displayed his willingness to perform Hashem's bidding at all costs, Hashem had one challenge left for him. This is very hard to understand. Why was it necessary to test Avraham again? Rabbi Moshe Eisemann explains that we have a tendency to expect that once we have proven ourselves, we believe we should receive an enthusiastic pat on the back for our efforts. If we are challenged again and again, the natural response would be one of indignation: "Have I not proven myself already? What more do you want!" The last trial of Avraham was to show the world his true mettle. He did not accomplish what he did for recognition or for the commendation of a job well done. He did so because it was Hashem's will. A servant of Hashem performs his tasks without regard as to how much his work is appreciated. Doing Hashem's will for His sake means to accept the challenges of life without regard to the frequency and difficulty of the endeavor. He stood firm in the last trial and did not question Hashem by asking, "Why are You doing this to me? Have I not proven my loyalty already?" We see that Avraham endured the last trial as perfectly as he had the previous trials. Avraham Avinu was the quintessential servant of Hashem, one who serves out of love for his Maker.

Parashas Toldos

The *Sedrah* begins:

> "And these are the generations of Isaac, son of Abraham: Abraham fathered Isaac. And Isaac was forty years old when he took Rebecca, daughter of Bethuel the Aramean, from Paddan Aram, sister of Laban the Aramean, as a wife for himself. Isaac pleaded with Hashem on behalf of his wife, because she was barren. Hashem allowed Himself to be entreated by him, and his wife Rebecca conceived."

Rashi comments: **"And these are the generations of Isaac:** Jacob and Esau, who are spoken of further on in the passage. Abraham fathered Isaac: Since the verse wrote 'Isaac son of Abraham,' it had to say, 'Abraham fathered Isaac,' for the scoffers of the generation were saying, 'Sarah became pregnant from Abimelech' [she was detained in his harem (Genesis 20:2), but Hashem warned him in a dream not to come near Sarah, for if he did his life would be forfeit]. 'For she had spent many years with Abraham as his wife, yet she did not become pregnant from him.' What did the Holy One, Blessed is He, do? He fashioned the form of Isaac's face to resemble Abraham's, and everyone attested, 'Abraham fathered Isaac.'"

THERE IS DIVISION BETWEEN THE COMMENTATORS ON THIS VERSE AND previous occurrences where the term *toldos*, literally "generations," appears. According to Rashi, it may stand also for experiences which either precede and follow a passage containing this term. Rashi's view is not totally in accord with that of Ramban. Ramban explains that the term refers to what follows — specifically, to children. Rashi's view is that in some, but not all instances, it may refer to posterity. However, a homiletical explanation may be offered that reconciles Rashi's position with Ramban's — in that worthy posterity can come only from people who live nobly and pursue experiences that are honorable. (See *Parashas Noach*.)

It is significant that our mothers — Sarah, Rivkah, and Rachel (excluding Leah, who was blessed with fecundity from the first) — were denied children for a long time after their marriage. Despite the fact that hundreds of millions of women bring children into the world in the normal course of nature, in the cases of all our mothers, including Leah, there was Divine involvement from the very inception of this blessing in order to show that children who are born into every family are a gift from Hashem Yisbarach, whether or not their parents realize it. Such a gift demands reciprocity, which entails training children to obey His Will.

> *Divine intervention on behalf of all our mothers is described in the Talmud. The Talmud teaches (Taanis 2a) that three "keys" remain in Hashem's hands and are not delegated to subordinates. One of the three is the "key of pregnancy." Hashem Himself decrees if a child will be conceived or not; this decree is not assigned to the angels. All the events of the natural world are administered by Hashem and are delegated to His ambassadors, the angels, to perform. On a day-to-day basis, the natural world order — such as the ecosystem, photosynthesis, and the food chain — do not require Divine intervention. But procreation among humans is not part of the natural order of the world. Contrary to popular belief, our sages teach us that procreation requires Divine intervention for every occurrence to come to fruition. Every child born is indeed a gift from Hashem, and as such we are obligated to express the proper appreciation to Him, and to care for this gift according to the instruction manual, the Torah. Therefore, it is incumbent upon every father and mother to train their children to obey His will, to love Him, His Torah, and His people.*

Parashas Vayeitzei

THE *SEDRAH* BEGINS:

"And Jacob departed from Beer-sheba and went to Haran. He encountered the place and spent the night there because the sun had set; he took from the stones of the place, put them around his head, and lay down in that place. And he dreamt, and behold! A ladder was set earthward and its top reached heavenward; and behold! angels of G-d were ascending and descending on it. And behold! Hashem was standing over him, and He said, "I am Hashem, G-d of Abraham your father and G-d of Isaac; the ground upon which you are lying, to you will I give it and to your descendants."

Rashi comments: **"And Jacob departed:** *Owing to the fact that because the daughters of Canaan were bad in the eyes of Isaac his father and that Esau went to Ishmael to take a wife, Scripture interrupted the subject of the episode of Jacob and wrote, 'And Esau saw that Isaac had blessed. . . .' And once Scripture made its point regarding Esau, it returned to its original topic, Jacob's departure. And Jacob departed: Scripture needed only to have written 'And Jacob went to Haran.' Why does it mention his departure? It tells us that the departure of a righteous person from a place makes an impression, for at the time that a righteous person is in the city, he is its magnificence, its splendor, and its grandeur. However, once he has departed from there, its magnificence, its splendor, and its grandeur have also gone away."*

Rashi further states that the place at which Yaakov arrived was Mount Moriah, as is stated at the *Akeidah*, "and he saw the place from afar" (*Genesis* 22:4), which was the destination, "the land of Moriah," to which Hashem directed Avraham to go (*Genesis* 22:2). Our Rabbis teach that Yaacov originated the *Maariv* (evening) prayers there.

At the *Akeidah,* Rashi comments that the land of Moriah is Jerusalem. By *halachah,* Jews are forbidden to set foot upon this sanctified ground because of our ritual impurity. Thus, Yaakov providentially stopped on this Mount.

Rashi states in *Genesis* 28:17 that the Heavenly Temple is situated immediately opposite the Earthly Temple. This is our assurance that this sacred shrine is not lost to us, but that *l'asid lavo,* in the future, it will be reconstituted in all its ancient glory, just as the Heavenly Temple cannot be touched or moved from its place. How this will come about is included in the promise that Hashem made to Yaakov in this *parashah*. As Ramban states, Hashem promises that He will be with Yaakov wherever he is, guard him, and rescue him from his old enemies, Edom and Ishmael. And then all nations will submit to His Will, "And Hashem shall be King over the earth, and on that day Hashem will be One and His Name One" (*Zechariah* 14:9).

It is interesting to contrast Yaakov's experience with that of his father, Yitzchak, in whose behalf Eliezer, the master of Avraham's household, went to the same place, Charan, in search of a wife for him. Eliezer took with him ten camels laden with the wealth of Avraham — precious stones and pearls. However, regarding Yaakov's travel to the same destination and for a similar purpose, Yaakov passed over the Jordan with his staff and nothing more to his name, save the clothes on his back, and a tremendous faith in the great destiny that awaited him. It was his determination to bring into the world a family who would be the ancestors of a unique nation, a nation that through all the vicissitudes of its checkered career has played such an important role in the spiritual development of mankind, that kept him going.

> *Yaakov Avinu left Beer-sheba empty-handed, as a Jew enters galus (exile). Rav Gedaliah Schorr (1910-1979) explained that this is the Sedrah of*

galus. When Yaakov reached Mount Moriah, he dreamed about the galus of his descendants. He foresaw the destruction of the Temple that would stand on that spot. That evening, as Yaakov rested on the sanctified ground, he absorbed its holiness and was fortified for his exile to Haran. For the duration of his sojourn he was attached by a spiritual tether to Mount Moriah, anchoring him to Israel and to all that is holy. This is the legacy which Yaakov Avinu instilled in his offspring. Every Jew at one time or another will find himself in his own Haran, a place where the ways of the Torah are challenged and attacked. Wherever he may be and whatever he may endure, the Jew tenaciously remains anchored to the Torah and its teachings. This is the gift of Yaakov Avinu to all those who proudly associate themselves with his name, B'nei Yisrael.

Parashas Vayishlach

The Sedrah begins:

"And Jacob sent messengers before him to Esau his brother in the land of Seir, the field of Edom. He charged them saying, 'Thus shall you say to my lord, to Esau: So said your servant Jacob: I have sojourned with Laban and have lingered until now. I have acquired oxen and donkeys, flocks, servants and maidservants, and I am sending to tell my lord to find favor in your eyes.'"

> *Rashi comments: **"And Jacob sent messengers** (Hebrew: malachim, a homonym which means 'messengers' or 'angels'): actual angels. I have sojourned (with Laban): I did not become a dignitary or a notable but remained a mere sojourner. It does not befit you to hate me over the blessings of your father who blessed me, 'Be a lord over your brothers,' for it has not been fulfilled in me. Alternatively, the numerical value of garti, 'I have sojourned,' is six hundred and thirteen, as if to say, 'I sojourned with Laban, the evil one, yet I kept the six hundred thirteen commandments and did not learn from his evil actions.'"*

THE WORD MALACH IS THE SAME WORD IN HEBREW FOR BOTH messenger and angel. That angels should be in the service of Yaakov, as Rashi interprets the word messenger, is a remarkable tribute to the greatness of the man and an indication of his spiritual purity. Can other mortals achieve such a degree of rectitude? If we conduct ourselves in conformity with the edicts of our sacred heritage, can we too expect Divine aid in our daily doings to achieve in excess of that which our own poor powers can accomplish? Is this what the Psalmist meant when he said, "It is vain for you to rise up early, to sit up late, to eat the bread of sorrows, for so He gives His beloved in sleep" (*Psalms* 127:2)? There was only one Yaakov, but all of us have the potential to merit Heavenly messengers to aid us in our deeds and strivings, despite our obvious frailties, and who will guide us to safety, security, and a fair share of happiness, individually as well as collectively in our national capacity. After all, the name Yaakov, as is pointed out by Ramban, is also a collective designation: "For the portion of Hashem is His people; Yaakov is the lot of His inheritance" (*Deuteronomy* 32:9).

> *As mentioned, Rashi explains, "the numerical value of garti, 'I have sojourned,' is six hundred and thirteen, as if to say, 'I sojourned with Lavan, the evil one, yet I kept*

the six hundred thirteen commandments and did not learn from his evil actions.'" Why is Rashi redundant? If Yaakov kept the six hundred thirteen commandments, is it not obvious that he did not learn from Lavan's evil ways? Why did Yaakov emphasize to Esav that he diligently kept the commandments and also that he did not learn from Lavan's deeds? Rabbi Yaakov Yitzchok Ruderman (1900-1987), founder of Yeshivas Ner Israel of Baltimore, answers these questions with penetrating insight. Rashi is teaching us that a person may properly fulfill all the commandments incumbent upon him and still conduct himself in a reprehensible fashion. Ramban (Vayikra 19:2) describes the phenomenon of the "naval b'rshus haTorah," a person who is an abomination while he remains within the framework of the Torah. Adherence to the letter of the law as described in the Torah does not guarantee righteousness. A righteous man is just as sensitive to the goals of the Torah and to the spirit of the law as he is to his commitment to adhering to the letter of the law. Without this sensitivity, it is possible to perform all the mitzvos and still remain as evil as Lavan. Therefore, Yaakov Avinu explicitly described to Esav, "Not only have I been firm in my commitment to the laws of the Torah, but I have also remained true to the spirit of the Torah and have not learned from the evil ways of Lavan."

Parashas Vayeishev

The *Sedrah* begins:

"Jacob settled in the land of his father's sojourning, in the land of Canaan. These are the offspring of Jacob: Joseph, at the age of seventeen years, was a shepherd with his brothers by the flock, and he was a youth with the sons of Bilhah and with the sons of Zilpah, his father's wives; and Joseph brought unto his father evil reports of them. Now Israel loved Joseph more than all his sons, since he was a child of his old age; and he made him a fine woolen tunic. His brothers saw that it was he whom their father loved most of all his brothers, so they hated him and were not able to speak to him peaceably."

Rashi comments: **"Jacob settled:** *After Scripture has written for you (the circumstances) of the settling of Esau and his offspring in a concise manner, it explains to you in detail the settling of Jacob and his offspring in a lengthy manner — for Jacob and his children are important enough before the Omnipresent to dwell at length about them. Similarly, you find regarding the ten generations from Adam to Noah, "So-and-so fathered So-and-so," but when it came to Noah, Scripture dwelled at length on him. Similarly, regarding the ten generations from Noah to Abraham, Scripture was brief about them, but once it got to Abraham, it dwelled at length on him. This can be compared to a pearl that fell into the sand. A person feels the sand and sifts it in a sifter until he finds the pearl. But once he finds it, he discards the pebbles from his hand and takes the pearl."*

MALBIM POINTS OUT THAT THIS NARRATIVE SHOWS THE ULTIMATE GOOD that Hashem has intended for our people, commencing with the descent to Egypt and the foundation of a powerful nation.

The pasuk states, "These are the offspring of Jacob: Joseph." Why does the verse limit the children of Yaakov Avinu by mentioning only Yosef? Rabbi Yisroel Meir Kagan (1838-1933), the Chofetz Chaim, explained that this episode is a microcosm of the Jewish experience throughout the ages, with Yosef representing all Jews. Yosef is torn away from his family in the prime of his life. Despite every effort to destroy him, he remains indestructible. Ultimately, he is sold as a slave in a heathen land, where the Egyptian culture is the antithesis of all that he learned at his father's side. It is only natural to assume that he would not survive in his new environment. Yet before long, Yosef ascends to unimaginable heights within the hierarchy of Pharaoh's Egypt, and eventually those who preferred to destroy him bow at his feet. This is the story of the Jews. Time and again, they were torn asunder from their homeland. Nation after nation attempted to eradicate the Jews and their Torah. Yet despite their attempts, the Jews endured and rose to the top. As we recite in the Haggadah, "In every generation there are those who attempt to destroy the Jews, and the Holy One, Blessed is He, saves us from their hands." With this faith we eagerly await the final redemption when we will attain the peak of our spiritual height and influence on the world so that we may teach the other nations the ways of Hashem.

PARASHAS MIKEITZ

THE *SEDRAH* BEGINS:

> *"It happened at the end of two years to the day: Pharaoh was dreaming that he was standing over the 'canal' [the Nile], when suddenly out of the Nile there emerged seven cows of beautiful appearance and robust flesh, and they were grazing in the swamp. Then seven other cows emerged after them from the Nile, of poor appearance and gaunt flesh; and they stood next to the cows on the bank of the canal. And the cows of poor appearance and gaunt flesh ate the seven robust cows of beautiful appearance — and Pharaoh awoke."*

> Rashi comments: **"It happened at the end:** The word *mikeitz* is to be understood as Targum Onkelos renders it — 'at the end.' And all words related to *keitz* mean 'end.'"

THE EXPIRATION OF TWO YEARS MENTIONED AT THE BEGINNING OF THE *Sedrah* is interpreted by Rashi as a reflection upon Yosef because he relied for his freedom upon the chief butler, whom he implored to secure help from Pharaoh; instead he should have relied on Hashem (*Rashi* on *Genesis* 40:23). Indeed, Rashi spares nobody in his quest for truth.

Rashi continues: **"Over the canal:** All other rivers are not called 'canals,' only the Nile. For the entire land is made into many man-made canals, and the Nile goes up into them and waters them (fills them with water) because rains do not regularly fall in Egypt as they do in other lands. Of beautiful appearance: It is a sign of days of abundance, when people appear nice to one another, for people are then not miserly toward each other."

Rashi's comment that in good times all are well disposed toward each other throws a light upon how anti-Semitism sometimes gains ground, for when times are bad, people will seek a scapegoat, and Jews are the convenient ones, as we well know!

Ramban elucidates further that the cows symbolize plowing; the ears of corn, harvest. Yosef understood the character of the dream — that there would be an abundance in Egypt and famine in all the surrounding lands. When after interpreting the dream, Yosef gave Pharaoh advice as to organizing machinery during the years of plentiful for the years of famine, it was not gratuitous advice: it was a part of the interpretation. This he gathered from the verse, "And the cows of poor appearance and gaunt flesh ate the seven cows of beautiful appearance and robust," which showed him that there would have to be plenty accumulated during the years of plenty if people were to survive during the lean years.

> The Midrash associates the verse, "It happened at the end of two years to the day: Pharaoh was dreaming," with the verse in Iyov (28:3), "He placed an end to the darkness." Hashem determined the duration of Yosef's incarceration, and when that time elapsed, Pharaoh had his dream. Rabbi Yosef Dov Soloveitchik (1820-1892), the Beis HaLevi, explains that this Midrash informs us that we live in a world of cause and effect. Logically, we would assume that Pharaoh's dream was the cause of Yosef's release from prison. However, the Midrash teaches us that the opposite is true. Yosef's release from prison caused Pharaoh's dream. Since Hashem predetermined the length of Yosef's imprisonment, when his sentence expired, Hashem made Pharaoh dream. Even though in appearance Pharaoh's dream triggered Yosef's release, in reality the need to free Yosef from prison initiated Pharaoh's dream. This is the lesson of the Midrash. The point of the verse, "It happened at the end of two years to the day," is that it was time for Yosef to be liberated and that, therefore, "Pharaoh was dreaming."

Parashas Vayigash

The Sedrah begins:

Then Judah approached him and said, "If you please, my lord, may your servant speak a word in my lord's ears, and may your anger not flair up at your servant; for you are like Pharaoh. My lord asked his servants, saying, 'Have you a father or brother?' And we said to my lord, 'We have an old father and a young child of his old age; his brother is dead, he alone is left to his mother, and his father loves him.' Then you said to your servants, 'Bring him down to me, and I will set my eye on him.' We said to my lord, 'The youth cannot leave his father, for should he leave his father he would die.'"

Rashi comments: **"Then Judah approached him ... 'may your servant speak a word in my lord's ears:'** *May my words enter your ears. And may your anger not flare up: From here you learn that Judah spoke to Joseph harshly. For you are like Pharaoh: You are as esteemed in my eyes as the king. This is the verse's simple meaning. And its exegetical interpretation is as follows: Your end will be to be stricken over Benjamin with tzaraas as Pharaoh was stricken through Benjamin's great-grandmother Sarah, for the one night that he detained her."*

THERE IS A LACK OF UNANIMITY AMONG THE COMMENTATORS ON HOW to view Yehudah's impassioned appeal to Yosef for the release of Binyamin. Yehudah, of course, knew that persuading Yosef was a difficult job. But he was faced with a terrible adversary, so it seemed to the brethren, and to extricate Binyamin from this man's clutches was a formidable task. Rashi tells us that Yehudah used a mailed fist encased in a silk glove.

Ramban's view is, "Yehudah's words are only to supplicate, to stir Yosef's compassion." For with all the cards being stacked against him, what else was there left for Yehudah to do?

Rabbi Samson Raphael Hirsch (*Genesis* 44:18) pauses on "speak a word in my lord's ears": A nice expression if one wants to give someone something to consider very deeply. I will not appeal to your feelings but direct myself to your mind and intelligence. Rabbi Hirsch's idea is, therefore, the opposite of Ramban's.

Rabbi J. H. Hertz provides a rhapsody of praise for Yehudah: "The pathos and beauty of Yehudah 's plea on behalf of Binyamin have retained their appeal to man's heart throughout the ages. The spirit of self-sacrifice which Yehudah 's speech reveals, offering to remain as a slave in Binyamin's place, has its parallel in the life story of Moshe, who besought G-d to blot out his name from the Book of Life unless the people of Israel were saved with him (*Exodus* 32:32)." Who would deny that this praise of Yehudah is well merited?

A modern, legalistic explanation may also be offered. Yehudah's problem was essentially a legal one, to defend his client who was libelously accused, the evidence being against him. In such a case, the advocate is well advised to recapitulate the well-known facts of the case, in the hope that something may develop in the course of his argument that will save his client. That is what Yehudah did. After all, everything that he said was known to Yosef for all intents and purposes.

> *Rabbi Yaakov Kamenetsky (1890-1986) addresses the contradiction in Rashi's comments. Rashi begins by explaining that Yehudah praised Yosef: "You are like Pharaoh: You are as esteemed in my eyes as the king." But Rashi continues with the Midrashic interpretation as follows: "Your end will be to be stricken over Binyamin with tzaraas as Pharaoh was stricken through Binyamin's great-grandmother Sarah." Where did the sages see in Yehudah's words a confrontation with Pharaoh? He simply attempted*

to supplicate, to stir Yosef's compassion, as Ramban explained. How do we reconcile the simple meaning with the Midrashic interpretation?

Rabbi Kamenetsky explained that first we must understand how Yosef appeared to Yehudah. Yosef was a man who single-handedly arranged the Egyptian economic system and the support of its neighboring countries. A brilliant leader possessing a magical goblet to divine the future, he was superior to Pharaoh. Indeed, if Yehudah intended to praise this man and stir his compassion, he would pour lavish praise upon Yosef by commenting on Yosef's profound wisdom and fear of G-d. Why did he limit his praise to "you are like Pharaoh"? Our sages understood that even though the simple message to Yosef was "you are as esteemed in my eyes as the king," there was another message: Yehudah conveyed to Yosef threats that he was sure would intimidate him. Therefore, it is possible to reconcile many different explanations of the verse, since Yehudah spoke to Yosef on several levels.

Parashas Vayechi

The Sedrah begins:

"Jacob lived in the land of Egypt seventeen years; and the days of Jacob, the years of his life, were one hundred and forty-seven years. The time approached for Israel to die, so he called for his son, for Joseph, and said to him, 'Please, if I have found favor in your eyes, please place your hand under my thigh and do kindness and truth with me.

Please do not bury me in Egypt. And I will lie down with my fathers, and you shall transport me out of Egypt and bury me in their grave.' He said, 'I will do in accordance with your words.'"

Rashi comments: *"**Jacob lived:** Why is this passage closed? Because once our forefather, Jacob, passed away, the eyes and heart of Israel were closed because of the suffering of the enslavement, for the Egyptians began to enslave them."*

IT WOULD SEEM THAT THE LONGEVITY OF THE FATHERS OF OUR PEOPLE WAS gradually lessening. Yitzchak lived the longest. Avraham, his father, was short of Yitzchak's age by five years; Rashi explains that this was Providential so that Avraham would not see the extent of Esav's corruption. Yitzchak appears to have been wondering whether he would reach the age of his mother, Sarah, one hundred twenty-seven or that of his father, Avraham, one hundred and seventy-five, so Yitzchak outdistanced his father by five years (*Rashi, Genesis* 27:2). Levi lived the longest of all Yaakov's children, one hundred thirty-seven years (*Rashi Exodus* 6:16). Yosef lived only one hundred ten years. This descending longevity may be explained by the diminishing ages of man after Adam's times. Also this longevity may have become shorter in proportion to an individual's trouble and grief. For example, Yaakov had experienced much strife and suffering owing to Esav, Dinah, and Yosef. Levi and Shimon were involved in the difficult Shechem controversy. Yosef from his early youth was a troubled man until he reached the age of thirty, at which time he was summoned to Pharaoh and named second in command — a formidable task indeed!

Why does Rashi assert that the closure of *Vayechi* accounts for the conclusion that with the passing of Yaakov the bondage of his children commenced? As long as one of the tribes was domiciled there, the oppression did not commence (*Rashi, Exodus* 6:16), certainly not as long as Yosef was viceroy, and he occupied that post for fifty-four years after Yaakov's passing. The answer is that the Torah is not referring to bondage per se, but to the change in the status of the Jews from visitors to citizens of the country, along with their assumption of all the corresponding obligations of citizenship.

> *Rabbi Shmuel Borenstein (d. 1926) comments in his work Shem M'Shmuel on Shemos that the slavery in Egypt occurred in two stages. First, the Jews slipped into a spiritual bondage. Afterwards, the physical bondage began. Rashi comments that when Yaakov died, "the eyes and heart of Israel were closed." This refers to the loss of their spiritual level. Later, when the last of those who traveled from Canaan to Egypt with Yaakov died, the physical bondage began. Hashem did not impose the rigors of physical slavery until they were already in the grips of spiritual atrophy. This concept is also described at the time of the destruction of the Temple. The Talmud (Sanhedrin 96b) teaches that when the Babylonians destroyed the first Temple, they "ground wheat which had been ground already," meaning that the spiritual Temple was already destroyed when the Romans destroyed the physical edifice. Similarly, the exile of the Jews was only the physical realization of the chasm already separating them from Hashem.*

SEFER SHEMOS
PARASHAS SHEMOS

THE *SEDRAH* BEGINS:

"And these are the names of the Children of Israel who came to Egypt with Jacob; each man and his household came: Reuben, Simeon, Levi, and Judah; Issachar, Zebulun, and Benjamin; Dan and Naphtali; Gad and Asher. And all the persons who emerged from Jacob's loins were seventy souls, and Joseph was in Egypt."

Rashi comments: **"And these are the names of the Children of Israel:** Although He counted them by their names in their lifetimes, He counted them again after their deaths to make known how precious they are to Him. The Children of Israel are counted by name because they are compared to the stars which He brings out and brings in by number and by their names, as it says (Isaiah 40:26), 'He Who takes out their hosts by number, He calls them all by name.'"

FOLLOWING RASHI'S VIEW, THE OPENING OF THE BOOK OF *SHEMOS* IS A paean of joy to Hashem for His love of our people, commencing with our father Avraham, continuing with the tribes;

throughout the wandering by our ancestors — already a numerous nation — in the wilderness; during the era of our national independence; during the period of the bitter *galus*; and as we confidently expect at the impending final redemption, speedily and in our days, when Hashem will continue with His unchanging love for our people. However, love of Hashem for His people, Israel, is a two-way street, as it were, for we are duty-bound to love Him reciprocally. From this also flows *Ahavas Yisrael*, love for our brethren, love for the sojourner and love for our fellow man. The entire relationship between Hashem and His people is a love story, as we find in the homiletic tradition of *Song of Songs*.

Hashem's love for His people recurs in numerous passages throughout the Torah. As it says in *Pirkei Avos* (5:4): "With ten trials our father Abraham was tried, and he stood firm in them all — to make known how great was the love of our father Abraham." This was the foundation of the love between Hashem and His people, followed by His love for the tribes, cited at the beginning of *Shemos;* similarly, in *Numbers* (1:1) we read, "Hashem spoke to Moses in the wilderness of Sinai, saying, 'Take a census of the entire assembly.' " Rashi notes that because Hashem loved his people, He counted them frequently. Thus we are continually made aware of the reciprocal love existing between Hashem and the Jewish people, which is the basis for man's obligation to his fellow man, as it is written: "You shall not hate your brother in your heart . . . . you shall love your fellow as yourself: I am Hashem" (*Leviticus* 19:17-18).

> As cited above, Rashi comments that "the Children of Israel are counted by name because they are compared to the stars which He brings out and brings in by number and by their names ... to make known how precious they are to Him." To whom does Hashem want to make it known? Rabbi Yehudah Aryeh Leib Alter (1847-1905), the Sefas Emes, explained that Hashem wanted to make B'nei Yisrael aware of how precious they are. Every one of them is endowed with enormous potential to light

up the world like the stars that illuminate the darkness of the night. Furthermore, just as each star has its own name and place in the solar system, so too does each Jew have a unique role: to brighten, in his own special way, the world around him with the truth of the Torah and the love of Hashem.

Parashas Va'eira

The *Sedrah* begins:

"And G-d spoke to Moses and said to him, 'I am Hashem. And I appeared to Abraham, to Isaac, and to Jacob as G-d Almighty; through My Name Hashem I did not become known to them.'"

Rashi comments: **"And G-d spoke to Moses:** He spoke to Moses with words of rebuke for speaking harshly and saying (Exodus 5:22), 'Why have You harmed this people?' **And He said to him, 'I am Hashem.'** With this declaration of His Name to Moses, Hashem wishes to say, 'I am faithful to pay a good reward to those who walk before Me. I have not sent you in vain; rather I have sent you to fulfill My words that I spoke to the forefathers.' "

Where did Rashi derive the fact that Hashem reproached Moshe for saying, "Why have You harmed this people; why have You sent Me?" Rabbeinu Eliyahu Mizrachi (d. 1525) explains that the Name "G-d" is mentioned here, which signifies the Divine Attribute of Strict Justice. Rabbi Yehudah Loewe, the *Maharal*

(1526-1609), explains (in *Gur Aryeh*) that it says "And G-d spoke," whereas the usual expression in the Torah is "and Hashem spoke." The terms "G-d" and "Hashem" are distinct in their use. The first describes the Deity, stressing His justice and rulership; the second emphasizes His lovingkindness. It is difficult to find other places in the Torah which detail Hashem's taking Moshe to task. In the present instance, both Moshe and the people were possessed of despair, in view of the additional hardships which Pharaoh decreed following Moshe's demand for their liberation. This undoubtedly accounted for Moshe's response.

Perhaps the nearest approach to this is when Hashem first commissioned Moshe for the task of liberation. Moshe tried energetically to withdraw from his appointed mission, and Hashem was correspondingly angry with him. These experiences testify that Moshe our teacher, who is described in the Thirteen Principles of Faith as "the father of all prophets, both those who preceded and those who followed him," is portrayed by our tradition as a human being. Our greatest personality — and Moshe was certainly that! — might err, but he rose to sublimest heights, as Hashem Himself said: "In My entire house he is trusted" (*Numbers* 12:7).

> *The Torah goes to great lengths to establish that Moses was indeed a human being. Later in this Sedrah (6:14-27), there is a detailed description of Moshe and Aharon's family tree. Why is the narration interrupted with their genealogical table? Rabbi Samson Raphael Hirsch (1808-1888) explains that until this point Moshe and Aharon's efforts were completely frustrated. However, from this point onward their unique triumphant mission commenced. Therefore, it became a real necessity, first of all, to establish their origin and their absolutely ordinary human nature. From the earliest times various societies invested certain men with a "godly" origin on account of their supposed "godlike" deeds. Our Moshe was a man, remained a*

man, and will always remain just a man. On the day when Hashem first spoke to him in Egypt, people knew his parents and grandparents, his uncles and aunts, and all his cousins — his origins and relations. They knew him for eighty years in his perfectly human nature, subject to all the failings and weaknesses, to all the limits and requirements, of human beings, just like all other men among whom he had been born and raised. Moshe and Aharon were men like all other men whom Hashem had selected for His great work.

Parashas Bo

The *Sedrah* begins:

"Hashem said to Moses, 'Come to Pharaoh, for I have made his heart and the heart of his servants stubborn so that I shall place these signs of Mine in his midst and so that you may relate in the ears of your son and your son's son the series of deeds which I have wrought upon Egypt and My signs that I have placed among them, that you may know that I am Hashem.' "

Rashi comments: **"Hashem said to Moses, 'Come to Pharaoh'** *and warn him."*

IN REFERRING TO THE DIRECTION GIVEN TO MOSHE — *Bo* ("come") to give Pharaoh a warning — Rashi is explaining to us that it relates to Hebrew jurisprudence, which demands that a person who is about to commit a crime must be warned of the consequences thereof before he is criminally liable, for there is a difference in degree of culpability between intentional and inadvertent offenses. The purpose of *hasra'ah* (warning), as the term is designated, is to give a prospective offender a chance to withdraw from his proposed course, lest he claim that he was not aware of its criminality. Such is not true in common law, which is based on the essential assumption that everyone is presumed to be aware of the law. A judge may use discretion in pronouncing sentence upon an inadvertent offender, but this does not change the nature of the crime. There are certain crimes which are designated by law or by statutory enactment as being of lesser degree if not due to malicious afterthought, but still ignorance of the law is not considered a valid excuse.

Thus, according to Rashi, the mission of Moshe our teacher to Pharaoh was to indicate to him that he was treading on dangerous ground, declaring to him the inevitable grave results of his actions.

The verse continues, "For I have made his heart and the heart of his servants stubborn so that I shall place these signs of Mine in his midst." This raises the perennial question: Was the Egyptian ruling class to blame for the oppression of our ancestors, since they would appear to have had no choice in the matter? Rashi answers in *Sedra Va'eira* (*Exodus* 7:3): " 'And I shall harden Pharaoh's heart': Now that Pharaoh has behaved wickedly and has brazenly opposed Me, and it has been revealed before Me that there is no goodness of spirit among idolatrous nations to set themselves wholeheartedly to repent, it is good that his heart should become hardened so that I may increase My miraculous signs against him — and you, Israel, will thereby recognize My might." This is the method of Hashem. He brings punishment upon the sinful nations so that Israel may hear of it and fear Him.

> *The concept mentioned above, that punishment is brought upon sinful nations "so that Israel may hear of it and fear Him," is based upon the teachings of the Talmud. The Talmud (Yevamos 63a) states that*

punishment is brought upon the world in order to prompt Yisrael to repent their sins. This idea is based on the prophecy of Zephaniah (3:6-7): "I have destroyed the nations; their roads and plazas are desolate... I said, 'Now you will fear Me and learn the lesson so that you will not be destroyed.'" However, the question lingers: Why shouldn't the sinful nations be punished, regardless of whether or not Israel will learn from their downfall? To explain this we must understand the difference between Divine retribution and the punishment dispensed by human governments. Human punishment for criminal activity is essentially a form of revenge. The criminal deserves to suffer commensurate with the suffering he meted out to his victim. In a kinder legal system, if a punishment is deemed cruel and unusual, it is replaced with incarceration, thus removing the criminal from society. Divine retribution is different. When Hashem punishes, it is not an act of vengeance. Hashem punishes in a fashion that can serve as a lesson to the criminal, to help him understand from the punishment the nature of his crime and to prompt him to repent (Berachos 5a). Evidently, this process does not work well with the nations of the world. They do not repent when faced with natural disasters and illnesses. Therefore, why should Hashem continue to punish them for their crimes? To answer this, the Talmud teaches us that the sinful nations are still punished even if they do not "get the message," because B'nei Yisrael are expected to take heed, increase their fear of Heaven, and repent whenever they hear of calamities around the world.

Parashas Beshalach

The *Sedrah* begins:

"It happened when Pharaoh sent the people that G-d did not lead them by way of the land of the Philistines because it was near, for G-d said, 'Perhaps the people will reconsider when they see a war, and they will return to Egypt.'"

Rashi comments: **"It happened when Pharaoh sent the people that G-d did not lead them:** The term *lo nacham* means "He did not lead them," similar to the word *nechei* in the phrase 'Go, lead the people' and to the word *tanche* in the phrase "As you go, it will lead you." **Because it was near:** And it is easy to return to Egypt by that route. **When they see a war:** Such as the war referred to in the verse 'And the Amalekite and the Canaanite descended, etc.' Had the Israelites gone out of Egypt by a direct route, they would have returned. If now, when He took them roundabout by a circuitous route, they said, 'Let us appoint a head and return to Egypt,' had He taken them by a straight one, all the more so would they have wanted to return to Egypt, since the direct route would have allowed a quicker return."

Rashi comments that Hashem did not lead them by way of the land of the Philistines, explaining the term *nacham* as coming from the word meaning "to lead and guide." There are two aspects of guiding the forward movement of a large group of people: one involves leading them, pure and simple; the other, promoting an ultimate goal. A common example of the first is when in normal times an army sergeant leads his men from place to place or from one location to the point of dispersion, both of which involve ordinary physical direction with no further involvement. However, when an Israeli officer took his men into battle, his slogan was *achari* ("follow me"), different from commands issued in other armies, when as often as not the commander orders his men to engage the enemy while he keeps at a discreet distance from the fray. This sort of leadership is in line with Rashi's interpretation of *nacham,* to lead and guide.

Going from the mundane to the sublime, so to speak, we read (*Exodus* 13:21): "Hashem went before them by day in a pillar of cloud to have them led along the way, and by night in a pillar of fire to give them light so that they could travel by day and by night." The same pillar of cloud moved from the lead to assume a position behind them at the Sea of Reeds when there was imminent danger of an attack by the Egyptian enemy, in order to confuse the Egyptians with darkness and finally to lead to their annihilation through Hashem's miraculous splitting of the sea. Such leadership or guidance, protection, and miracles all rolled together can be brought about only through Divine intercession.

This loving care and provision for the security of our ancestors in the wilderness is fitly memorialized by Moshe Rabbeinu in *Deuteronomy* 32:10,11: "He encircled him; He made him comprehending; He guarded him like the pupil of His eye. Like an eagle arising from his nest, hovering over its young." May it be His will that we may experience His lovingkindness in our day and age to lead us from this *galus* (Exile) to the land of our fathers "with our youngsters and with our elders..."

> *Rabbeinu Yaakov (c.1275-c.1340), the author of the Tur Shulchan Aruch (Code of Jewish Law), writes that the mitzvah of dwelling in a succah during the festival of Succos is a reminder of the protective clouds provided by Hashem that surrounded the Jews as they traveled from Egypt through the wilderness on their way to Israel. The question is asked: Why do we commemorate the clouds and not the manna that fell from the skies for forty years to nourish the Jews in the wilderness? Why do we commemorate the clouds*

and not the well of Miriam that followed the Jews throughout their travels to provide them with life-sustaining water? Of these three — the clouds, the manna, and the well — only the protective clouds were unnecessary. B'nei Yisrael could not survive without food and water, but the clouds were not life sustaining; they provided only comfort and protection from the elements. Hence, we must recognize that Hashem in His lovingkindness provides us with everything, not just with the necessities.

Parashas Yisro

The Sedrah begins:

"Jethro, the priest of Midian, Moses' father-in-law, heard all that Hashem did to Moses and to Israel, His people, and that Hashem took Israel out of Egypt ... Jethro rejoiced over all the goodness that Hashem had done for Israel."

Rashi comments: **"Jethro heard:** *What report did he hear that had such a great effect on him that he came? He heard about the dividing of the Sea of Reeds and the war with Amalek."*

It is noteworthy that of all the miracles, signs, and wonders that Hashem had wrought, Rashi comments that Yisro heard only of the splitting of the Sea of Reeds and the war with Amalek, with no reference to Hashem's visitations upon the Egyptians, from the extraordinary manifestation of the staff's turning into a serpent in front of Pharaoh to the ten devastating plagues that followed. The final one, that of the destruction of the firstborn, brought the Egyptians to their knees. Rashi then clarifies what was in Yisro's mind when he rejoiced in Hashem's goodness, noting that his rejoicing, according to the words of our sages (*Sanhedrin* 94a), was not an unmixed joy. Though he was a righteous proselyte, he experienced pricks of horror on his flesh brought about by his grieving — because of his heathen ancestry — at the disaster that had befallen his former non-Jewish comrades.

The Talmud (*Sotah* 11a) teaches that Yisro, Iyov, and Balaam were joint contemporaries and joint counselors of Pharaoh at the beginning of his oppression of the Jews. Perhaps Pharaoh's obstinacy in disobeying Hashem's message as conveyed by Moshe, which brought about the repeated punishment of the Egyptians, was in a measure due to the personalities of the members of that trio. Balaam's evil attitude toward the Jews we learn from Balak. Iyov is portrayed in the book bearing his name as a man of exemplary faith, piety, and righteousness, but in the accumulated experience of our various exiles, some of our "best friends" may join with those who basely and falsely deprecate our people. Iyov may thus have been likewise misled. Yisro's solidarity with the Egyptians, as implied by Rashi's comments above, may have exerted a special influence upon him before he became a true believer. Nevertheless, he wanted to erase the past from his mind, so he conveniently began his rejoicing from the miracle at the Sea of Reeds.

> *A further elaboration of the Talmudic discussion above is found in the writings of Rav Moshe Schreiber (1762-1839), the Chasam Sofer. Yisro traveled to join the camp of Yisrael after hearing of both the splitting of the sea and the ensuing battle with the Amalekites. Why did he wait to hear about the battle? Yisro should have embarked as soon as he heard the news of the splitting of the sea! The*

Chasam Sofer explains that Yisro sinned when he was an adviser to Pharaoh because he did not stop the evil decrees issued against the children of Yisrael. He fled to Midian rather than remain part of Pharaoh's oppressive regime. Nonetheless, he shouldered some of the responsibility for the Jews' suffering, since he did not intercede on their behalf. When Yisro heard about the splitting of the sea and the subsequent drowning of the Egyptians, he learned Hashem's method of judgment — midah k'neged midah ("measure for measure"). Therefore, he resolved to mend his ways and offer advice on Yisrael's behalf the next time he was consulted. However, if his opinion was not sought out, he felt that it was unnecessary to initiate and advocate pro-Jewish positions. He rationalized that since his sin was passive, one of omission, he need not actively look for ways to correct his earlier infraction. Then he heard about the battle with the Amalekites, who had traveled many miles to engage the newly liberated Jewish nation in battle. They did not wait until the Jews approached their territory but pursued them in their zeal to destroy them. Yisro learned from the Amalekites that it was inadequate to wait until he was approached to become an advocate for the Jews. He took the initiative and traveled to the camp of Yisrael in order to mend his ways completely. As a member of the Jewish camp, he actively offered his counsel to aid the Jewish people.

Parshas Mishpatim

The author wishes to dedicate this column to the memory of his father, Menachem Mendel ben R' Zvi Merzon of blessed memory, who departed this life in a Russian shtetl on Shabbos, the 29th day of Shevat, which occurred, as does the *yahrzeit* this year, on Shabbos *Mishpatim*. May he rest in the sphere reserved for the righteous, may he be a *meilitz yosher* (a steadfast advocate) for my family and me, for our embattled brethren in Israel, and for *Klal Yisrael* as a whole. May his *z'chus* bring near the redemption of our people from the *galus* so that Israel may dwell in tranquillity. May my father's soul be bound up in the bond of eternal life and prevail upon the *Kisei Hakavod*, the Throne of Glory, to endow our brethren in their dispersion with the firm determination that the time has come to liquidate the *galus* and proceed to Israel, as we are told: "With our young and with our elders shall we go; with our sons and with our daughters, with our flocks and our cattle shall we go" (*Exodus* 10:9).

The Sedrah Begins:

> *"And these are the ordinances that you shall place before them."*
>
> Rashi comments: **"And these are the ordinances:** *Wherever it says 'these' in the Torah, it rejects that which has been stated previously. Wherever it says 'and these,' as it does here, it adds on to that which has been stated previously. The Ten Commandments are from Sinai, and these too are from Sinai. And why was the section that deals with judicial cases juxtaposed with the preceding passage that deals with the Altar? To tell you that you should place the Sanhedrin (the Supreme Court) adjacent to the Beis HaMikdash (the Temple)."*

R ASHI COMMENTS THAT WHEN THE WORD "THESE" IS USED, THE preceding subject concludes, and a new subject begins. On the other hand, when "and these" is used, the prior subject is tied to the new one. Just as the Ten Commandments were given at Sinai, so too were "the ordinances ... set before them."

Rashi's views may be summarized: Thus this incomparable civil and criminal code is of equal authority to the Ten Commandments themselves. The administration of justice and the establishment of courts of law are a supreme function of government — and generally speaking, an understanding of and knowledgeability about the laws constitute the sine qua non of learning Torah.

Rabbi Hertz states it succinctly: "The Torah recognizes no strong line of demarcation between the Decalogue and the civil laws in the chapters that follow it. All alike disclose the will of G-d. His Torah treats every phase of human and national life — civil, religious, physical, and spiritual."

The administration of justice is considered by the Torah as if engaging in it were tantamount to participating in a Divine function. It states, "I commanded your judges at that time saying, 'Listen among your brothers, and judge righteously between a man and his brother or his disputant. You shall not show favoritism in judgment; small and great alike shall you hear; you shall not fear before any man, for the judgment is unto G-d" (*Deuteronomy* 1:16-17).

Other than commandments termed *chukim,* statutes which we are bidden to obey unquestioningly — whether or not we grasp their underlying reasons — we are not only allowed but urged to question. We are enjoined to learn and to try to reach the level of understanding and evaluation reflected in the verse of the Psalmist: "The statutes of the Hashem are right, rejoicing the heart; the commandment of the Hashem is pure, enlightening the eye" (*Psalms* 19:9).

> *Rabbi Gedaliah Schorr (1910-1979) asks why Rashi comments that "just as the Ten Commandments were given at Sinai, so were the rest of these laws."*

Why is this commentary necessary? Would anyone think that these laws were not from Hashem? Rabbi Schorr answers that there are laws whose meaning lies beyond our understanding (chukim), and there are laws that are logical and within our grasp (mishpatim). The possibility exists that one could err and think that the mishpatim are incumbent upon us only because they are logical and not Divine orders. Therefore, the verse begins *"And these are the ordinances"* in order to teach us that just as we know that the Ten Commandments were given by Hashem at Sinai and that they reflect His wisdom, so too the mishpatim were given by Hashem and likewise reflect His wisdom.

Concerning the end of the verse *"the ordinances which you shall set before them,"* Rashi explains: *"Before them, and not before non-Jewish courts. Even if you know that in a particular case the civil courts judge the same as does the Torah, do not go to their courts, because one who litigates before a civil court desecrates the name of Hashem."* Why is it a desecration of the name of Hashem to present a case in the civil courts instead of in a Beis Din (a Jewish court)? The explanation is that a civil legal system is a man-made convention to benefit society. However, as logical as man can reason, his conclusions are not Divine. A Beis Din legislates Hashem's law, Hashem's wisdom, Hashem's Torah. A decision of a Beis Din is an insight into Hashem's will, and one who would rather abide by the decision of a civil court than learn Hashem's wisdom indeed desecrates God's Name.

Parashas Terumah

THE *SEDRAH* BEGINS:

"Hashem spoke to Moses, saying: 'Speak to the Children of Israel that they take for Me a portion; from every man whose heart will motivate him you shall take My portion.'"

Rashi's comments: **"They shall take for Me a portion:** 'For Me' means dedicated to My Name. **A portion:** *That is, something set aside. They should set some of their money aside for Me as a contribution."*

RASHI EXPLAINS THAT THE TAKING OF THE *TERUMAH* IN HONOR OF Hashem is significant as regards the relations between Him and the people of Israel. Does Hashem desire those things we are conceivably able to do for Him? The answer must be yes, since man was created in His image. Like Hashem, man is endowed with the ability to exercise freedom of will. Rambam says in *Hilchos Teshuvah* 5:1: "To every man is given the freedom, if he so wishes, to incline to the good path and become a *tzaddik* (saint). He has also the freedom to incline to the evil path and become a *rasha* (wicked person). It is this which is written in the Torah: 'Behold, the man is become as one of us to know good and evil, and now lest he put forth his hand and take also of the tree of life and eat and live forever' (*Genesis* 3:22). Thus the species of man is unique in the world, and he does whatever he wants; there is none that can prevent him from doing good or evil — therefore 'lest he put forth his hand...' "

A consequence of this principle is that we find that "Hashem saw that the wickedness of man was great upon the earth and that every product of the thoughts of his heart was but evil always. And Hashem reconsidered having made man on earth, and He was pained in His heart" (*Genesis* 6:5-6). If Hashem can experience grief, He can also experience joy. Hashem created the

Jewish people with high hopes: "And now, if you hearken well to Me and you keep My covenant, you will be a treasure to Me from among all the peoples, for all the earth is Mine. You will be to Me a kingdom of priests and a holy nation" (*Exodus* 19:5-6). The "Me" in these excerpts is comparable to the "Me" in our *Sedrah*. Hashem wishes to extend the utmost beneficence to our people, but that depends on us. If we honor Him by devoting our actions and endeavors to serving Him, but above all to "hearken well to Me," then He in turn will deem us His treasure. That is what we can do for Him, so He reciprocally will stand by us in all life's exigencies. The choice is ours!

> *Rabbi Chaim of Volozhin (1749-1821) writes in the first section of his classic Nefesh HaChaim (Chapter 3) that Hashem created man to control the destiny of the world through his freedom of choice. Man's good deeds, words, and thoughts strengthen and maintain the world, thereby perpetuating holiness throughout the universe. And if, Heaven forbid, he engages in evil deeds, words, and thoughts, he weakens and destroys the world, thereby defiling the entire universe. This embodies the concept of man's image resembling that of Hashem, so to speak. Just as Hashem created the universe and continuously guides its destiny, He created man in His image with the power to strengthen or undermine the universe. If man acts in accordance with the will of Hashem, he magnifies Hashem's presence in the world, as the verse states: "Give strength to Hashem" (Psalms 68:35). If man does not act in consonance with the will of Hashem, Heaven forbid, the presence of Hashem is diminished in the world, as the verse states: "You have weakened the Mighty One Who bore you" (Deuteronomy 32:18).*
>
> *Rav Shimon Schwab (1908-1995) writes that if a person harmed the universe through his sin, he*

has an opportunity to repair that damage through teshuvah (repentance). When he does teshuvah, he rebuilds a more magnificent and sturdy edifice than the one he tore down with his sin. With this thought in mind, we can understand the directive to build the Mishkan (Tabernacle). After the Sin of the Golden Calf, the universe suffered a terrible blow. The Jewish people were told that in order to make amends, a Mishkan should be constructed that would utilize their resources and skills. This dedication to construct the Mishkan was tantamount to the reconstruction of the world as it stood prior to the Sin of the Golden Calf. The gift of teshuvah grants us a second chance to make a choice that might elevate the universe to an unprecedented level of sanctity. Even after making a poor choice, we still retain the ability to choose again.

Parashas Tetzaveh

The author wishes to dedicate this column to the memory of his mother, Teuba bas R' Moses of blessed memory, who departed this life in a small town in Russia on the eleventh day of Adar, on Shabbos *Tetzaveh,* when the author was barely 15 years old. May her soul rest in the sphere reserved for the *tzidkanios* (righteous women). May she be a *meilitz yosher* (steadfast advocate) for my family and me, for *Medinas Yisrael,* and for all of *Klal Yisrael.* May our redemption from the *galus* come nearer through her *z'chus,* uniting us with our brethren in Israel and bringing us to devote our powers to Torah, *mitzvos,* and *ma'asim tovim* (good deeds). May my mother's soul be bound up in the bond of eternal life.

THE *SEDRAH* BEGINS:

> *"And you shall command the Children of Israel that they take for you clear olive oil, crushed for illumination, to light a lamp continuously. In the Tent of Meeting, outside the dividing-curtain that is near the [Ark of] Testimony, Aaron and his sons shall arrange it from evening until morning, before Hashem — an eternal decree for their generations — from the Children of Israel."*

> *Rashi comments:* **"And you shall command ... clear:** *Without sediments, as we learned in Tractate Menachos (86a), 'He leaves it [the olives] to ripen at the top of the olive tree, etc.'* **Crushed:** *That is, the olives. He would crush the olives in a mortar, and he would not grind them in a mill so that there would be no sediments in the oil. After he extracts the first drop of oil, he puts the olives into a mill and grinds them. The second oil is unfit for use in the Menorah but is fit for meal-offerings."*

RASHI EMPHASIZES THE SANCTITY OF THE MENORAH, THE SYMBOL OF Israel. This *Sedrah* deals with the requirements of those who were to minister in the Sanctuary. Of these duties, the tending of the Menorah was of utmost importance. One of the reasons is that even though the Sanctuary was transient, the Menorah would forever be perpetuated through the observance of Chanukah and the lighting of the Chanukah menorah.

Ramban comments on the opening phrase "And you shall command" which was directed to Moshe Rabbeinu so that he could guide the people as to the bringing of the oil. That is, Moshe was to receive the olives from the populace, and he was to supervise the processing of the olives into oil for the lighting of the Menorah, as was the case with the construction of the

Tabernacle until its completion. In these two cases we encounter techniques of modern management, in which an executive's role is to deputize and supervise.

> As stated above, the Menorah is the symbol of Israel. Rabbi Naftali Zvi Yehudah Berlin (1817-1893), the Netziv, explains that it is important to appreciate the symbolism of the Menorah. The Menorah is the symbol of Yisrael because it is a symbol of Torah. The light of the Torah was projected from the Menorah, emanating from the Sanctuary outside to the world at large. The intricate design of the branches represented the intricate structure of Torah novellae (original thoughts on Torah subjects). As the Talmud (Berachos 57a) states, "One who sees olive oil in a dream should anticipate the light of Torah."
>
> Why was it necessary for Moses Rabbeinu personally to oversee the processing of the oil for the Menorah? Couldn't he have trusted others with this responsibility as he entrusted them with the other tasks of the Sanctuary? Moses was the pre-eminent scholar, the wise mentor, the father of all Torah novellae. Accordingly, it was necessary and fitting for him personally to oversee the production of the oil that would brighten the world through the illumination of the Torah.
>
> In light of this explanation, we can appreciate why the production of the oil was performed so meticulously so as to avoid any impurities. Only select drops of oil were used from each olive. This olive oil would be used to cast the light of Torah: just as the Torah is pure and true, so too the oil designated for the Menorah had to be pure and holy, as Rashi explains.

Parashas Ki Sisa

The Sedrah begins:

"Hashem spoke to Moses, saying: 'When you will take a census of the Children of Israel according to their numberings, every man shall give Hashem an atonement for his soul in their being counted, and there will be no plague among them when counting them. This is what they shall give — everyone who passes among the counted — half a shekel (by the holy shekel — the shekel is twenty geirah), half a shekel as a portion to Hashem. Every one who passes among the counted from the age of twenty years and up shall give the portion of Hashem."

Rashi comments: **"When you will take [a census]:** *The word tisa means 'taking,' as it is rendered by Targum Onkelos. The verse is saying that when you will wish to take the total of their number, to know how many they are, do not count them by heads. Rather let each one give a half-shekel, and you will count the shekalim; you will thereby know their number.* **And there will be no plague among them:** *Otherwise there would be a plague, for the evil eye can affect that which has been counted, and pestilence can come upon them, as we find in the days of David."*

Rashi comments that when the B'nei Yisrael were to be counted, it was not to be done by census but through the giving of a half-shekel. This was done to avoid a plague, for numbers are subject to the influence of the evil eye, and pestilence may befall the people being counted, as we find happened in the days of David (*Samuel II* 24:10, 15).

Rabbi Hertz comments upon this idea that giving the half shekel by each man 20 years old and upward is termed a ransom for his soul. He explains that the counted were intended to be mustered for war. A potential taker of life, even though he may be justified in doing so, nevertheless needs atonement. It may also be added that giving money to good causes has at all times been deemed a protection against evil. Incidentally, this is the *z'chus* (merit) of American Jewry, whose generosity toward all Jewish causes at home and abroad is one of our most laudable accomplishments. Charity is a great savior.

> The concept that charity is a great savior is described in both the Written and Oral Torah. King Solomon wrote in Mishlei (10:2): "Charity protects from death." The Talmud (Shabbos 156b) tells a story about Rabbi Akiva's daughter. When she was born, astrologers announced that she would die on the day of her wedding. As she approached matrimony, Rabbi Akiva was consumed with worry and anxiety. On the day of the wedding, the bride took her hairpin and stuck it between the stones of the wall. She did not realize that a venomous snake was in the crack and that the pin had impaled the serpent. The next morning, she took her pin from the wall and dragged the dead snake from the hole, still attached to the pin. Rabbi Akiva said to her, "What did you do to merit such a salvation?" She explained that right before the wedding, a pauper had come to the door but went unnoticed owing to the hustle and bustle in the house. She got up and gave the poor man food from the wedding feast. Rabbi Akiva exclaimed, "And charity protects from death!"
>
> The Talmud teaches (Bava Basra 10b) that Moshe Rabbeinu asked Hashem how the Jewish people will achieve spiritual prominence. Hashem answered him, "With Ki Sisa." Rashi comments: Whenever the people are counted, take from them a ransom for charity. Rabbi Moshe Yechiel Epstein (1890-1971) in his work Be'er Moses asks how we

derive from "ki sisa" a donation to charity. After all, the purpose of the collection of the half-shekels described in Ki Sisa was to gather funds for building the Mishkan and later to purchase animals for offerings in the Mishkan. Charity, on the other hand, is to aid the indigent!

    Rabbi Epstein explains that Rashi reveals the principle underlying Ki Sisa. The uniform donation of a half-shekel symbolizes the interdependence of mankind. The wealthy and poor give the same amount, a half-shekel, for everyone needs each other, regardless of financial status. A half coin is used and not a whole shekel because each person is incomplete when taken alone. Therefore, the funds could be directed to the Mishkan or to charity. The message of Ki Sisa is to teach us to realize that at the time of counting, precisely when we consider each individual a unique entity, he is still dependent on the other members of Klal Yisrael.

PARASHAS VAYAKHEL

THE *SEDRAH* BEGINS:

"And Moses assembled the entire assembly of the Children of Israel and said to them: 'These are the things that Hashem commanded, to do them: For a period of six days, work may be done, but the seventh day shall be holy for you, a day of complete rest for Hashem; whoever does work on it shall be put to death. You shall not light fire in any of your dwellings on the Shabbath day.'"

> Rashi comments: **"And Moses assembled:** On the day after Yom Kippur, when he descended from the mountain. **For a period of six days:** Moses first told them the prohibition of working on the Shabbath before he told them the commandment regarding the construction of the Mishkan in order to emphasize that the work of the Mishkan does not override the Shabbath."

It should be noted that Rashi's specification of the time as after Yom Kippur appears in *Parashas Yisro* (*Exodus* 18:13), where Moshe's father-in-law advised him about decentralizing the administration of justice. There Rashi says, "It was the day after Yom Kippur. It had to be done after Moses' descent from the mountain, for before the giving of the Torah it would have been impossible to say, 'And I made known the statutes of Hashem.' Moshe descended from the mountain on Yom Kippur when Hashem was fully reconciled to our ancestors after the Sin of the Golden Calf. The significance of this fact is that in the previous case, the task of Moshe was the administration of impartial justice as a prime essential of Torah teaching. However, the later instance in this *Sedrah* emphasizes the observance of Shabbos as the bottom line of Jewish adherence to the Torah. The two are inseparable. A person cannot be a loyal Jew unless he follows the Torah and couples this with the active pursuit of justice.

> Rabbi Shlomo Ephraim Lunshitz (1550-1619), the *Kli Yakar*, comments that on the day after Yom Kippur, Moshe Rabbeinu gathered B'nei Yisrael to discuss with them the Torah's judicial system and the instructions for the receipt of donations for the construction of the Mishkan. Why were both of these issues addressed on the same day? The Kli Yakar explains that Moshe was concerned that someone might donate material for the Mishkan that was not legally his, even though he thought it was rightfully his own. Certainly, Hashem would not reside in the

Mishkan if any of the construction materials were stolen. Therefore, Moshe gathered B'nei Yisrael to resolve any financial disputes through jurisprudence, and only afterwards did he outline the process for the collection of materials for the construction of the Mishkan. The Mishkan, where man serves Hashem, cannot exist if someone does not fully respect the rights of his fellow man.

The association between Shabbos observance and the enforcement of justice is found in the Talmud. The Talmud teaches us (Shabbos 10a): "Every judge who judges the absolute truth is considered as if he were a partner with Hashem in the creation of the world" (see Rashi on Exodus 18:13). Similarly, the Talmud teaches (Shabbos 119b): "Everyone who attests to the creation of the world by Hashem and observes Shabbos is considered as if he were a partner with Hashem in the creation of the world." This connection between the execution of justice and Shabbos observance does not exist between any other mitzvos. What is the unique relationship between these two mitzvos that their fulfillment pairs the performer with Hashem in the creation of the world?

The Mishnah in Pirkei Avos (1:18) lists the administration of justice as one of the three things that preserves the existence of the world. King Solomon writes in Mishlei (29:4): "The king through justice established the land." The Midrash teaches (Bereishis Rabbah 14:1): "The King, the King of kings, through justice established the land: He created the world with justice." Just as the observance of Shabbos attests to the creation of the world by Hashem, so too does the administration of justice perpetuate the purpose inherent in creation. The observance of Shabbos firmly establishes man's relationship with Hashem, whereas *the administration of justice establishes the framework of a person's relationship with his fellow man. A person cannot be a loyal Jew unless he understands and fulfills his obligations to Hashem and his fellow man, follows the Torah, and actively pursues justice.*

Parashas Pekudei

The *Sedrah* begins:

"These are the accountings of the Mishkan, the Mishkan of the Testimony, which were counted at the word of Moses; the work of the Levites under the hand of Ithamar, son of Aaron the Kohen. Bezalel, son of Uri, son of Hur, of the tribe of Judah did all that Hashem commanded Moses."

Rashi comments: ***"These are the accountings:*** *In this passage, all the weights of the contributions to the Mishkan have been listed — for the silver, for the gold, and for the copper. And all its implements were counted for all its service.* ***The Mishkan, the Mishkan:*** *The word is stated twice, an allusion to the Beis HaMikdash which was taken as collateral in its two destructions for the sins of Israel."*

The Torah foresees in numerous places future deviations of Israel from the right path, seemingly prophesying future disasters as inevitable. However, it is a part of Jewish fundamental doctrine that there is nothing which is inevitable. All is the will of Hashem and a reflection of the loyalty of the *B'nei Yisrael* to Him and their adherence to His commandments.

This answer can be corroborated by a passage in the Talmud. The Talmud teaches (Avodah Zorah 5a) that when the Torah was given on Mount Sinai, B'nei Yisrael reverted to the greatness of Adam before the sin of eating the forbidden fruit of the Tree of the Knowledge of Good and Evil. In their perfection they became immortal, and only with the subsequent Sin of the Golden Calf did they lose their invulnerability before the Angel of Death. The Talmud asks: Why, if B'nei Yisrael were immortal when they received the Torah, could the Torah include laws of inheritance and Yibum, the marriage of a childless widow to her brother-in-law. The Talmud answers that these laws were included in the Torah on a conditional basis. If B'nei Yisrael remained worthy, these laws would never apply to them. But if they sinned, these laws would become effective immediately. Similarly, whenever the Torah alludes to events that occur as a result of sin, we understand that such events were included conditionally in the Torah.

SEFER VAYIKRA
PARASHAS VAYIKRA

THE *SEDRAH* BEGINS:

"He called to Moses, and Hashem spoke to him from the Tent of Meeting, saying: Speak to the Children of Israel and say to them: When a person from among you will bring an offering to Hashem — from the animals, from the cattle, and from the flocks you shall bring your offering."

Rashi comments: **"He called to Moses:** *'Calling' preceded every statement, and every saying, and every command. It is the language of affection, language that the ministering angels use, as it says, 'One called to the other and said, "Holy…"' But as for the prophets of the other nations of the world, He revealed Himself to them in language of transitoriness and impurity, as it says, 'G-d happened upon Balaam.'* **He called to Moses:** *The voice of Hashem would go and reach Moses' ears, but all Israel would not hear it."*

RASHI OBSERVES THAT HASHEM'S CALLING MOSHE PRIOR TO HIS speaking to or commanding him was a unique expression of affection for him. Furthermore, when Hashem called, He spoke only to him; none of the people except Moshe heard what was said.

Not only on this occasion, comments Rashi, but whenever a Divine communication was made to Moshe, it was preceded by a call. We find this term specifically used at other times. Thus when Hashem came down upon Mt. Sinai, He called Moshe "to the top of the mount, and Moshe went up" (*Exodus* 19:20); "And Hashem came down in a pillar of cloud and stood at the door of the tent, and He called Aaron and Miriam, and they both came forth" (*Numbers* 12:5); "Then Moshe called to the elders and told them to prepare the Passover lamb" (*Exodus* 12:21). The first call was to summon Moshe to the supreme event of our heritage. The second was to reprimand Aharon and Miriam for speaking ill of Moshe. The third was a directive by Moshe while our ancestors were still in Egypt and preparatory to their liberation. The first of the three cited was a call to distinction; the second, a call to a task; the third, a delegated call from Hashem to Moshe — and from him, in turn, to the people. All of them, it must be concluded, were accompanied by a feeling of love, even the second one, despite the fact that it was a call of criticism. This teaches us a lesson, for we are bidden to emulate Hashem in our conduct, in that even while administrating a reprimand, it should usually be done with kindness.

> *The proper method of reprimand is described in the Talmud. The Talmud (Sotah 47a) teaches us that in order to properly rebuke "one must distance with his left hand and simultaneously draw near with the right hand." A reprimand should never ostracize. Only when a person is motivated by a feeling of love for the offender will his rebuke be accepted. Indeed, the Mishnah states (Pirkei Avos 1:12): "Hillel said: 'Be a student of Aharon... who loves people and brings them close to the Torah.' " Rabbi Chaim Shmulevitz (1902-1979) wrote (Sichos Mussar 5731, Chapter 26) that just as love is necessary when introducing people*

to the Torah, so is love also necessary in even greater measure when the need arises to reprimand and to discipline. The Talmud (Yoma 54b) teaches that when the Temple was destroyed, the gentiles entered the Holy of Holies and found the cherubim in a warm embrace. Rabbi Shlomo Eidels (the Maharsha, 1555-1632) comments that the embrace of the cherubim signified the love and affection between Hashem and His children, B'nei Yisrael. If the Jews did not live up to Hashem's expectations, the cherubim turned away from each other. Therefore, when the Temple was destroyed and Hashem punished the Jews for their sins, why were the cherubim embracing each other? Rabbi Shmulevitz answered that when Hashem reprimands and punishes B'nei Yisrael, He is full of love and affection for them. This explains why the cherubim were lovingly embracing one another at the time of the destruction of the Temple. Ultimately, we must understand that when Hashem rebukes and disciplines us, He has not forsaken us but instead is full of love for His children.

PARASHAS TZAV

The *Sedrah* begins:

"Hashem spoke to Moses saying: Command Aaron and his sons, saying: This is the law of the olah-offering: It is the olah-offering [that stays] on the flame, on the Altar, all night until the morning, and the fire of the Altar shall be kept burning on it."

> Rashi comments: "**Command Aaron:** 'Command' can be meant only to express an urging on — for the immediate moment and for future generations. The Tanna R' Shimon said, 'Scripture must especially urge in a situation where there is a material loss involved.'"

Rashi notes that the term "command" indicates Hashem's urging or encouragement of both present and future generations. The term "*tzav*" is used in the Torah in other instances — for example, in *Numbers* (5:2), where Hashem tells Moshe to "command the Children of Israel to send away from the camp every leper." We may draw a comparable conclusion that there too a mitzvah which comes to our hands should not become soured; rather we should act promptly. The relationship between Hashem and His people must be amenable to a sense of urgency and promptness. And if we do our share, even if only to initiate it with a show of sincere effort, He does His share.

> As described above, alacrity in the performance of mitzvos is part and parcel of the mitzvah. Rabbeinu Yaakov (c. 1275-c. 1340), the author of the Tur Shulchan Aruch (Code of Jewish Law), begins his work with the words of the Tanna Yehudah ben Tema (Pirkei Avos 5:23): "Be strong as a leopard, light as an eagle, swift as a stag, and mighty as a lion to do the will of your Father in Heaven." Before we begin to study the Code of Jewish Law, we must recall the words of Yehudah ben Tema — "swift as a stag" — so that we will neither procrastinate nor hesitate in matters of the performance of our duty.
>   Rabbi Chaim D. Rabinowitz explains in his book Daas Sofrim that we are expected to perform every mitzvah quickly, without hesitation or procrastination, even if the verse does not say tzav. The emphasis in the verse quoted above, as Rashi explains, is only because of a concern for financial

loss. We need extra encouragement in situations involving an expense. When we serve Hashem with alacrity and zeal, it is evident that we desire to serve Him. This is conceptualized in the Mishnah (Pirkei Avos 2:4): "Do His will as you would your own will so that He may do your will just as He does His will." Rabbi Samson Raphael Hirsch (1808-1888) explains that "we are asked to identify our will entirely with that of Hashem so that we may perform joyously and willingly whatever is pleasing to Him as being in accord with our own wishes. If we have no other wishes but those identical with the wishes of Hashem, we will have a greater right than anyone else to hope that our own wishes will be fulfilled, and we will have less cause than others to fear that such wishes may be inimical to our welfare." If we exert a proper show of effort and identify our will with His will, Hashem will always do His share.

Parashas Shemini

The Sedrah Begins:

"It was on the eighth day that Moses called to Aaron and his sons and to the elders of Israel. He said to Aaron: 'Take yourself a calf, a young male, for a sin-offering and a ram for an olah-offering, unblemished, and offer them up before Hashem. And to the Children of Israel speak as follows: Take a he-goat for a sin-offering and a calf and a sheep in their first year, unblemished, for an olah-offering.'"

> Rashi comments: *"**And to the elders of Israel**: To let them hear that in accordance with the statement of G-d, Aaron enters and officiates in the office of Kohen Gadol, and they should not say that he enters the office of Kohen Gadol on his own. **Take yourself a calf**: To inform Aaron that the Holy One, Blessed is He, grants atonement for him through this calf for the matter of the golden calf that he made."*

THERE ARE TWO REASONS FOR MOSHE'S CALLING THE ELDERS OF ISRAEL: to ward off any complaints that Aharon was a self-starter and to bear witness to the fact that his call came from the Highest Authority. However, these reasons did not stop the archrebel Korach from attempting to stimulate sentiment among the people precisely on the false charge that Aharon was a usurper. History is replete with such instances. That our people should be subject to similar aberrations is indeed a source of deep sorrow.

Aharon's part in the golden-calf incident is a moot point — whether he acted his peaceful nature in order to gain time or out of fear of the common elements among the people. Such elements among all of the nations from time immemorial during periods of stress promote excesses. In any event, the forgiving Father in Heaven cleared Aharon from the onus of this calamity. The lesson is clear: sin must be averted at all costs, but no man, even if he be a *tzaddik,* is free from it. But there is a saying that there is more rejoicing in Heaven when a sinner turns penitent than when a *tzaddik* stays righteous. Indeed, in Jewish tradition, a confession that one has sinned provides a way out of one's moral dilemma as well as a firm resolve not to sin again.

> *Rabbeinu Bachya (1263-1340) comments that the calf of Aharon and the calf of B'nei Yisrael were both offerings to atone for the sin of the golden calf. However, the offerings were not identical. Why did Aharon bring a calf as a sin-offering and B'nei Yisrael a calf as an olah-offering? Rabbeinu Bachya explains that the offerings reflect the crimes committed. A sin-*

offering was brought if a person sinned inadvertently; the activity was prohibited, but there was no intention to rebel. An olah-offering was brought when a person thought of committing a crime but took no action. Aharon was prescribed a sin-offering for his part in the sin of the golden calf. The Torah is teaching us that even though his actions were criminal, his motive was pure. Aharon's sin is likened to the inadvertent sin: the activity was prohibited, but there was no intention to rebel. B'nei Yisrael, on the other hand, were prescribed an olah-offering. The ranks of B'nei Yisrael who actively participated in the sin of the golden calf were already punished. There remained only those who considered joining the rest but did not act on their evil thoughts. Since their sins were only in thought, not in action, their atonement required an olah-offering.

The Talmud (Berachos 34b) teaches that in Heaven, the place reserved for the penitent sinner is beyond the place reserved for the righteous. Perhaps Aharon merited more than his brother, Moshe, to serve as the high priest precisely for this reason. After Aharon's atonement for his part in the sin of the golden calf, the place reserved for him was beyond that of his brother Moshe, who had no part in the sin.

PARASHAS TAZRIA

THE *SEDRAH* BEGINS:

"Hashem spoke to Moses, saying: Speak to the Children of Israel, saying: When a woman conceives and gives birth to a

male, she shall be impure for a seven-day period; during the days of her menstruant infirmity shall she be impure."

Rashi comments: **"When a woman conceives:** *The Amora R' Simlai said that just as the fashioning of man came after that of all cattle, beasts, and fowl in the Torah's account of the Creation, so too is his law explained after the law of the beast and the fowl."*

STRICTLY SPEAKING, THE PREVIOUS SECTION TO WHICH RASHI HAS referred in regard to the law of the lower beings is related to the dietary laws commanded to us with respect to the consumption of animal flesh, limiting it, among other things, to cattle that have cloven hooves and chew the cud. The section follows with the designation of those lower creatures whose contact renders one unclean, and with comparable regulations. And significantly enough, the section does conclude with "This is the law of the animal, the bird, and every living creature that moves in the waters and of every creature that creeps on the ground. In order to distinguish between the impure and the pure and between the creature that may be eaten and the creature that may not be eaten" (*Leviticus* 11:46-47). And the motivation for this law is "For I am Hashem Who has brought you up from the land of Egypt to be a G-d unto you; you shall be holy, for I am holy" (*Leviticus* 11:45).

The Torah describes the difference between those animals which are pure and those which are impure and between those which may be eaten and those which may not be eaten in order to imbue us with holiness, for Hashem is holy. Therefore, our obedience to these laws of Hashem are more than a mere dietary edict or abstaining from uncleanliness. The animal world is dignified through a spiritual dimension. The juxtaposition of the command concerning human births is intended to enhance the supreme duty of man to serve Hashem. Just as man's creation, following that of the lower creatures, was the masterful culmination of the fashioning of the world, so too regard for the proper utilization of the latter by man is a precondition for him to attain holiness. Man's obvious elevation in the creative process entails his obligation to pursue yet greater holiness.

> *In Gur Aryeh, Rabbi Yehuda Loewe (1526-1609), the Maharal of Prague, asks about the logic of recording the laws of animals and the laws of man parallel to their order in Creation. He explains that the laws of the Torah are the ultimate completion and perfection of the entire universe. Therefore, since the animals preceded man at the time of Creation, their laws follow the identical sequence. The laws pertaining to man are not incidental to his existence: they perfect his existence. Since the mitzvos complete the Creation process, those which pertain to animals precede those which pertain to man.*
>
> *The laws of the Torah are the Tikun Olam, the ultimate perfection of all Creation. This thought is clearly expressed by the 18th-century master Rabbi Moshe Chaim Luzzato (1707-1747). He writes (Mesillas Yesharim, Chapter 1): "If you delve into the matter, you will see that the world was created for man's use. However, man is at the center of a great balance. If he is drawn after worldly pursuits and alienates himself from his Creator, he corrupts himself and ruins the world around him. But if he rules over himself and unites himself with his Creator, [thus] availing himself of the world as an aid in the service of his Creator, he elevates himself, and the world is uplifted with him. For all creatures are greatly uplifted when they are used in the service of the perfected man who is sanctified through Hashem's holiness." Proper utilization of the world by man is thus a prerequisite of man's holiness, for it imparts holiness to the world in which he lives and functions.*

Parashas Metzora

THE *SEDRAH* BEGINS:

"Hashem spoke to Moses, saying: This shall be the law of the metzora on the day of his purification: He shall be brought to the Kohen. The Kohen shall go forth to the outside of the camp; the Kohen shall look and determine that the tzaraas affliction has healed from the metzora. The Kohen shall then command; and for the person being purified, there shall be taken two live pure birds, cedarwood, a crimson (tongue of) wool, and hyssop."

Rashi comments: **"This shall be the law of the metzora on the day of his purification:** *This teaches us that they do not purify him at night."*

THERE ARE OTHER REFERENCES IN THE TORAH WHERE RASHI EXPLAINS that the word "day" is to be taken literally. For example, where the Torah notes: "In the selfsame day (was Abraham circumcised)," Rashi comments: "During the daytime and not at night." Contrast this with the opening of the Torah where "day" means a twenty-four-hour period — thus the repetitions following the various acts of Creation: "There was evening and there was morning one day. . . . a second day. . . . the sixth day." We find as well instances in which "day" is synonymous with light, which is a favorite metaphor for Judaism: Isaiah speaks of Israel's being a light unto the nations; the Menorah as the symbol for the very essence of our beliefs. Moreover, when the plague of darkness enveloped all Egypt, "all the Children of Israel had light in their dwellings."

Why is the mitzvah of purifying the metzora relegated to the daytime? What is the significance and symbolism of this requirement? Rabbi Samson Raphael Hirsch (1808-1888) explains (Collected

Writings, III, pp. 86-96) that darkness is the expression of the absence of individuality, for the existence of individual objects cannot be discerned. On the other hand, light is the expression of complete existence. During the daylight hours, man masters the world around him. It is the time of his independence and activity. During the night, however, he is chained in the bonds of earthly elements, a time of yielding and passivity. By day, man is in power and the world is his product. By night, man is himself the product and the universe has become the power that restrains and molds him.

Night or day — in which of these two phenomena must man seek his G-d? To many, the quest for G-d is expressed in sorrowful supplication, in pleading for deliverance from the powers of evil in the world. Only through the tribulations of life's nighttime experiences does man seek out G-d.

Judaism teaches that whether night or day, man has the free-willed, G-dly power with which he can subdue both the world around him and the world within his own heart. Man should serve G-d as a vigorous, happy, free, and active individual, and thereby exercise his dominion over the rest of the world. He is capable of mastering his inclinations and of controlling his destiny. Pleasure, life, strength, freedom, and rejoicing lead man to G-d. Hence, most mitzvos that are relegated to a specific time are designated for daytime, not for night.

The Torah especially specifies daytime for those acts which could erroneously be associated with the nighttime aspects of life. Which laws are so easily relegated to the dark sphere of night as those *regarding ritual impurity? Precisely in this area, the Torah prescribes the daytime to show that the service of G-d comes about through man's exercising his free will in order to control his dark side for the good and for the service of the Almighty.*

Parashas Acharei Mos

The *Sedrah* begins:

"Hashem spoke to Moses after the death of Aaron's two sons, when they approached before Hashem and they died. And Hashem said to Moses: Speak to Aaron, your brother: He may not come at all times into the Sanctuary, within the Curtain, in front of the Cover that is upon the Ark, so that he will not die, for with a cloud I appear upon the Ark-Cover."

Rashi comments: **"Hashem spoke to Moses after the death of Aaron's two sons:** Why did the Torah say this? The Tanna R' Elazar ben Azaryah explains with a parable. This may be compared to a sick person treated by a physician. The doctor said to him, 'Do not eat cold food and do not lie in a damp, chilly place.' Another doctor came and said to him, 'Do not eat cold food and do not lie in a damp, chilly place so that you will not die the way So-and-So died.' This second doctor roused him to follow his instructions more than the first [by adding 'so that you will not die']. This is why the Torah adds 'After the death of Aaron's two sons.'"

Citing "when Nadav and Avihu drew near before Hashem and expired" from the opening verse, Rabbi Samson Raphael

Hirsch (1808-1888) states that "therein lay the cause of their demise, a complete overestimation of their own importance." This calamity was an object lesson for all Israel — that we must never enlarge upon nor inflate our importance — not only before our fellow man, but before Hashem as well.

> Rabbi Shlomo Ephraim Lunshitz (1550-1619) in Kli Yakar on Vayikra 10:1 asks why Nadav and Avihu had to die by a Heavenly fire that consumed their souls. He explains that the reason for their unique deaths is consistent with the adage of our sages (Vayikra Rabbah 7:6): "Anyone who is haughty will be judged by fire." The haughty man seeks to rise higher and higher, just as the nature of flames is to rise higher and higher. Since he aspires to emulate fire, fire consumes him. Nadav and Avihu were consumed by fire because they exhibited a degree of pompous behavior unbefitting men of their stature. They taught Yisrael the lesson that people should never overestimate their own importance.
>
> Aharon's sons Nadav and Avihu were righteous men. The Talmud Yerushalmi (Yoma 1:1) asks why the deaths of Nadav and Avihu are mentioned near the Yom Kippur offerings. The Talmud answers: to teach us that the death of the righteous atone just like the Yom Kippur offerings. Nadav and Avihu were great men with the best intentions, but they did not consult their father, Aharon nor their uncle, Moshe Rabbeinu, about their plans. They did not consider the need to seek the advice and counsel of the leaders of the Jewish nation. (See Rabbi Hirsch's commentary to Vayikra 10:1.) Rabbi Shimon ben Elazar said: "If the elders advise to demolish [a building] and the young advise to build, demolish it, because the demolition of the elders is constructive, while the building of the young is

destructive" (Megillah 31b). It is imperative for young leaders to follow the guidance of the Sages, whose wisdom directs our nation.

Parashas Kedoshim

THE SEDRAH BEGINS:

"Hashem spoke to Moses, saying: Speak to the entire assembly of the Children of Israel and say to them: You shall be holy, for holy am I, Hashem, your God. Every man shall revere his mother and his father, and you shall observe My Sabbaths: I am Hashem, your God."

Rashi comments: **"And you shall observe my Sabbaths:** *The verse juxtaposes observance of the Shabbath to reverence for one's father in order to indicate that although I have enjoined you about revering a father, if your father should say to you, 'Desecrate the Shabbath,' do not listen to him. And so too with regard to other commandments."*

NOTING THE PROXIMITY OF THE COMMANDMENT TO FEAR ONE'S PARENTS to that of keeping the Shabbos, Rashi observes that even though one must fear and obey his father, should his father require him to profane Shabbos, he must not listen to him, for he is then voiding Hashem's words. Indeed, the same is true for all the commandments, as it is said: "I am Hashem, your [in the plural] G-d: both you and your father are equally bound to obey Me."

As mentioned above, both times the Torah mentions the mitzvah of honoring parents, the Torah juxtaposes the mitzvah with the mitzvah of keeping Shabbos. Here they appear in the same verse, and in the Ten Commandments the mitzvah of Shabbos is the fourth commandment, while honoring parents is the fifth. Why are these two mitzvos connected to each other? Rabbi Chaim D. Rabinowitz (Daas Sofrim) explains that when a person aspires to spiritual greatness, his course includes perfecting his service to man, along with perfecting his service to Hashem. The main path to sanctity through serving Hashem comes about through keeping Shabbos, which imbues man with a holy spirit that accompanies him throughout the week. The path to sanctity through serving one's fellow man is achieved by honoring his parents. Just as Shabbos imbues man with a holy spirit, so too do parents imbue their children with the spiritual direction that permeates their being and guides them through the challenges of life. Shabbos and parents together thereby constitute the keys to spiritual greatness.

But the parents' guidance must conform with Shabbos, with the path to sanctity defined by serving Hashem. When the parents' wishes conflict with serving Hashem, they have abdicated their role as spiritual guides for their children, and their wishes must not be obeyed.

There are two categories of mitzvos in the Torah. There are mitzvos whose meaning is beyond our understanding — chukim — and there are mitzvos that are logical and fall within our comprehension — mishpatim. Both chukim and mishpatim are necessary for our spiritual growth. The mitzvah to honor and obey parents is a mishpat, the category of mitzvos that are logical and rational. Yet we are ordered to fulfill these mitzvos simply because Hashem has commanded Yisrael to perform them — and not because they are acceptable to our sensibilities. The Torah is teaching us this principle here in conjunction with Shabbos observance. The intent and goal of honoring parents is to fulfill Hashem's command to do so and thereby ascend the ladder of sanctity. If Hashem's authority is challenged by parents, however, we are not permitted to comply with their wishes. Our dedication to Hashem must become the driving force behind all the mitzvos that we perform.

EMOR

THE *SEDRAH* BEGINS:

"Hashem said to Moses: Say to the Kohanim, the sons of Aaron, and you shall say to them: To a dead person he shall not become impure among his people; except for his relative who is closest to him, to his mother and to his father, to his son, to his daughter, and to his brother — and to his virgin sister who is close to him, who has not been unto a man; for her he shall make himself impure."

Rashi comments: **"Say to the Kohanim:** *The Torah uses the redundant wording of 'say' followed by 'and you shall say' to caution adults with regard to minors."*

THIS *SEDRAH* SHOWS THAT THE SUBJECT MATTER COVERED IS ENVELOPED in *kedushah,* sanctity, both as regards the Kohanim to whom the direction is given as well as to all Israel affected by the commandment. The tribe of Levi, who fathered the Kohanim and the Levites — the elite of our nation to this very day, obviously owing to their dedication to Temple service — were endowed with sanctity. The purpose of these regulations was to safeguard that holiness.

From the inception of our nation in the Egyptian *galus,* in which the elders maintained the positions of leadership; to Moshe Rabbeinu's appointment of various classes of leaders according to Yisro's counsel; to the organization of the Temple services by Aharon and his sons (to whom the Levites were "given . . . from the Children of Israel" [*Numbers* 3:9] and taken by Hashem in place of the firstborn of the Children of Israel in recognition of the Levites' faithful stand during the golden-calf apostasy, while the firstborn did not fulfill that test); to the princes of Israel, the heads of their fathers' houses for the twelve tribes, who officiated at the dedication of the Altar; to the designation of Yehoshua as successor to Moshe Rabbeinu: All were moved by a sense of sanctity shared by our entire people.

The respect which tradition dictates ought to be accorded to the dead of our people is reflected in the Psalmist's comment (*Psalms* 6:6): "For in death there is no remembrance of You; in *She'ol* (the underworld) [see glossary] who shall give You praise?" Since when we are alive we are required to praise Hashem, when life ceases, the sanctity that was once there is gone, thus leaving the lifeless body the main source of ritual uncleanliness. Hence, we say in *Hallel* (*Psalms* 115:17): "The dead cannot praise G-d!"

We may well ask: Why does the opening verse relating to priestly posterity and their extraordinary care in the performance of their priestly duties touch *at this point* on the inevitable that must come to all? Could this not have been reserved for another section dealing with people of advanced age? When we contemplate children, we think of life, hope, and flowering. It may be that the Torah indeed wants us to have in mind life and its necessary continuation. And children are our witnesses that the *Ribbono Shel Olam,* Master of the Universe, has "eternal life planted within us." We do not pass from the scene of existence but live on in our children — providing, of course, that they are worthy by reason of their proper training not only to succeed us in whatever good we have attempted to do in our lifetime, but even to improve upon it. For those who unfortunately may be childless, tradition tells us that those who teach Torah to the children of others are considered as though they fathered them, and they therefore continue to live on through their students.

> *The Sefer HaChinuch (attributed by many to Rabbeinu Aharon HaLevi, 13th century) explains in the beginning of our Sedrah (Mitzvah 263) that the Torah prohibits a Kohen from defiling his sanctity through contact with a corpse, with the exception of the enumerated relatives, because the Kohanim were designated to serve Hashem. The corpse is the epitome of ritual impurity, the earthly remains without the Divine spark that we call the soul. If the Kohen is to succeed in preserving his sanctity, he must exercise due diligence to distance himself from anything that would diminish his holiness and his ability to serve Hashem.*
>
> *The Torah exhorts the Kohen to protect his son also from impurity. Even though the child is a minor, without the yoke of the Torah's obligations on his shoulders, his parents must strive to maintain his purity, his holiness, and his readiness to join the ranks of the adults in their service of Hashem. This mitzvah must become the sine qua non of rearing children. A parent should never underestimate the potential of his child, and a parent should never underestimate how a negative influence during a child's formative years will stunt his spiritual development in the years to come.*

Parashas Behar
Parashas Bechukosai

THE *SEDRAH* BEGINS:

"Hashem spoke to Moses on Mount Sinai, saying: Speak to the Children of Israel and say to them: When you come into the land that I give you, the land shall observe a Sabbath rest for Hashem. For six years you may sow your field, and for six years you may prune your vineyard, and you may gather in its crop. But on the seventh year a complete rest there shall be for the land, a Sabbath for Hashem: Your field you shall not sow and your vineyard you shall not prune."

Rashi comments: **"On Mount Sinai:** *What is the matter of shemittah doing next to Mount Sinai (that is, why does the Torah say "on Mount Sinai" specifically in the context of the laws of shemittah, as opposed to that of other laws)? Were not all the commandments stated at Sinai? But it is written here to teach that just as with shemittah its general rules and its fine points were stated at Sinai, so too with all the other commandments: Their general rules and their fine points were stated at Sinai. And it appears to me that this is the explanation: Since we do not find a passage on shemittah of lands which was repeated at the Plains of Moab in Mishneh Torah (Deuteronomy), we have learned that its general rules and its details were all stated at Sinai. And Scripture comes and teaches us here about other Divine statements that were made to Moses — the commandments given to Moses by Hashem — that they were all from Sinai, both as regards their general rules* *and their fine points, and that they were reiterated at the Plains of Moab."*

THE *SIFSEI CHACHAMIM* (RABBI SHABSE SHTRIM, D. 1719) elucidates further: "The *shemittah* mentioned there (*Deuteronomy* 15:1) is only the general rule — 'At the end of every seven years you shall make *shemittah*' — but the specific details are stated here to teach us that they were promulgated at Sinai. All the details of the other commandments which were mentioned in the Plains of Moab had been given before at Sinai."

In the Talmud we often meet with the expression *Halachah L'Moshe MiSinai:* The stated rule of law was received by Moshe Rabbeinu at Sinai, which is supported by tradition and not by any reference in the Torah (see the Rambam's introduction to his commentary on the *Mishnah*). We know, of course, that the entire body of the Oral Law originated at Mount Sinai. The Rambam (introduction to the *Yad Hachazakah*) writes that the Written Law was given in the basic, succinct form that we have before us today. The detailed meaning and explanation remained for oral transmission. The Oral Law was later reduced to being written down, first as the *Mishnah* and later as *Gemara*.

BECHUKOSAI BEGINS:

> "If you will go in My decrees and observe My commandments and perform them, then I will provide you rains at their proper time, and the land will give its produce, and the tree of the field will give its fruit."

> Rashi comments: *"If you will go in My decrees:* One might be able to think that this refers to fulfillment of the commandments. When it says 'and observe My commandments and perform them,' note that the fulfillment of the commandments has already been stated.

> *What then do I maintain is meant by 'if you go in My decrees?' That you should be laboring in the Torah."*

THE SIFSEI CHACHAMIM ELUCIDATES ON THIS: "SCRIPTURE IS INTERPRETED thusly: 'If you will go in My decrees': When you shall occupy yourselves with Torah, to understand and know it, you shall learn it so that you may 'observe My commandments and perform them.'"

It may well be that our Sages, of blessed memory, chose these two *Sedrahs* to be combined on one Shabbos because *Behar* commences with a reference to Sinai, and *Bechukosai* begins by referring to the obligation to perform the commandments given at Sinai. Taken together, these two *Sedras* present in logical sequence the essence of *Yiddishkeit*, which is predicated on the injunction to remember the Egyptian exodus as a prelude to receiving the Torah at Sinai — which was the ultimate purpose of the liberation of our ancestors from *galus*.

> *Why does the Torah select the mitzvah of shemittah to teach us that the entire Torah, and specifically all its mitzvos, were given at Sinai? Rabbi Moshe Feinstein (1895-1986) explains that the mitzvah of shemittah teaches us that those who trust and rely on Hashem will be blessed and become prosperous. Even though the fields are left unattended during the shemittah year, Hashem blesses the crops of those who trust Him and who keep the mitzvah of shemittah. Similarly, we can apply the lesson of shemittah to all the other mitzvos. Anyone who puts his trust and faith in Hashem and performs His mitzvos will be blessed with all the blessings enumerated in Bechukosai.*

Sefer Bamidbar
Parashas Bamidbar

THE *SEDRAH* BEGINS:

"Hashem spoke to Moses in the wilderness of Sinai, in the Tent of Meeting, on the first of the second month, in the second year after their exodus from the land of Egypt, saying: Take a census of the entire assembly of the Children of Israel according to their families, according to their fathers' house, by number of the names, every male according to their head count."

Rashi comments: **"Hashem spoke to Moses in the wilderness of Sinai:** Because of Israel's dearness before Him, He counts them at all times. When they departed from Egypt, He counted them. And when they fell at the sin of the golden calf, He counted them to determine the number of those who remained. And here, when He came to rest His Divine Presence upon them, He counted them. On the first day of the month of Nisan, the Tabernacle, the site of the revelation of the Divine Presence, was erected. And on the first day of Iyar, the following month, He counted them."

RASHI ENUMERATES ALL THE PLACES WHERE OUR ANCESTORS WERE counted, from the exodus in *Shemos* to the present count in

Bamidbar and beyond, as evidence of the love that Hashem bears His people, Israel. In *Vayikra*, Rashi makes a similar comment, but there it is based on a "call," *vayikra,* and is equated with the call of angels one to the other: "Holy, holy, holy is the Lord of hosts"; without expressly stating it, angels relate to each other with love.

The purpose of counting generally revolves around wealth, to take stock of resources and plan ahead in the field of economy. It will bring satisfaction to a person if the totals "work out" for whatever plans he may have. It may create anxiety if the opposite seems to be the case. Indeed, there is a class of people whose counting of money constitutes an aberration, an unnatural relish for money. The sound approach, however, would seem to be that money is meant to be invested for economic security and, when that is achieved, spent for future needs — or perhaps the other way around — and within the parameters of these two categories one should use it for whatever good he can do with it.

The counting of our forefathers at the direction of Hashem was not just an expression of the love He had for them, but perhaps it was primarily a sign of Hashem's expectation that our people should carry aloft the torch of the Torah as Hashem's beacon of light for all mankind. The comparison of His love to that of angels for one another imparts the idea that humans can emulate that example only if we are capable of fulfilling the edict "You shall not hate your brother in your heart .... you shall not take revenge and you shall not bear a grudge against the members of your people; you shall love your fellow as yourself: I am Hashem" (*Leviticus* 19:17).

References to the love which Hashem has for His people, derived from the several countings and other comparable passages in the Torah, disclose three aspects of that love. Hashem loves all mankind, but primarily Israel; His love encompasses each individual; and He loves the institutions ordained by the Torah, the first of which is Shabbos, "the first of the holy convocations."

> *The Midrash (Bamidbar Rabbah 2:3) teaches that Hashem demonstrated His affection to B'nei Yisrael*

by dividing them into Degalim, distinct camps each with its own distinctive ensign. In the division of the camps, each tribe became conspicuous and unique — as a sign of the pleasure which Hashem took in them. They marched in formation as in a parade, for they were Hashem's pride and joy. The Midrash describes this through an analogy to a wealthy man who inspected his wine cellar. To his dismay, he discovered that all the barrels of wine had soured. As he turned to leave the cellar, he noticed one barrel that had fermented into a fine wine. All his efforts were justified for that single valuable barrel. Similarly, Hashem was disappointed with the behavior of the world, but he took solace in the behavior of Yisrael. Therefore, B'nei Yisrael received special attention and marched in formation.

The Midrash (Bamidbar Rabbah 2:19) also teaches us that Hashem repeatedly counts B'nei Yisrael and takes great pleasure in doing so. Again, the same reason is given: Of all the nations in the world, Hashem focuses on Yisrael. Hashem expresses His love for Yisrael because Yisrael express their love for Hashem in their commitment to His Torah and in their dedication to their duty as the bearers of Torah as a light for all mankind.

Torah Reading for Shavuos

The Torah reading
on the first day of Shavuos begins:

> "In the third month from the Exodus of the Children of Israel from Egypt, on this day they arrived at the wilderness of Sinai" (Exodus 19:1).
>
> Rashi comments: "**On this day:** That is, on the first of the month. It should not have written 'on this day,' but 'on that day,' because the Torah is relating the events after they have happened. What is meant by 'on this day'? That the words of Torah should be as new to you as if it had been given today."

Ramban says that the Israelites went forward to receive the Torah with joy, gladness, and great anticipation. Thus on this holiday of Shavuos, we celebrate *Matan Torah,* the Giving of the Torah, as *Toras Emes,* the Law of Truth, something which in this day and age is not so abundant in the world and something which could solve many a perplexing problem.

On the second day of Shavuos, the Torah reading begins: "Every firstborn male that is born in your cattle you shall consecrate to Hashem your G-d; you shall not work with the firstborn of your ox, and you shall not shear the firstborn of your flock" (*Deuteronomy* 15:19).

Rashi brings down two references to sanctification and concludes that the dedication here involves the redemption of the owner's interest in the animal, the money subsequently going to the Temple's treasury. However, as for the sanctification of the firstborn — from among the Israelites and from among their animals as well — the Torah seems to be emphasizing the miraculous nature of life, its beginning and development, for in actuality the firstborn constitutes the first inkling of a new life.

> *Rabbi Yehuda Loewe (1526-1609), the Maharal of Prague, in Gevuros Hashem (Chap. 46) explains that the three major festivals — Pesach, Shavuos, and Succos — follow an agricultural cycle. Pesach occurs in the spring as the first barley crops ripen, Shavuos occurs when the first fruits ripen sufficiently and are brought to Jerusalem as Bikurim, and Succos is the time of harvest before the onset of the rainy season. The time the first fruits ripen is relative to the time of the initial sprouting during Pesach. That is why the Bikurim are always brought for exactly fifty days, beginning with the second day of Pesach. Similarly, on a spiritual plane, Shavuos is inexorably tied to Pesach. On Pesach the Jews left Egypt, and a new nation was born. The purpose of this new nation was realized at Matan Torah, on Shavuos. Just as the creation of the world depended on the Torah to be completed and perfected, so too the new nation of Israel required the Torah in order to realize its completion and perfection (Sedrah Tazria).*
>
> *Shavuos is the festival in which the sanctification of the first fruits, marking their perfection at the time of ripening, coincides with the sanctification of Yisrael, marking their perfection at the time of Matan Torah. The joy and appreciation the farmer experiences as he makes his pilgrimage to Jerusalem with his Bikurim offering is rivaled only by the joy and appreciation that the Jew experiences in accepting the Torah of truth, Toras Emes, as he makes his ascent to spiritual perfection.*

Parashas Nasso

The *Sedrah* begins:

> "Hashem spoke to Moses, saying: Take a census of the sons of Gershon, them as well, according to their fathers' house, according to their families. From thirty years of age and up until fifty years of age shall you count them, everyone who comes to join the legion to perform work in the Tent of Meeting."

Rashi comments: "Take a census of the sons of Gershon, them as well: As I commanded you regarding the sons of Kehath, to see how many there are who have reached the category of those old enough for Temple service."

Levi had three sons: Gershon (the oldest), Kehas, and Merari. Kehas was the most distinguished of his sons. His first-born son, Amram, was the father of the master of all prophets, Moshe Rabbeinu; his brother Aharon, the first High Priest; and their sister, the prophetess Miriam. Kehas was also the progenitor of the demagogue, Korach, who led a revolt against the authority of Moshe Rabbeinu, seeking thereby to wrest that authority from the Divinely appointed leader, and was soundly punished for his attempt. However, Korach's sons were saved from the debacle according to Rashi (*Numbers* 16:7), and they later became authors of numerous psalms included in the book of *Tehillim*. This happy reversal for the sons of Korach shows the power of *teshuvah*, repentance, a lesson for our people. Thus the sons of Korach reestablished the prestige of their forefather Kehas.

The tribe of Levi was assigned vital tasks in the Sanctuary, commencing with the Tabernacle in the wilderness and continuing throughout the days of the Holy Temple which King

Solomon built. They also dismantled the Tabernacle before Israel journeyed and reassembled it when they rested. Finally, the Levites sang psalms and played musical instruments in the course of the priests' activities.

As well as the priests, the Levites were a privileged group. Forty-eight cities were designated for their occupancy (*Numbers* 35:7). The intent of the scattering of the Levites may have been to allow them to blend with the rest of the nation, since they were a privileged group, in accordance with the direction given to our father Abraham: "Go out of your country... to the land that I will show you" (*Genesis* 12:1), so that his excellence might be widely promulgated.

Tradition has it that the tribe of Levi wielded substantial influence even while in the Egyptian *galus* so that they were not subjected to servitude. Evidence of this belief appears to be the fact that Moshe and Aaron, who were of that tribe, could come and go as they pleased (see Rashi's commentary on *Exodus* 5:4). The freedom of the Levites from the oppression forced upon the rest of the nation is explained as follows: In his evil mind, Pharaoh conceived the idea of utilizing the originally honored guests of the state, the children of Israel, in his building frenzy. But he hesitated to apply compulsion at the beginning. So he issued a call to all patriotic residents of the state, natives and otherwise, to volunteer for such tasks. Our forefathers felt a debt of gratitude to him for having offered them shelter in time of need. In a burst and show of loyalty, they came out en masse, together with other elements of the population who were probably privy to Pharaoh's scheme of directing the plan exclusively at Israel. But the tribe of Levi held back. They were wary of Pharaoh's intentions and chose not to volunteer. After a time Pharaoh contrived to let all other people go free from their labors, but not Israel. Because of their initial rejection of the bait, the Levites remained free. However, the rest of the nation could not wiggle themselves out of the predicament, since they had initially volunteered. This teaches us caution and deliberation in all realms of activity.

The Midrash (Shemos Rabbah 5:16) teaches us that the tribe of Levi was exempt from the labor forced upon the rest of B'nei Yisrael in Egypt. The early commentaries suggest different reasons as to why they were exempt. The Ramban explains that every nation exempts their wise men and scholars from national service; therefore, the tribe of Levi — the scholars and statesmen of Yisrael — were exempt from hard labor.

Based on the Talmud (Sotah 11a), Rabbeinu Chizkiyah Chizkuni (13th century, France) explains that initially even Pharaoh joined the work detail in order to enjoin all the able-bodied men to share in this national service. It is very probable that great rewards were promised to those who joined the work effort. However, the tribe of Levi remembered what their ancestor Yaakov had ordered at the time of his passing. Yaakov had requested his sons to carry his remains out of Egypt for internment in Hebron; all his sons were included, except Levi. Since Levi was destined to serve in the Tabernacle, Yaakov restricted Levi from engaging in any other, mundane service. Therefore, the tribe of Levi did not engage in Pharaoh's workforce, despite the fact that they were compromising their patriotism and resisting the great rewards offered to all the laborers. According to the Chizkuni, we learn from the tribe of Levi to exercise discipline so that we may desist from impulsiveness.

Parshas Beha'aloscha

The *Sedrah* begins:

"Hashem spoke to Moses, saying: Speak to Aaron and say to him: When you kindle the lamps, toward the face of the Menorah shall the seven lamps cast light."

Rashi comments: *"**When you kindle:** Why was the passage dealing with the kindling of the Menorah put next to the passage dealing with the contribution and offerings of the princes? Because when Aaron saw the inauguration of the princes (the contributions and offerings made by the princes at the inauguration of the Tabernacle), he felt bad, for neither he nor his tribe was with them at the inauguration. The Holy One, Blessed is He, said to him: I swear by your life! Your role is greater than theirs, for you kindle and prepare the lamps."*

RAMBAN ELABORATES UPON AND ELUCIDATES RASHI'S COMMENT. The kindling and setting the lamps in order, which we would normally view as a mere menial chore, is of supreme significance — so much so that it exceeds in this respect the dedication of the princes. While on the face of it, there might have been more substantial performances by Aharon and his sons and their descendants that could be deemed praiseworthy — such as the sacrifices which the priestly order was destined to perform during services in the Holy Temple, or the seven-day consecration of Aharon and his sons at the time of the erection and the centralizing of the Tabernacle or the services that the High Priest would perform on Yom Kippur, or his ascent to the pinnacle of sanctity in order to be able to enter the Holy of Holies on that day — in reality the care, kindling, and arrangement of the lights turned out to be far more laudable. Ramban concludes that the encouragement Hashem gave Aharon is in reality an allusion to the Chanukah dedication of lights which the Hasmoneans were to inaugurate after their victory — and the lights of the Chanukah festival will shine forever, although the tenure of the Holy Temple will come to an end. The Hasmoneans, the heroes of the festival, were priests, descendants of Aaron. The image of light used by Isaiah, together with its irresistible illumination of the surrounding darkness, is in reality the Menorah itself, the favorite symbol of Israel (see *Sedrah Metzora*).

We of this generation have witnessed the bestial onslaught by a degenerate Nazi Germany against our helpless brethren — men, women, and little children. We have also been privileged to witness the reestablishment of the Jewish State with the beautiful Menorah as its emblem. May this great and miraculous event, granted us by the *Ribbono Shel Olam*, be a precursor of the rebuilding of the Holy Temple on its holy mountain speedily in our days.

> *Rashi and the Ramban deal with Aharon's feelings when the princes of each tribe offered contributions for the Tabernacle and he did not. Hashem comforted Aharon with the mitzvah of lighting the Menorah. Rabbi Yehoshua Heschel Rabinowitz, the late Rebbe of Manestritch (1860-1938), explains the underlying meaning in his work Divrei Yehoshua with the following introduction: When a group of people form a community, they must appoint leaders who will tend to their physical welfare. Authority is vested in this leadership, and an infrastructure is created to facilitate commerce and justice and to guarantee the safety of the community. These appointees devote themselves to enhancing the quality of life in the physical sense. However, there must also be spiritual guidance. In a Jewish community, the Rabbinical leadership, charged with the religious education and spiritual welfare of their*

community, hold a higher office than their counterparts charged with the physical well-being of that community. After all, spiritual gains are eternal, while physical benefits are only temporal. Aharon and the princes of the twelve tribes were all leaders. Aharon is described by the Mishnah (Pirkei Avos 1:12) as "loving peace, loving people, and bringing them closer to the Torah." He was the paradigm of religious leadership. The princes, however, were leaders who tended to the physical welfare of their tribes. When the princes calculated the weight of the disassembled Tabernacle, they dedicated wagons and oxen to transport the heavy load. They were motivated by the love of their fellows and a desire to help alleviate their burden. When Aharon saw the princes' dedication, he was consumed with doubt and concern: Perhaps he was not serving his fellow man within his realm as well as he could. If he were more involved in the physical world, like his counterparts, maybe he could have made a greater contribution. Hashem therefore explained to Aharon that within his realm he contributed more than did the princes. To this end, Aharon was given the mitzvah of lighting the Menorah, the symbol of the Torah's guiding light, since spreading the light of Torah is the ultimate accomplishment.

Parshas Shelach

The *Sedra* begins:

> "Hashem spoke to Moses, saying: Send forth for yourself men, and let them spy out the Land of Canaan that I am giving to the Children of Israel; one man each from his father's tribe shall you send, every one a leader among them."

> Rashi comments: "**Send forth for yourself men:** The term 'for yourself' means 'by your discretion.' I do not command you to do so, but if you wish, send forth. Since Israel came and said, 'Let us send men ahead of us,' as it says (Deuteronomy 1:22), 'All of you approached me and said, "Let us send men ahead of us, etc.,"' Moshe consulted the Shechinah. G-d said: I told them that the Land is good, as it says (Exodus 3:17), I shall bring you up from the affliction of Egypt, etc. I swear by their lives that I give them room to err through the words of the spies so that they shall not take possession of it."

RAMBAN DOES NOT TAKE AS STRINGENT A VIEW AS RASHI, SINCE Moshe was agreeable to the venture apparently without any objection. However, Ramban points out that Moshe had in mind for the spies to bring back a verification of the "good land"; also, when the Israelites asked to send spies, their intent was to achieve a military objective. They wished the spies to become acquainted with the lay of the land and to determine where the first assault should be made, to see the "nakedness of the land" so that the spies could then lead in the invasion as the vanguard. The conclusion may legitimately be drawn that the spies brought a truthful report in accordance with their findings and that their dissenters, Yehoshua and Calev, were just a bit unrealistic.

The sin of the spies, according to Ramban, based on our Sages in the Talmud (*Sotah* 34b), was that the majority of the spies, as well as the people themselves, should never have requested nor entered upon the venture but followed Hashem implicitly, just as they had been guided in the wilderness by His clouds. As it is written (*Deuteronomy* 1:30): "Hashem, your G-d Who goes before you, He shall fight for you." When Moshe Rabbeinu said that the enterprise pleased him well, it was with much reluctance, seeing the frame of mind of our ancestors at the time.

Rashi points out that the spies were initially worthy men (*Numbers* 13:3). However, this would seem to be at variance with Rashi's commentary on the verse (*Numbers* 13:26): "**They went and came:** To compare their going with their coming; just as their coming was with an evil scheme, so too was their going with an evil scheme." Similarly, the Talmud (*Sotah* 34b) states that Rabbi Chiya bar Abba declared that from the very beginning the spies had the intention to report only the disadvantages of the land of Israel. So how could Rashi comment earlier that they were worthy men? One answer is that on the scale of worthiness, intentions do not count — only actions. As long as the spies were open to persuasion by their colleagues Yehoshua and Calev to desist from giving an evil report and fulfill their mission in accordance with the rectitude expected of them, they were not deemed perverters of the truth. But in the long run, it is action that counts. Thus it is always not the theory that matters so much as the deed, even (to quote a non-Jewish writer, Longfellow) "heart within and G-d o'erhead."

A question may be asked on Rashi's comment, "I swear by their lives that I give them room to err through the words of the spies so that they shall not take possession of it." Might not this be antithetical to the concept that before the blind one should not place a stumbling block, both in the physical and moral sense? As it is written (*Genesis* 18:25), "And shall the Judge of all the world not do judgment?" One possible answer is that Hashem foresaw what the people had been up to and, as is the way of Divine guidance, if one is righteous, Hashem aids him in that course, and if regretfully he proves ornery, he is confirmed in that situation as well. The choice is ours.

> Rabbi Yaakov Yitzchok Ruderman (1900-1987), founder of Yeshivas Ner Israel of Baltimore, asks how the spies, worthy men of great stature, changed their colors so quickly and caused one of the greatest debacles in Jewish history. He answers with the words of our Sages in the Talmud (Succah 52b). Man's yetzer harah, his evil inclination, attempts to overcome him every day. Were it not for Divine assistance, man would be overwhelmed by his yetzer hara. As it is written in Psalms (37:32-33), "The evil (inclination) seeks to kill the righteous, but Hashem does not allow him to fall." Accordingly, since Hashem did not explicitly order the expedition into Canaan, the spies were not imbued with the Divine assistance to shield them from their yetzer hara. And obviously, without Divine assistance, even the greatest of men will be overpowered in short order by his evil inclination. For this reason we make in our daily prayers a special request: "Do not let my evil inclination overcome me." Hence, we can explain the words of Rashi: "I give them room to err through the words of the spies so that they shall not take possession of it." Rashi does not mean that Hashem will cause them to stumble. Rather, without Divine aid, there will always be room to err.

Parashas Korach

THE *SEDRAH* BEGINS:

> "Korah son of Izhar son of Levi, with Dathan and Abiram, sons of Eliab, and On son of Peleth — sons of Reuben — took ."

> Rashi comments : "**Korah took:** This passage is beautifully expounded in the Midrash of Rabbi Tanchuma."

A QUESTION MIGHT BE ASKED CONCERNING THE USE OF THE TERM "beautifully" in Rashi's comment, "This passage is *beautifully* expounded in the *Midrash* of Rabbi Tanchuma." Here was an example of a perfidious rebellion with potentially disastrous consequences for the people. How does "beautifully" fit in with the tragedy even by way of objective comment? One possible answer is that the translation of the term used by Rashi, "*yafah*," is not always "beautifully"; it may mean "good" or "well"; i.e., the matter is expounded well in the *Midrash*.

> Rabbi Dovid ben Shmuel HaLevi (the Taz, 1586-1667) asks in his work Divrei Dovid how Rashi could comment that this passage is expounded beautifully or well in the Midrash. Our Sages teach us that it is forbidden to comment that a particular law is nice and another one is not. By commenting that this particular Midrash is "beautiful," it is implied that other portions of the Midrash are not beautiful, Heaven forbid. The Taz answers that typically there is a simple interpretation of a verse and a Midrashic (homiletic) interpretation. However, this verse can be understood only with the Midrash, since there is no simple explanation for the words "and Korach took," since the verse does not tell us

> what he took. Therefore, Rashi explains that on this verse the Midrash explains beautifully, meaning to say that here we must rely on the Midrash even for the simple explanation.

Rashi continues: "**Korach took:** This means he took himself off to one side to be separate from the assembly of Israel by raising objections regarding the priesthood. This is why Onkelos rendered "and he took" as "and he separated himself," as if to say that he separated himself from the rest of the assembly by sustaining a dispute. Alternatively, "Korach took" means he drew heads of courts who were among them to himself with words; i.e., he persuaded them to support him, as it says, 'Take Aaron,' and 'Take with your words.'"

It should be noted that the Hebrew text does not have the apparent grammatical requirement of an object for the verb "*took*" ("Korach took"). Perhaps what is emphasized in Rashi, in part borne out by Ramban, is that the verb "took" is best understood as a reflexive: he took himself in his own demagogic fashion to cause trouble and in some way to aggrandize himself. Such a course of action has been repeated time and again throughout history.

The commentaries fluctuate between supplying an object for the word "took" to make it grammatically sound and not doing so. *Midrash Rabbah* and *Midrash Tanchuma* explain the word "took" in two different ways. First, it could mean that he separated himself; he became a loner, intending to influence other disaffected people — or those easily led astray — in order to establish an opposition to Moshe and Aharon. In response, Moshe challenged the Korachites to a test. They were to assume the function of priesthood by bringing incense before Hashem, Who would then indicate His choice. Of course, the outcome was a foregone conclusion, but Korach could not refuse to undergo this test.

Second, "take" could mean to win over and to find favor. No man is above being pleased when something good is said to his face about him or even "behind his back." Thus Korach directed his attention to the heads of the Sanhedrin, the top echelon of the nation. And when he found that someone else seemed to speak in similar terms, he was surprised how another could be endowed with similar talents. Such was the case with Korach: He plumbed his own mind and heart and found that he was really a "great guy," although he was actually infected with a goodly dose of egotism, vaulting ambition, and jealousy. He decided to cast the dice.

However, the Ramban has a third explanation. "Taking" is also used in Scripture in the sense of bestirring oneself. In such case, it needs no object, for it is purely reflexive, as Ramban cites: "Now Avshalom in his lifetime had taken and reared up for himself a pillar which is in the valley of the King" (*Samuel II* 18:18). Hashem should rescue us from such self-styled saviors.

> The Taz points out that the Ramban explains "Korach took" to mean that his heart took him. Perhaps Rashi also means that Korach's heart took him and led him away from the rest of Israel. The point of this modification of Rashi's explanation is that there is a difference between a crime committed on the spur of the moment and a crime that is premeditated. By indicating that Korach's heart took him to separate from the rest of Israel, we learn that Korach planned and schemed his rebellion. His rebellion did not ignite suddenly; rather it was premeditated.

Parashas Chukas

The *Sedrah* Begins:

> "Hashem spoke to Moses and to Aaron, saying: This is the statute of the Torah, which Hashem has commanded, saying: Speak to the Children of Israel that they shall take

to you a perfectly red cow, which has no blemish, upon which a yoke has not come."

Rashi comments: **"This is the statute of the Torah:** *Because Satan and the nations of the world aggrieve Israel by saying, 'What is this commandment?' and 'What reason is there to it?' therefore, Scripture wrote of it 'statute,' which implies that 'it is a decree from before Me; you do not have the right to question it.'"*

RASHI EXPLAINS THE USE OF THE *CHUKAH* (STATUTE), AS A RESPONSE to the nations of the world who might taunt *B'nei Yisrael*: "What is this commandment and what is its reason?" It is thus described as "a decree from before Me, and you do not have the right to question it." This remarkable statute emphasizes that which is truly inexplicable; the purpose of the ashes of the red heifer is to cleanse those who are unclean, yet it defiles all who handle the ashes. To dispel any criticism of a seeming contradiction, Hashem began by saying: "This is the statute of the Torah." It is a statute promulgated by the Divine Lawgiver, and as is the case of every statute, it must be observed, even if we cannot fathom its meaning.

Where, however, do we find that the nations take sufficient interest in so intimate a matter as how a Jewish person serves his G-d? Rarely do the nations of the world take an interest in, or show any knowledge of, how the Jew worships his G-d. At times they inquire about the mitzvos we are commanded to keep, but generally speaking, the world at large is fairly oblivious to Jewish religious practices. The meaning of the reference may be intended as a hint to the Jewish attitude, "What will the *goyim* say?" We should have learned by now, as reinforced by this *Sedrah*, that we should let them say whatever they want — and we should pay no heed at all!

A question might be asked as to Satan's involving himself in this speculation. It is understandable that he notoriously fishes in troubled waters and that this lack of comprehension on the part of the obedient may be his entry. For on "And these are the ordinances which you shall place before them" (*Exodus* 21:1), Rashi points out that this direction indicates that the laws of the Torah should not only be rehearsed but also explained as to their reasons so as to make them palatable as is a table set with sumptuous foods. Here, however, quite the contrary is taught — that we accept the directive on faith and implicit observance. Satan can involve himself only when a Jew is too confused to be able to distinguish the difference between these two approaches.

Consequently, whether or not we, either collectively or individually, are aware of Satan's meddling depends upon our proper attunement to such a collective or individual consciousness so as to be able to spot that evil agency and recognize it for what it is, a motiveless malignity. The remedy is not to become flustered but to treat it with the utmost patience; then Satan is sure to lose. We are using figurative language, because no matter how one designates the impediments that frequently appear in our course of life, such drawbacks unquestionably exist. Whether or not our response is to pray, "Remove Satan from before us and after us," or we tell ourselves, "Smile, Buddy, you will overcome this also," an attitude of being calm, cool, and collected will contain and isolate that "no-goodnik." As to the conclusion of Rashi, we accept the decree from Above and endeavor to abide by it implicitly.

> *We are taught in Pirkei Avos (5:23-24): "Yehudah the son of Tema said: 'Be brazen as a leopard to do the will of your Father in Heaven." He continued to say that the impudent is destined for Gehinnom. Rabbi Samson Raphael Hirsch (1808-1888) explains that the preceding Mishnah teaches that firmness and defiance in the face of obstacles is praiseworthy when it comes to fulfilling the will of Hashem. But such conduct is not necessarily beneficial in our relationship with our fellow man and in the*

attainment of objectives which a man willingly sets for himself. Rabbi Moshe Isserles (1525-1573) incorporates this idea into his introductory comments on the Code of Jewish Law and writes (Orach Chaim 1:1) "One should not be embarrassed before those who scoff at his worship of Hashem." The trait of impudence has its proper time and place — when it is necessary to ignore the taunts of those who attempt to divert us from our service of Hashem.

Parashas Balak

The Sedrah begins:

"Balak son of Zippor saw all that Israel did to the Amorite. Moab was very frightened of the people because they were formidable, and Moab was disgusted in the face of the Children of Israel. Moab said to the elders of Midian, 'Now the congregation will chew up our entire surroundings, as an ox chews up the greenery of the field.'"

[Balak is afraid of being overrun by B'nei Yisrael and so appeals to Balaam:] "Please come and invoke a curse upon this people for me, for it is more powerful than I am; perhaps I will succeed; we will strike at it, and I will drive it away from the land. For I know that whomever you bless is blessed and whomever you curse is accursed."

Rashi comments: "**Balak son of Zippor saw all that Israel did to the Amorite:** He said to Moab, 'These two kings, Sihon and Og, in whom we had confidence, did not stand up before the B'nei Yisrael. How much more so that we, who are weaker, cannot stand up before them.' Therefore, Moab was very frightened. **To the elders of Midian:** But had they not always hated each other, as it says, 'who struck Midian in the field of Moab,' for Midian had come against Moab for war? But out of their fear of Israel, they made peace between themselves. And what did Moab see that led them to take advice from Midian? Since they saw Israel emerging victorious in an extraordinary manner, they said, 'The leader of these Jews grew up in Midian. Let us ask them what his unique trait is.' The Midianites said to them, 'His power is in nothing but his mouth.' The Moabites said, 'We too will come against them with a person whose power is in his mouth.'"

RAMBAN DWELLS UPON WHAT BALAK HAD IN MIND WHEN HE SAID THAT B'nei Yisrael were "more powerful than I am." He knew that our ancestors were not going to attack Moab (*Deuteronomy* 2:19), but his fear was that the prowess of Israel would cause havoc among *B'nei Yisrael's* enemies, resulting in the humiliation of Moab and perhaps in the eventual subservience of Moab to B'nei Yisrael.

A comparison between Balak of ancient Moab and the Arabs of our own day might be instructive. Why are the Arabs opposed to us? Did Israel dispossess any of them? On the contrary, Israel's provisional government at the time of the Declaration of Independence pleaded with the Arabs to stay put and work together for the good of the country, but the Arabs chose the path of war.

When Nasser of Egypt formed what he thought was a strong alliance against Israel in 1967 in order to launch first a blockade and then a vicious land attack, he found himself so outwitted that he had to make the strange statement that Israel was aided by America. He finally succumbed physically owning to the failure of his plans.

What do the Arabs still fear? They see that Israel is victorious as if through a miracle and are oppressed by the thought of their continued humiliation. But Israel has taught them the *Sedrah* of *Balak*, and they should know it by now.

> *Rabbi Meir Leibush ben Yechiel Michel (the Malbim, 1809-1879) asks why Balak resorted to the unconventional plan of invoking a curse upon B'nei Yisrael. A king in his situation has two choices: either to muster his troops and engage the enemy in battle or to dispatch a diplomat to negotiate a peaceful relationship in order to allay his fears. Why were these conventional options neglected? The Malbim answers that the Torah addresses this question. Balak could not start a war with B'nei Yisrael because he "saw all that Israel did to the Amorites." Even though Balak was a powerful monarch, he recognized the superior might of B'nei Yisrael. Furthermore, "Moab was very frightened of the people because it was formidable." Balak knew that it would be an exercise in futility to engage the enemy with his frightened troops. The alternative, then, would be to negotiate a peaceful relationship, but "Moab was disgusted in the face of the Children of Israel." The Moabites could not bring themselves to offer B'nei Yisrael the olive branch because they hated them. The religion of the Jews — the Chosen People — and their exalted place in the universe created an irreversible animosity. There is no hatred like the hatred engendered by religious differences. Therefore, Balak had to resort to unconventional warfare, and he attempted to have B'nei Yisrael cursed. Only through the agency of Balaam did Balak learn "How can I imprecate? G-d has not imprecated" (Numbers 23:8).*

PARASHAS PINCHAS

THE *SEDRAH* BEGINS:

"Hashem spoke to Moses saying: Phinehas son of Elazar son of Aaron the Kohen turned back My wrath from upon the Children of Israel when he zealously avenged My vengeance among them, so I did not consume the Children of Israel in My vengeance. Therefore, say: Behold! I give him My covenant of peace."

Rashi comments: **"Phinehas son of Elazar son of Aaron the Kohen:** *Because the tribes were humiliating him, saying, 'Did you see this son of Puti whose mother's father fattened calves for idolatry, yet he killed the prince of a tribe of Israel!' This is why Scripture comes and traces his ancestry to Aaron.* **When he zealously avenged My vengeance:** *This means when he avenged that which had to be avenged for Me, when he expressed the rage with which I should have been enraged.* **My covenant of peace:** *That it should be for him as a covenant of peace, like a person who feels thankful to one who does him a favor. Here too, the Holy One, Blessed is He, declared to him His feelings of friendship."*

RASHI EMPHASIZES THE DISPARAGEMENT OF PINCHAS BY HIS CRITICS. They contended that he took the law into his own hands to execute judgment against a leader of the community, whereas Pinchas's father, Elazar, married a daughter of Putiel, identified as Yisro, who before his conversion was an idol worshiper (see *Rashi Exodus* 6:25). But the same Rashi also says that Putiel may refer to Yosef, who overcame his passion. This interpretation stems from the Hebrew word for "overcame," which shares the same root as "Putiel," as does the Hebrew word for "fatten" (calves) — to hint at idolatry (fattening calves for idolatry).

Rashi emphasizes the "covenant of peace" given by Hashem through Moshe Rabbeinu as Pinchas's reward because he was a true descendant of Aharon, a man of peace, and because he saved the honor of Israel by performing the deed on behalf of Hashem. Ramban, on the other hand, stresses the covenant of eternal priesthood as the consequence of his unsparing zeal in avenging what Hashem might have avenged Himself. Thus, according to Ramban, Pinchas brought about expiation for the people rather than some untoward calamity which might have otherwise befallen our ancestors.

The stirring, regretful, and exciting drama associated with Pinchas may be viewed from several different angles. Essentially, the deed of Pinchas was an act of national atonement. It arrested the moral plague that threatened to destroy the character of our people through idolatrous worship and lewd behavior. The despicable rites associated with idol-worshiping nations and their accompanying moral laxity have been the major factors in the destruction of ancient peoples. It is a source of deepest concern for our people in today's day and age, when having entered the mainstream of some of the progressive nations of the world — including this, our blessed America — we may become influenced by the deterioration of the moral fiber of such nations.

It is in these areas where our *Yeshivos Gedolos, Yeshivos Ketanos,* and Hebrew Day Schools have done a yeoman's job of moving our Jewish youth away from the backsliding tendencies which have afflicted our society. May Hashem strengthen those who are active in promoting these sacred institutions.

> *Rabbi Elimelech of Lizhensk (1717-1787), the Noam Elimelech, ponders Rashi's commentary: "The tribes were humiliating him, saying, 'Did you see this son of Puti whose mother's father fattened calves for idolatry, yet he killed the prince of a tribe of Israel!' This is why Scripture comes and traces his ancestry to Aharon." Didn't everyone*

know that Pinchas was the grandson of Aharon? And this knowledge notwithstanding, they still berated him! So what is gained by tracing his roots back to Aharon? To answer this question, the Noam Elimelech explains that many of us are uncertain in specific situations as to whether or not a particular activity is a mitzvah. As with every moral dilemma, the evil inclination blinds us from seeing clearly the proper path to pursue. But, when we see a tzaddik embark on this course, we can learn by his example that this is in fact an opportunity to perform a mitzvah. Before Pinchas killed Zimri, the prince of the tribe of Shimon, no one knew what to do (see Rashi, Numbers 25:6). Would it be a mitzvah to kill him or not? After Pinchas killed Zimri, however, it became clear to everyone that it was a mitzvah to stand up for Hashem — even if it meant killing the prince of a tribe. But no one could understand how Pinchas knew that it was a mitzvah. "Did you see this son of Puti whose mother's father fattened calves for idolatry!" How did he know that it was a mitzvah? "This is why Scripture comes and traces his ancestry to Aharon." There is nothing unusual here: Pinchas was the grandson of Aharon, and in his grandfather's merit he perceived the proper course of action that eluded all the others. According to this explanation, the tribes were not humiliating Pinchas; rather they were proclaiming their surprise at and admiration for his quick response, while at the same time questioning their own hesitation.

Parshas Mattos
Parshas Masei

THE *SEDRA* BEGINS:

"Moses spoke to the heads of the tribes of the Children of Israel, saying, 'This is the matter that Hashem has commanded: If a man takes a vow to Hashem or swears an oath to prohibit a prohibition upon himself, he shall not profane his word; according to whatever comes from his mouth shall he do.'"

Rashi comments: **"The heads of the tribes:** *He accorded honor to the princes by teaching them first, and only afterward did he teach all the rest of the Children of Israel. And from where do we know that the other statements of G-d were also taught in this manner? The Torah says (Exodus 34:31-32), 'And Aaron and all the princes of the assembly returned to him, and Moses would speak to them; after that, all the Children of Israel would approach.' Why does Scripture see fit to bring this statement here? It teaches us that the nullification of vows can be performed by an individual who is an expert, and if no individual who is an expert is available, one can nullify his vows with three common people."*

THERE ARE SEVERAL TYPES OF VOWS. ONE IS A SOLEMN PROMISE TO consecrate something to Hashem, made at a time of distress in order to secure Divine help. Another type is an expression of gratitude for Divine aid. Then there is an *issur*, a negative vow, a self-imposed pledge to abstain from doing or enjoying something that is otherwise perfectly allowable.

The essential requirement when one has made a vow is that "he shall not break his word" (*Numbers* 30:3), except those commitments which may be legally annulled. Special regulations apply to women who have undertaken vows, viz. (1) a young unmarried woman under her father's guardianship; he may annul such a pledge the day he hears of it; (2) a married woman may have certain types of her self-assumed obligations nullified by her husband — again only on the day he hears of it; (3) widows and divorced women are independent, and their vows are fully binding.

Perhaps the reason for the investiture of a father and husband with the authority to cancel the vows of women under their respective jurisdictions — in which instances the Torah says, "And Hashem will forgive her" — is for the sake of *shalom bayis*, domestic tranquillity.

S\ED\RAH M\ASEI opens with the journeys of the Children of Israel during their forty years in the wilderness. Rashi explains that these journeys were listed to make known the acts of kindness of the Omnipresent. Lest it be thought that the thirty-eight years of the remaining forty years of wandering in the wilderness were exacting and exhausting, the recapitulation of the journeys shows the contrary. It may be suggested that the placing of this *Sedrah* after *Mattos*, usually both read together on a single Shabbos, is a *remez*, a hint, that where there is *shalom bayis*, a house where peace and contentment reign, there also do His mercy and lovingkindness dwell.

> *As mentioned above, there are three types of vows. The first type is a vow uttered during a time of distress to secure Divine help. Yaakov Avinu (Bereishis 28:20) set the precedent when he made a vow to Hashem to secure His protection as he fled from his parents' home on account of Eisav's wrath. Tosafos (Chullin 2b) states that we learn from Yaakov Avinu to act accordingly. The second type,*

an expression of gratitude for Divine aid, had taken the form of a sacrifice brought in the Temple. The owner would "vow" to bring an animal as a sacrifice. Today, a pledge to charity is a substitute for a sacrifice. The third type of vow is an issur, a self-imposed pledge to abstain from doing or enjoying something that is otherwise perfectly allowable. Our Rabbis have taught us that it is inappropriate to make such vows. As the Talmud (Nedarim 22a) teaches, one who makes a vow, even if he fulfills it, is an evil person! The Talmud Yerushalmi rebukes the man who makes such vows: "The Torah's prohibitions are not enough for you that you feel compelled to add more!" The Torah is teaching us that the gift of speech is very powerful and that a prohibition created by man's words is as severe as the Torah's prohibitions. As with all of Hashem's gifts to man, we must be careful not to abuse our power of speech.

SEFER DEVARIM
PARASHAS DEVARIM

THE *SEDRAH* BEGINS:

"These are the words that Moses spoke to all Israel, across the Jordan; in the wilderness, in the Plain, opposite the [Sea of] Reeds, between Paran and Tophel and Laban, and Hazeroth, and Di-zahab."

Rashi comments: **"These are the words:** *Because they are words of rebuke and because Scripture lists here all the places in which they caused anger before the Omnipresent, this is why it put "the words" vaguely and mentioned them through intimation, because of the honor of Israel.* **To all Israel:** *Had he rebuked only a part of them, those in the market who were not present at the rebuke would have said, 'You heard from the son of Amram and did not respond at all from such-and-such a point. Had we been there, we would have answered him.' This is why Moses gathered all of them and said to them, 'See now, you are all here. Whoever has a refutation of my words, let him respond.'"*

A SUMMARY OF THE IMPLIED MEANING OF THE PLACES IS GIVEN IN Onkelos' version of this verse: "... He reproved them because they sinned in the desert. They angered Him in the plain of Moab, facing the Sea of Reeds. In Paran they derogated the manna, and in Hazeroth they angered him on account of meat, and because of the golden calf."

Rashi's comment notes that since these are words of reproof, Moshe sets forth all the places where Israel angered Hashem. Out of respect for Israel, however, he alludes to these events by their location. Nonetheless, he includes all Israel, singling out no one, absenting no one from the words to follow through which he elucidates the significance of the places mentioned.

Moshe Rabbeinu never hesitated to call Israel onto the carpet. Why then the circumspection here? When he came down from Sinai with the Tablets of the Law, in sight of the golden calf, he shattered the Tablets in righteous anger and called out, "Whoever is for Hashem, let him come to me," and when the Levites obeyed the call, he ordered them to execute summary judgment on the sinners. Three thousand men immediately paid with their lives (*Exodus* 32:28).

Further, "And you should know that not because of your righteousness does Hashem, your G-d, give you this good land to take possession of it, for you are a stiff-necked people" (*Deuteronomy* 9:6). And further (*Deuteronomy* 9:24), "You have been rebels against Hashem from the day that I knew you!"

Perhaps the sharp language used by Moshe was due to extreme provocation — at the sight of the terrible deed of the sin of the golden calf. When Moshe recapitulated in *Deuteronomy* the forty years' experience in the wilderness and recalled the instances of backsliding on the part of our ancestors, he could mince no words in utter condemnation. But here in *Sedrah Devarim* he was calm, cool, and collected as he sought to mollify the Israelites rather than reprimand them, following the dictum of Rashi (*Numbers* 12:13): "When one seeks something from another, he should say a few niceties first and then present his request." In other words, Moshe Rabbeinu fulfilled one of the teachings of the Torah: *Derech Eretz*, or *Menschlichkeit*.

Rabbeinu Ovadiah of Bertinoro (1440-1516) also addresses the method of Moshe Rabbeinu's rebuke. In his work Amar Nekei he showed that Moshe Rabbeinu rebuked B'nei Yisrael in strong terms many times, as it says (Deuteronomy 9:7-8): "You have been rebels against Hashem," and "at Horeb you provoked Hashem." In these instances Moshe did not take into consideration the honor of Yisrael, so why did he concern himself with it here? Rabbeinu Ovadiah answers that since this is the beginning of a book of the Pentateuch, Moshe did not publicly want to express his rebuke in such a manner that the Book of Devarim would open with the disgrace of Israel. Similarly, Rashi comments at the mitzvah of Pesach Sheni (Numbers 9:1), "And why did the book not begin with this passage? Because this passage is to the discredit of Israel, in that the entire forty years that Israel were in the wilderness, they sacrificed no pesach offering but this one alone."

Rabbi Leib Chasman (1869-1935) comments that this Parashah gives us an insight into how great and holy were the Jews of this period. Most people tend to believe that they were fine, upstanding individuals, having little need to improve. Rarely did they have to take the time to introspect. Nothing could be further from the truth. When Moshe spoke to B'nei Yisrael, he rebuked them in code, without explicitly describing their flaws, yet each one of them heard his chastisement! How sensitive they must have been to their true spiritual level, ever searching for ways to improve — to the extent that even an ambiguous statement of reproof had real meaning to them! We should learn from this episode to attempt to gauge our spirituality realistically, rather than go through life in a fantasy of assumed perfection.

Parashas Va'eschanan

THE SEDRAH BEGINS:

"I implored Hashem at that time, saying, 'My Lord Hashem, You have begun to show Your servant Your greatness and Your strong hand, for what power is there in the heavens or on earth that can perform according to Your deeds and according to Your mighty acts? Please let me cross and see the good land that is on the other side of the Jordan, this good mountain and the Lebanon.' But Hashem became angry with me because of you, and he did not listen to me; Hashem said to me, 'It is much for you! Do not continue to speak to Me further about this matter.'"

Rashi comments: **"I implored:** *Forms of the word chinun, imploring, in all places in which they appear in Scripture mean nothing but granting or requesting a gift for free. Although the righteous could make their requests dependent on their good deeds and would be justified in requesting things as the reward they deserve, they seek from the Omnipresent nothing but a gift without payment. Because Hashem told Moses, 'And I will show favor to whom I shall show favor' (Exodus 33:19), Moses spoke to Him with the language of 'I implored.'"*

Concerning Rashi's comment, Ramban remarks that the plea was on the basis of being "merciful in judgment." It seems that Rashi meant that Moshe Rabbeinu's plea to Hashem was that if he was justly entitled to have the decree in question reversed — good — and if not, then the plea should be granted out of Divine mercy.

However, the following consideration must be kept in mind. The terms "My Lord Hashem" is pronounced in Hebrew as if written Hashem *Elokim,* though in the text it is written with *Aleph-Dalet* and *Yud-Hei,* which according to the Rabbis yields

140 / Raising the Bar

Ramban's view, of Divine justice preceding Divine mercy. If however we use the pronunciation in the usual course of reading it, then we have a Rashi elsewhere which would support his interpretation here.

On the verse "In the beginning of G-d's creating the heavens and the earth" (*Genesis* 1:1), Rashi says that "it does not state 'Hashem created' because at the beginning Hashem intended the world to be placed under the attribute of strict justice, but He realized that the world could not then endure. Therefore, He gave precedence to Divine mercy which is combined with Divine justice. It is thus written later (*Genesis* 2:4): "On the day of Hashem's, *Elokim*'s, making of earth and heavens." In our present discussion, too, we pronounce the first word Hashem and the second, Elokim — which signifies the order used by Rashi, Divine mercy preceding Divine justice.

Learned people perennially inquire why the severe decree was made against Moshe Rabbeinu for having struck the rock that yielded water to the thirst-oppressed Israelites instead of speaking to it as Hashem had commanded him to do (*Numbers* 20:7-11). The acceptable explanation is based on the verse, "And Hashem was angry with me for your sakes." "For your sakes" is understood by Rabbi Samson Raphael Hirsch to mean "for your good." Had Moshe's disbelief (that the rock would produce water by merely speaking to it) gone unpunished, the people would have become hardened in their transgression. For their sake, therefore, it was impossible for Hashem to overlook it. This explanation underscores the fact that Moshe Rabbeinu's life was not only one of extraordinary service and dedication to the people of Israel but also one of self-sacrifice.

The Talmud (Sotah 14a) teaches that Rabbi Simlai explained why Moshe Rabbeinu wanted to enter Eretz Yisrael so desperately. Moshe Rabbeinu yearned for the opportunity to fulfill those mitzvos that are performed exclusively in Eretz Yisrael. Hashem responded to Moshe's request as follows:

Since you are concerned only with receiving the rewards of the mitzvos fulfilled in Eretz Yisrael, it will be considered as if you actually did the mitzvos, and you will receive the commensurate rewards.

However, the question lingers as to why this was Moshe's desire. Does not the Mishnah in Pirkei Avos (1:3) teach that we should perform the mitzvos as a servant who is not motivated by rewards. Rabbi Chaim of Volozhin (1749-1821) answered (Ruach Chaim on Avos) that Hashem's master plan when creating the world was to extend His beneficence to the inhabitants of the world. Ultimately, the highest form of Divine service would be to perform mitzvos in order to provide Hashem an opportunity to grant reward. But when a person wants to receive the rewards for his own selfish reasons, his service appears less than exemplary. The test of one's true intentions is whether he would do the mitzvah in order for someone else to receive the reward. Now we can understand the exchange between Moshe Rabbeinu and Hashem as described by Rabbi Simlai. Moshe's service was on the highest level. He performed the mitzvos so that Hashem could extend His kindness to His creation. Therefore, Moshe desired to enter Eretz Yisrael to fulfill those mitzvos that are applicable only there. Hashem responded that since Moshe's real concern was solely to generate reward for the mitzvos, it would be considered as if he had performed the mitzvos, and he would be granted the accompanying reward.

Parashas Eikev

The *Sedrah* begins:

> "And it will be because of your listening to these ordinances and your observing and performing them that Hashem, your G-d, will safeguard for you the covenant and the kindness that He swore to your forefathers. He will love you, He will bless you, and He will multiply you, and He will bless the fruit of your womb and the fruit of your land; your grain, your wine, and your oil; the offspring of your cattle and the herds of your flock — on the land that He swore to your forefathers to give you. You will be the most blessed of all the peoples; there will be no infertile male or infertile female among you or among your animals."

> Rashi comments: *"And it will be because of your listening:* If the relatively light commandments that a person tramples with his heels and does not take seriously enough 'you shall listen to,' then 'Hashem, your G-d, will safeguard for you the covenant'; in other words, He will keep His promise to you."

Rashi uses the picturesque, if not somewhat strange, image of easy-to-observe commandments as those upon which a person treads with his heels in order to emphasize their "lightness." Ramban states that the word *eikev* means "heel" or "footprint," and when used in connection with obedience to the edicts of the Torah, it refers to those mitzvos that people regard lightly and consider their reward to be trivial. Ramban adds that Rashi's meaning is that such people are mistaken, since in the subsequent verses cited above, Scripture points out the magnificent reward one receives for doing these mitzvos — prosperity, vitality, and health.

Ramban further explains that the term *eikev* is used strictly as "because" in another connection (*Genesis* 26:5) where Hashem appears to our father Isaac, promising him that his posterity will be as the stars in the heavens, that He will give them "all these lands" (the land of Canaan) and that all the nations of the earth will be blessed in his seed "because (*eikev*) Avraham listened to My voice, and kept My charge, and My commandments, My ordinances, and My laws." Our father Avraham, we may derive from here, knew the Torah and observed the entire gamut of what Torah expects of us. Another instance of the word *eikev* used as strictly "because" is found at the *Akeidah* (*Genesis* 22:18): "And the nations of the earth shall bless themselves in your seed because (*eikev*) you listened to My voice."

Support for the significance of so-called light commandments is also found in *Pirkei Avos* (Chapter 2:1): "Rabbi [Yehudah the Prince] said: ... 'be attentive to a light precept as to one which seems important, for you do not know the reward for each precept,'" and (Chapter 4:2): "Ben Azzai said, 'Hasten to do even a light precept and flee from transgression.' " It is noteworthy that the Tanna uses the imagery of movement in connection with precepts, which may perhaps explain Rashi's use of "heel" as the meaning of *eikev*, for this part of the anatomy is indicative of the firmness with which we conclude our steps, as if to say that in our performing mitzvos we do so with firmness and determination.

> *Rabbeinu Bachya (1263-1340) explains that there are many different lessons that are conveyed through Scripture's choice of the word eikev. The Torah describes in our Parashah the rewards for obedience to Hashem, while our Sages teach us that this earthly world cannot possibly deliver the actual reward earned by mitzvah observance. Rather, the rewards described here are merely the eikev, the heel, the lowest and most insignificant form of reward earned by fulfilling Hashem's mitzvos. The ultimate reward is reserved for the World to Come, where our souls will bask in the Divine Presence. Another point to consider is that*

*there are many mitzvos that begin with the eikev, the heel. For instance, walking to the synagogue for services, going to the Beis Medrash to study Torah, visiting the ill, or accompanying the deceased to their resting place: All of these great mitzvos are performed with the "heel," and our Parashah is emphasizing the importance of observing these mitzvos. And the way one goes to perform these mitzvos is also significant. Does he proceed at a swift gait, anxious to perform the mitzvah, or does he stroll in a leisurely manner, eventually getting around to doing the mitzvah? Our Parashah teaches us that reward is meted out not only in consideration of the quantity of mitzvos performed but also in regard to the quality of those mitzvos — **how** they were performed. The Torah guarantees us full reward in this world and in the next for our performance of mitzvos with anticipation and joy.*

Parashas Re'eh

The Sedrah Begins:

"See, I present before you today a blessing and a curse. The blessing — that you listen to the commandments of Hashem, your G-d, that I command you today .... You shall place the blessing on Mount Gerizim and the curse on Mount Ebal" (Deuteronomy 11:26-29).

Rashi comments: **"See, I present (before you today) a blessing and a curse:** *Those said upon Mount Gerizim and*

> *Mount Ebal. The blessing: on condition 'that you listen.'*
> **You shall place the blessing:** *This is to be understood as Targum renders it, which means 'those who bless.'"*

RAMBAN IS IN SHARP DISAGREEMENT WITH RASHI, AND IPSO FACTO WITH Targum, both of whom explain that the word "blessing" is to be read "those who bless." Ramban argues that Scripture (*Deuteronomy* 27:12 ff.) gives a graphic representation of this rite: Six tribes are poised on Mount Gerizim as a token of blessing, and six tribes on Mount Ebal, implying the curse. And the Levites begin the declarations, commencing with the blessings as Rashi explains in the cited passages above, only afterwards resorting to the execrations. Thus the ceremony in its completeness is only set up here. According to Ramban, then, the language cited from the current *Parashah* is to be construed simply that Hashem presents to our ancestors two ways: one is the road to blessings; the other, to the opposite.

The first word of the quoted verses, *re'eh*, "see," is the imperative form of the verb "to see." We find a number of other passages which open with this direction, such as (*Deuteronomy* 4:5) "*Re'eh*, see, I have taught you statutes and ordinances as Hashem, my G-d, commanded me to do in the midst of the land to which you come to take possession of it." "*Re'eh*, see, I have placed before you today life and good, and death and evil" (*Deuteronomy* 30:15). Grammatically speaking, all these passages could have been opened, without the introductory word *re'eh* and still convey the same message. Perhaps the reason for this form's being used is to stress the challenging nature of these directions, to bring out a most vital aspect of Jewish observances — freedom of choice.

Ramban (*Deuteronomy* 30:15) puts it in a most remarkable manner: "See, I have placed before you today life and good [and the alternative]. Two courses are in their hands: life and good [and the opposite], and it is in their power to walk in whichever way they desire, and there is no power below or above that will hold them back and stop them." The Rabbis have said it with the exhortation (*Kesubos* 30a), "All is in the hands of Heaven except the fear of Heaven."

Attention should be drawn to the words "or above" — that even Hashem Himself will not redirect the human choice from one course to the other. We know that Hashem is often spoken of as affirming a man in his evil ways, as at the Exodus, in the hardening of the heart of Pharaoh, or the indication that the spies whom Moshe *Rabbeinu* sent to reconnoiter the Holy Land were not prevented from giving their erroneous report. This is because the sinners have first chosen to sin, and they are now merely given "plenty of rope," as the saying goes.

> *Rabbi Eliyahu Kramer, the Vilna Gaon (1720-1797), comments that the Torah writes, "See, I present before you today" employing a grammatical contradiction. Re'eh, "see," is in the singular form, as opposed to the plural form re'u," while "before you" is written lifneichem, in the plural form, instead of "lifanecha," the singular form. The Vilna Gaon explains that a person may ask himself, "Why should I choose to be good when I live in a decadent world where evil prevails? How can I possibly succeed when faced with so many obstacles? And what can I possibly accomplish when surrounded by evil influences?" To counter these thoughts the Torah writes re'eh in the singular form, to teach us **not** to look at other people's choices. We have to observe for ourselves and subsequently ignore our corrupt environment. We are accountable only for our own choices and actions; the impact of our decisions is for Hashem to mold and not for us to dwell upon.*

Parashas Shoftim

The *Sedrah* begins:

> "Judges and officers shall you appoint in all your cities which Hashem your G-d gives you for your tribes, and they shall judge the people with righteous judgment. You shall not pervert judgment, you shall not take notice of someone's presence, and you shall not take a bribe — for a bribe will blind the eyes of the wise and make the words of the righteous crooked. Righteousness, righteousness shall you pursue so that you will live and take possession of the land which Hashem your G-d gives you" (Deuteronomy 16:18-20).

> Rashi comments: "**Judges and officers:** Judges who pronounce sentence and officers who impose authority over the people, following the orders of the judges, with stick and with strap until one accepts upon himself the verdict of the judge. **In all your cities:** In each and every city. **For your tribes:** It refers to 'shall you appoint.' The verse is read: 'Judges and officers shall you appoint for your tribes in all your cities which Hashem, your G-d, gives you.' This teaches us that we must establish judges for each tribe separately and in every city."

THE DIVISION OF THE FUNCTIONS OF GOVERNMENT, AS EXPLAINED BY Rashi, is a virtual preview of what takes place in a modern democracy, particularly as we know it here in the United States. Fundamentally (and this is supposed to be within the knowledge of every humble citizen and those who apply for citizenship), the American system comprises, according to the Federal constitution, Congress which makes the laws, the administration which enforces the law, and the Supreme Court which determines the legality of the enactments or the conduct of the government.

The foreshadowing of this setup may be seen in the opening of this *Sedrah* and the laws promulgated in Scripture. Our constitution is obviously *Toras Moshe*. All conduct, whether private or public, is tested as to its compliance with the Torah. Further legislative power was vested in the Sanhedrin, the Supreme Court of the ancient Jewish commonwealth, whose seat was in the sacred precincts of the Temple. It consisted of seventy judges, presided over by a chief justice, and they had the power, within halachic limitations, to add to the requirements set forth in the Torah (*Yevamos* 21a) in order to set up safeguards for the mitzvos. At times they would abrogate certain regulations (*Yevamos* 90a: *Beis Din* [the Sanhedrin] suspended performance of some mitzvos on particular occasions). During the time of the monarchy, the king, like the United States president, was the commander-in-chief of the armed forces and simultaneously head of the civil government. The Sanhedrin enacted important litigation, the determination of which was binding on all, from the king to the lowest subject.

Malbim points out that this passage is an elaboration of *Exodus* 21:6, with relation to a Hebrew servant who does not wish to go out free at the end of six years: "The master shall bring him unto the judges," who would confirm the servitude by boring the servant's ear; we see also an elaboration of *Exodus* 22:8 on bailments: In case the bailed article is stolen or lost, both bailor and bailee "shall come before the judges" and determine the guilt or innocence of the bailee. In these passages the presumption obtains that there was in ancient Israel a duly designated and functioning judiciary. In this *Sedrah*, the judiciary is portrayed as part of the overall system of government, within which the administration of justice in the Hebrew commonwealth is of prime importance.

We must of course note that in *Exodus* (18:25), in the portion "And you shall select" (credited to Yisro, on whose advice Moshe Rabbeinu effected a decentralization of the personnel of the judicial system in the ancient Hebrew commonwealth), judges must be "able men, who fear G-d, men of truth, [who] hate unjust gain" (*Exodus* 18:21). No other detail of location and knowledgeability are indicated, as they do in this *Parashah*. As an aside we might mention that at the time of the Exodus there were approximately 600,000 "men on foot, besides children" (*Exodus* 12:37) and presumably women. It may be estimated that the total population may have been about 1.5 million souls. The total number of judges that Moshe Rabbeinu appointed on the advice of his father-in-law (proportionate to the size of the population) must have been upwards of fifty thousand. This is approximately the number of judges in the entire United States, which has a population of 220 million. A query: Were our ancestors so addicted to litigation that they needed that many judges? The answer may be that like Moshe himself, they were more than judges: "And I make them know the statutes of Hashem and His laws" (*Exodus* 18:16). These men were also teachers, and of such there can *never* be too many.

> The Sedrah begins: "Judges and officers shall you appoint in all your cities," when it could have written: "Judges and officers shall be appointed in all your cities." Why did Scripture include the personal reference "shall you appoint" in the verse? Rabbi Chaim Ibn Attar (1696-1743), the Or HaChaim HaKadosh, comments that the populace may expect the judges they appoint to treat them lightly and forgo due diligence in prosecuting their offenses. Therefore, the verse states "shall you appoint," meaning that they shall be appointed "over you," indicating the recognition that these judges will exercise their judicial powers in order to punish all crimes to the fullest extent of the law.
>
> Rabbi Moshe Feinstein (1895-1986) explains that the verse is teaching us to judge ourselves. We must conscientiously judge our actions to see whether our conduct and direction are correct. Furthermore, we must diligently police our activities to ensure that we pursue the path we have resolved to take. We must also be contemptuous of bribery in order to keep ourselves from succumbing to pleasures that we know we should avoid.

Parashas Ki Seitzei

The *Sedrah* begins:

> "When you will go out to war against your enemy and Hashem, your G-d, will deliver him into your hand, and you will capture its people as captives, and you will see among its captivity a woman who is beautiful of form and you will desire her, you will take her to yourself for a wife. You shall bring her into the midst of your house; she shall shave her head and let her nails grow. She shall remove the garment of her captivity from upon herself, and she shall sit in your house, and she shall weep for her father and her mother for a full month; thereafter, you may come to her and live with her, and she shall be a wife to you."

Rashi comments: "**When you will go out to war:** The verse speaks of an optional war, for in the war of the Land of Israel it cannot be said, 'And you will capture its people as captives,' for it has already said, 'You shall not allow any person to live.' **And you will capture its people as captives:** To include Canaanites who are in it even though they are from the seven nations. **A woman:** Even a married woman. **You will take her to yourself for a wife:** The Torah spoke only regarding the drive toward evil, for if the Holy One, Blessed is He, would not have made her permissible, he would marry her in a forbidden manner. But if he will marry her, his end will be to hate her, for it says after this passage: 'If a man will have two wives, one beloved and one hated.' And his end will be to father from her 'a wayward and rebellious son.' This is why these passages were juxtaposed."

THE VARIOUS DETAILS WHICH APPLY TO THE WOMAN'S BECOMING acclimated in the man's home are all intended to make her odious in his eyes, thus making him ask himself why he needs to be bothered with her when he can marry instead an Israelite maiden who is beautiful and full of life. But he is not allowed to treat the captive woman contemptuously; he must provide for her departure, if that is his choice, in a humane fashion.

The foregoing explanation fairly clamors for *darsheini* — for an elucidation culled from the commentators — and perhaps a logical exegesis. The principal source of Rashi's comments above, as indicated elsewhere, is in the Gemara (*Kiddushin* 21b and 22a). On "you will see among its captivity a woman who is beautiful," the Torah provides for human passion, and permission to take the captive as a wife is granted only if she was originally taken for lust, not if she was taken for enslavement. Thus, according to Rav, "The Torah provides for man's evil passion." The intriguing question may be asked: If so, then *ein ledavar sof* — there is no end! Where would this end? How far may this approach be pursued, and where do we draw the line?

Perhaps a partial answer may be that the important matter involved in this *Sedrah* at this point is not so much how to treat a woman taken captive in war, important as that may be, but rather the topic of matrimony generally — the choice of a mate — which may be derived obliquely from this discussion.

In *Exodus* 6:23, it is stated, "Aharon took Elisheva, the daughter of Amminadab, the sister of Nachshon, as a wife." Rashi comments that in choosing a wife one must have regard for what kind of person the perspective bride's brother is. It is the simple approach that was used by our fathers in the *shtetl*: the father of a woman looked for a *ben-Torah* for his daughter, while the father of the man was concerned about *yichus,* the kind of family from which the woman came. When one views the crop of divorces which infest American society today (and, unfortunately, we Jews, for whom the sanctity of marriage has historically made divorce a rarity, have also succumbed to this plague), one sees the virtue of living in a *shtetl.*

Thus in the Torah passages we have referred to above, we are taught that though Holy Writ frowns upon selecting a wife by passionate impulse, which is perhaps the major cause of modern divorces, yet if the warrior will take the woman into his home, endow her with the inspiring attributes of the Jewish *akeres habayis,* the joyful mother who abides by tradition, she might yet rise to become an exemplary Jewish wife and mother.

> *Rabbi Samson Raphael Hirsch (1808-1888) explains that the laws of the captive woman allow, as an exceptional case for exceptional circumstances, purely sensual impressions as the guiding basis for choosing a wife. However, the time between her capture and their marriage is meant to allow the Jewish soldier time to judge her character and time enough for her to give up her idolatry and heathen practices. For such a marriage, based solely upon the dictates of passion, is by no means approved of, and the results thereof are warningly pointed out in the immediately attached cases of discord in married life and in the unsuccessful rearing of children which can be expected from all unions whose matchmakers were not reason and suitability but solely passion. As Rashi comments: "If he will marry her, his end will be to hate her, for it says after this passage, 'If a man will have two wives, one beloved and one hated.' And his end will be to father from her 'a wayward and rebellious son.'"*
>
> *Furthermore, this section teaches us the laws of human rights and marriage rights through the treatment prescribed for criminals and the poorest of poor girls. The treatment prescribed for a captive woman proclaims the safeguarding of every woman against the passion of men and secures her from careless misuse. After a month in captivity, his duty is either to marry her, through which she becomes a full Jewess and his legal wife with all*

the rights that pertain to a Jewish wife, or to set her entirely free. He may neither misuse her in any way, keep her in his service, nor sell her to pass her on to somebody else.

Parashas Ki Savo

THE *SEDRAH* BEGINS:

"It will be when you enter the land that Hashem, Your G-d, has given you as an inheritance and you take possession of it and dwell in it, that you shall take of the first of every fruit of the ground that you bring in from your land that Hashem, your G-d, has given you, and you shall put it into a basket and go to the place that Hashem, your G-d, will choose to make His Name rest there."

Rashi comments: **"It will be when you enter [the land] and take possession of it and dwell in it:** *This tells us that they were not obligated concerning the commandment of bikurim, the first fruits, until they conquered the land of Canaan and apportioned it.* **Of the first [of every fruit]:** *But not the entire first, for not all fruits come under the obligation of Bikurim, just the seven species alone [as mentioned in Deuteronomy 8:8].* **Of the first:** *A man goes down into his field and sees a fig that has begun to ripen. He wraps a reed around the first fruit as a sign and says, 'This is hereby consecrated as bikurim.'"*

THE *BIKURIM* ARE BROUGHT TO THE PRIEST AT THE SANCTUARY, accompanied by a protocol of thankfulness for the mercies of Hashem to His people in which the donor gives a capsule history of our early years as a nation. The seven kinds of fruits referred to are wheat, barley, grapes, figs, pomegranates, olives, and dates.

Malbim concentrates upon the first word of the first verse, *vehayah*, "and it will be." He points out that in a similar reference about the entry of our ancestors into the Land of Israel, this introductory word is lacking. And comparing it thusly, the commentator (citing Vayikra 19:23, and Bamidbar 15:2, Devarim 17:14, 18:9) draws two conclusions: The first substantiates Rashi that the liability for *bikurim* does not arise until our ancestors will have conquered and divided the Land of Israel. This division includes the lands lying east of the Jordan River (present-day Jordan), the kingdoms of Sichon and Og whom Moshe dispossessed. These were lands assigned to the tribes of Reuven, Gad, and half of Menashe. Then they marched to the west side of the Jordan River, modern-day Israel, and that portion was divided between the remaining nine-and-one-half tribes. The total time it took to fulfill this objective was fourteen years.

Further, Malbim explains: "The duty to bring the first fruits would come into force only after the Jews had settled in the Promised Land, but their willingness to accept the duty before they entered the land was the merit that resulted in their conquest of the land." This is comparable to the assurance that Hashem gave Moshe Rabbeinu at the Burning Bush. When Moshe inquired of Hashem what merit his people possessed to deserve redemption, Hashem answered, "When you will have redeemed the people from Egypt, you shall serve G-d on this mount." This is a future condition for a present boon. Here too, the reference by Malbim is a challenge to *bitachon*, to faith. We are asked now to trust in Him that He will ensure that all conditions will be favorable for us, so we shall now perform what He is asking of us.

> The Talmud (Taanis 28a) relates that at one time the Roman governor of Jerusalem decreed a ban on the *bikurim* offering. To that effect, he stationed guards at the

crossroads leading to Jerusalem to inspect travelers and their packages to ascertain that no bikurim were being smuggled into the Holy City. Many G-d-fearing individuals contrived a scheme to fool the guards. They packaged the bikurim in baskets beneath large quantities of figs and carried a pestle in their free hand. When they reached the roadblock, they were questioned, "Where are you going, and what are you bringing with you?" They answered that they were going to the mill in order to grind the figs with their pestle into cakes of pressed figs, a common practice in those days. Satisfied with the response, the guards allowed them to continue on their way without suspicion. Once they were beyond the guards' scrutiny, they removed the figs and adorned the bikurim in the baskets. In this fashion, they continued to offer the bikurim in the Beis HaMikdash.

We can learn this portion of the Talmud and marvel at the courage, ingenuity, and dedication of those Jews who risked their lives in order to perform the mitzvah of bikurim. But there is also a question: "Why?" Why did they willingly risk their lives to smuggle in the bikurim in defiance of the government decree? The Torah does not sanction performance of the mitzvah of bikurim if there is a risk of life and limb, so why did they engage in this dangerous operation, seemingly without regard for their own lives?

The answer may lie in the essence of the mitzvah of bikurim. The bikurim constitute a thanksgiving offering. In recognition of Hashem's hand in assuring their crops' bounty, our forebears were compelled to express their gratitude. The Midrash (Shemos Rabbah 4:2) teaches that one must be willing to sacrifice his life on behalf of a person who has extended him a kindness. If the debt of gratitude is such that the recipient of a kindness must be willing to sacrifice his life on behalf of his benefactor, then it follows that to perform the mitzvah of bikurim — an expression of gratitude to the Benefactor of the entire universe — one must be willing to sacrifice his very life. That is why the Jews under Roman rule were willing to risk everything in order to fulfill the mitzvah of bikurim.

Parashas Nitzavim

The Sedrah begins:

"You are standing today, all of you, before Hashem your G-d: your heads, your tribes, your elders, and your officers, all the men of Israel; your small children, your women, and your convert who is in the midst of your camp; from the hewer of your wood to the drawer of your water; for you to pass into a covenant of Hashem, your G-d, and into His oath that Hashem, your G-d, forges with you today in order to establish you today as a people to Him and that He be a G-d to you, as He spoke to you and as He swore to your forefathers — to Abraham, to Isaac, and to Jacob" (Deuteronomy 29: 9-12).

Rashi comments: "**You are standing:** This teaches us that Moses gathered them before the Holy One, Blessed is He, on the day of his death, to bring them into the covenant. **Your heads, your tribes:** This means, the heads of your tribes. **Your elders and your officers:** The more prominent, the closer to the front of the assembly, and afterward, 'all the men of Israel.' **From the hewer of your wood:** This teaches us that Canaanites came to convert in the days of Moses in the manner that the Gibeonites came in the days of Joshua."

THERE ARE THREE BASIC IDEAS FLOWING FROM THE FOREGOING: FIRST, the message was addressed to the leaders and to the entire people; second, they would enter into a covenant with Hashem by an oath they made for themselves and for endless generations to come (v. 13); third, we are inextricably bound to Him as He is bound to us — as He had sworn to Avraham, Yitzchak, and Yaakov.

A similar theme is mentioned earlier (Devarim 27:9): "Moshe and the Kohanim (the Levites) spoke to all Israel, saying, 'Be attentive and hear, 0 Israel: This day you have become a people to Hashem, your G-d.' " Rashi (Bamidbar 30:2) speculates that wherever Moshe Rabbeinu spoke to the heads, it may also be presumed that he addressed the entire nation.

Malbim comments on this week's *Sedrah*: " 'You are standing today, all of you': He informed them that just as they came together to sustain for themselves and posterity all that is stated in the Torah, so Hashem went out to meet them." This is reflected also in *Pirkei Avos* 2:4: "Make His will as your will so that He may make your will as His; nullify your will before His so that He may nullify the will of others before yours." On the final clause, Bartenura comments, "As if it were written, 'that He may nullify His will before yours.'"

To enter into a covenant does not imply coercion but the assumption of an obligation. Hashem thus goes out of His way to impress upon us our obligation because He wants us to realize the great consequence of doing so: that we should be His people and He should be our G-d. For this is an irrevocable bond; therefore, we dare not provoke Him.

Why does this *Sedrah* follow the one containing the most terrible prophecy of destruction in the event of our disobedience (in the *Sedrah Ki Savo*)? Moshe *Rabbeinu* sought thereby to appease the people. Though they had been provoking the Omnipresent, yet here they were safe and sound before Him, and thus it shall ever be. The Torah here speaks of those present at the momentous occasion of the receiving of the Law, as well as countless generations of our people to come.

> The Sedrah begins by describing the various castes
> among the Jews in the plural form of the word

"you." "Atem, You are standing today, kulchem, all of you, before Hashem Elokeichem, your G-d: Rashaichem, your heads, shivteichem, your tribes, zikneichem, your elders, v'shotreichem, and your officers." But then it reverts to the singular form, kol ish Yisrael, literally, all the "man" of Israel. Rabbi Meir Simchah HaKohen of Dvinsk (1843-1926) explains that the Torah is teaching us the unity of Israel. Even though there are many castes among the Jews, there is a unity that binds all Jews to one another, that justifies the reference to all men of Israel rendered in the singular form ish. Particularly at this juncture, when all the segments of Israel joined to accept the covenant with Hashem, they were fused together, because our covenant with Hashem binds all Jews to one another. Like the spokes of a wheel that are connected to each other by virtue of their bond with the center of the wheel, so too are all Jews bound to each other through Hashem, the center and focus of all their endeavors. As the Midrash (Vayikra Rabbah 4:6) states, the children of Yaakov who serve one G-d are considered to be one soul. By virtue of each Jew's commitment to serve Hashem, all Jews become inexorably united and committed to each other.

Parashas Vayeilech

The *Sedrah* begins:

> "Moses went and spoke these words to all Israel. He said to them, 'I am a hundred twenty years old today; I can no longer go out and come in, and Hashem has said to me, "You shall not cross this Jordan." Hashem, your G-d, will cross before you .... Joshua will cross over before you, as Hashem has spoken.'"

> *Rashi comments:* "**I can no longer go out and come in:** One might be able to think that his strength had waned. To teach us otherwise, the Torah says, 'His eye did not dim, and his moisture did not leave him.' But what then is meant by 'I can no longer'? I am not allowed, for the authority has been taken away from me and given to Joshua."

Rashi explains that Moshe could no longer go out, not because his physical strength had failed him, but because authority was being taken from him and given instead to Yehoshua. Then Moshe called Yehoshua, and with the encouraging command "Be strong and firm," he told him that he, Yehoshua, must go with the people into the land which Hashem had sworn to our fathers to give their children as an inheritance.

Ramban states that when Moshe concluded the preceding *Parashah*, all returned to their tents. Here, in order to deliver this final message, he went out to his fellow Jews to bid them farewell, a mark of his humility.

> As mentioned above, we see the mark of Moshe Rabbeinu's humility in this Sedrah. Rabbi Zalman Sorotzkin (1881-1966) in Oznayim L'Torah points

out another example of Moshe's humility in this Sedrah. The Talmud (Berachos 55a) teaches that a leader must have the acceptance of the masses before he is appointed. Following this dictum, Moshe Rabbeinu approached B'nei Yisrael before he died in order to consult with them about his successor. He did not want to make this inquiry in Yehoshua's presence, since he would not elicit an honest response in front of Yehoshua. Therefore, Moshe went to B'nei Yisrael and explained to them that he would not cross the Jordan but that Yehoshua would lead them in his stead. However, only after he consulted with them did he confirm that Yehoshua would lead them into Eretz Yisrael. But why did Moshe have to go to them? Immediately prior to this event, everyone stood together to make a covenant with Hashem. The opportunity was ripe for Moshe to address the assemblage concerning their next leader. Why did Moshe send them home and then personally visit them before his death? Rabbi Sorotzkin explains that we see from here the enormousness of Moshe Rabbeinu's humility. Why didn't Moshe send Yehoshua to tend to some task while he sought the people's opinion of Yehoshua? Why did Moshe trouble himself to the extent of visiting the tents of B'nei Yisrael personally to make this inquiry, when he could have dispatched Yehoshua on some errand and thus not had to journey to the people to consult with them?! Such humility has not been witnessed among other heads of state from the time of Creation until this very day!

TORAH READING FOR ROSH HASHANAH

The opening verse of the Torah reading on the first day of Rosh Hashanah is "Hashem had remembered Sarah as He had said; and Hashem did for Sarah as He had spoken" (Genesis 21:1).

Rashi comments that the relationship of this section to the preceding one in which Abraham prayed for Abimelech and his prayer was answered lends credence to our Sages' declaration that "he who prays for others will likewise be answered for his own needs."

A QUESTION MAY BE ASKED HERE: WHY IS THE TERM "REMEMBERED" used in connection with the fulfillment of this promise? In *Pirkei Avos* (4:29), we learn, "Rabbi Elazar HaKappar used to say that we have to know that He is G-d .... Blessed is He, with Whom there is no unrighteousness nor forgetfulness." The reference to "remembered" would thus appear superfluous. Perhaps we may say that as far as we mortals are concerned, we must continually act in such a manner as to be worthy of the assurance of Hashem's covenant.

The opening verses of the Torah reading of the second day of Rosh Hashanah state: "And it happened after these words that G-d tested Abraham and He said to him, 'Abraham,' and he said, 'Here I am.' And He said, 'Please take your son, your only one, whom you love, Isaac; go to the land of Moriah and bring him up there as an offering upon one of the mountains which I shall tell you' " (Genesis 22:1-2).

*Rashi comments: "**After these words:** After the words of Satan, who made accusations against Abraham before*

> Hashem, saying, "From all the feasts that Abraham made, he did not bring a sacrifice to you of a single bull or a single ram.' Hashem replied, 'Abraham's feasts were for his son's sake. If I were to say to him, "Sacrifice him [Isaac] before Me," he would not refrain.'"

ABRAHAM WAS ENDOWED WITH PROPHETIC VISION (SEE *BEREISHIS* 22:6). Rashi says, "Abraham, who was aware that he was going to slaughter his son, was going with the same eagerness and joy as Yitzchak, who was unaware of the matter." And yet Avraham prophesied that both he and Yitzchak would return (*Rashi* 22:5). Is there any contradiction between the two manifestations of Avraham's mind at the crucial time during which he was hoping for a miracle to happen so that Yitzchak would not be sacrificed? At the last moment of the drama, Yitzchak *was* saved; that Avraham was determined that Hashem's Will be done, whatever it be, cannot be questioned. Language, however, has a dynamic of its own, for Avraham did prophesy that the supreme sacrifice would not occur. This is proof that in our utterances, whatever the occasion be, we speak of things (sometimes without knowing) that are good for us.

> As mentioned above, language has a dynamic of its own, as we learn from Avraham Avinu at the Akeidah. When Avraham set out to fulfill Hashem's will, he went with Yitzchak, Eliezer, and Yishmael to Mount Moriah. Scripture says, "And Avraham said to his young men, 'Stay here by yourselves with the donkey, while I and the lad [Yitzchak] will go up to here; we will worship and we will return to you' " (Berieshis 22:5). Even though Avraham Avinu had every intention of killing Yitzchak, he never enunciated his intention. He said, "We will return to you," and his words were fulfilled as stated. The Talmud describes this principle in Moed Katan 18a: Bris kerusah

l'siphasayim — there is a covenant made with the lips that whatever is uttered may come to pass. Rabbi Yochanan asked how we know that there is a covenant made with the lips. Since it says in Scripture, 'And Avraham said to his young men ... and we will return to you' — and it happened as he said that they both returned — we learn that there is a covenant made with the lips. This verse teaches us that the G-d-given power of speech, unique to mankind, is not to be taken lightly. A positive expression can bring forth significant results. Similarly, a negative utterance may cause harm, Heaven forbid, even though no harm was intended. This is described in the Talmud (Berachos 19a): "Do not open your mouth to Satan," which means that one should not give Satan an opportunity to take ones words and act upon them by turning an unwitting comment into an excuse to see that it indeed comes to pass. The gift of speech must be cherished and guarded, and we are required to be very selective in our choice of words. Therefore, whatever the occasion may be, we should always speak of things that are good for us.[1]

---

1. *Editor's note: Mr. Merzon lived by this credo. He opposed the use of expressions such as "That person is crazy" or "I'm dead!"*

Parashas Ha'azinu

The *Sedrah* begins:

> "Listen, heavens, and I will speak! Earth, hear the words of my mouth! May my teaching drip like the rain; may my speech flow like the dew, like storm winds upon vegetation and like raindrops upon grass. When I proclaim Hashem's Name, praise Hashem for His greatness."

Rashi comments: "**Listen, heavens:** That I am giving warning to Israel and be witnesses to the matter, for I told Israel that you shall be witnesses. And similarly, this is the meaning of 'Earth, hear.' Why did Moses call the heavens and the earth as witnesses against them? Moses said, 'I am flesh and blood. Tomorrow I will be dead. If Israel were to say, "We did not accept the covenant upon ourselves," who could come and contradict them?' This is why he called as witnesses against them the heavens and the earth, witnesses who last forever. And furthermore, if Israel will be meritorious, the witnesses will come and give Israel's reward. As it is stated (Zechariah 8:12), 'The vine will yield its fruit, and the earth will yield its produce, and the heavens will give their dew.' And if Israel will be found guilty, the hand of the witnesses will be the first against them, as it says (Deuteronomy 11:17), 'He will restrain the heavens, and there will be no rain, and the ground will not yield its produce,' and afterwards, 'and you will be swiftly banished' by the nations."

Ramban comments on Moshe Rabbeinu's twofold framing of the introductory verses to his farewell "May my teaching drip like the rain," which refers to the written Torah, which comes from Heaven. "May my speech flow like the dew" refers to the oral Torah, sanctioned by the same High Authority.

The underlying idea that our people are to be on trial is emphasized by the character of the objects which Moshe has invoked to serve as witnesses. This is different from the general earthly practice of requiring witness participation in verdict compliance, as is stated in *Devarim* 17:7, "The hands of the witnesses shall be first upon him [the convicted]." But Moshe's promise is that the witnesses will be equally as energetic to help supply us with an abundance of good things as (unfortunately) they will to help in applying severity and punishment. The choice is ours.

> As described in Rashi, the heavens and earth serve as witnesses to the covenant between B'nei Yisrael and Hashem. The unique quality of these witnesses is that they will also punish or reward B'nei Yisrael depending on the degree of their fidelity to the covenant. The Talmud (Avoda Zarah 3a) teaches us that when B'nei Yisrael will be challenged by the nations of the world as to whether or not they were faithful to their covenant, Hashem will direct the heavens and earth to give testimony that B'nei Yisrael fulfilled the mitzvos. The other nations will respond that the heavens and earth are invalid witnesses, for they are indebted to B'ne Yisrael. After all, B'nei Yisrael's commitment to the Torah is the reason why the heavens and earth were created. At Mount Sinai, had B'nei Yisrael refused to accept the Torah, the world would have returned to the emptiness and void that preceded Creation. Hence, we learn from the words of our Sages that the heavens and earth depend on B'nei Yisrael. Accordingly, when the heavens and earth dispense reward or punishment, they act from their own vested interest to assure the commitment of B'nei Yisrael to their covenant with Hashem, for only through this covenant does the world continue to exist.

TORAH READING FOR YOM KIPPUR

THE TORAH READING
ON THE MORNING OF YOM KIPPUR BEGINS:

> *"Hashem spoke to Moses after the death of Aaron's two sons, when they approached before Hashem and they died. And Hashem said to Moses: 'Speak to Aaron, your brother: He may not come at all times into the Sanctuary, within the Curtain, in front of the Cover that is upon the Ark — so that he will not die, for with a cloud I appear upon the Ark-cover. With this shall Aaron come into the Sanctuary — with a bull, a young male of cattle, for a sin offering, and a ram for an olah-offering'"* (Leviticus 16:1-3).

> Rashi comments: **"Hashem spoke to Moses after the death of Aaron's two sons:** *Why did the Torah say this? The Tanna R' Elazar ben Azaryah explains it with a parable. It can be compared to a sick person whom a doctor entered to treat. The doctor said to him, 'Do not eat cold food and do not lie in a damp, chilly place.' Another doctor came and said to him, 'Do not eat cold food and do not lie in a damp chilly place so that you will not die the way So-and-so died.' This second doctor roused him to follow his instructions more than the first (by adding 'so that you will not die ...'). This is why it adds 'after the death of Aaron's two sons.'"*

RASHI'S CITATION OF RABBI ELAZAR'S PARABLE FITS IN WELL WITH THIS season's soul-searching, particularly the prayer *Unesaneh Tokef* ("we will express the mighty holiness .... [and]

who shall live and who shall die"). While the latter relates to the Divine Judgment, Rashi's practical cast of mind (in compliance with the dictum "Only take heed to yourself and keep your soul diligently" [*Devarim* 4:9]) is averse to both fatalism and bravado. On matters involving health — that is, the continuation of life rather than risking the opposite — Rashi holds that hope must ever spring eternal in the human breast, not yielding to what may appear to be inevitable. At the same time, one must take no chances but must instead follow the direction of competent medical guides.

Elucidating Rashi's comments, Ramban is of the opinion that the opening verses do not present a chronological sequence but rather one of cause and effect. Hashem tells Moshe Rabbeinu to instruct Aharon, in light of what happened to his sons Nadav and Avihu, to use extreme care in the manner in which he enters the Holy of Holies on Yom Kippur and in the performance of the ritual sacrifices connected therewith, in order to assure for himself the desired protection from Above.

The Torah reading
during Minchah (the afternoon service) begins:

> "Hashem spoke to Moses, saying: Speak to the Children of Israel and say to them: I am Hashem, your G-d. Like the practice of the land of Egypt in which you dwelled, do not do, and do not perform the practice of the land of Canaan to which I bring you, and do not follow their statutes. Carry out My judgments and observe My decrees to follow them: I am Hashem, your G-d" (Leviticus 18:1-4).

> Rashi comments: "I am Hashem, your G-d: I am the One Who said at Sinai, 'I am Hashem, your G-d,' and you accepted upon yourselves My sovereignty. Now accept My decrees."

WE ARE REQUIRED TO DO THREE THINGS: OBEY HIS WILL, FOLLOW THE Torah, and assimilate its teachings into our lives.

The Talmud Yerushalmi (Yoma 1:1) asks why the deaths of Nadav and Avihu are mentioned near to the Yom Kippur offerings. The Talmud answers: to teach us that the deaths of the righteous atone just as the Yom Kippur offerings do. Our Rabbis teach that just as Yom Kippur atones for our transgressions, so too does the death of a tzaddik, a righteous man or woman. Rabbi Meir Simchah HaCohen of Dvinsk (1843-1926) explains these words of our Sages to mean that Yom Kippur is a unique time of year when Hashem's beneficence is extended to atone for those who repent. Similarly, the time of a tzaddik's death is a unique time when this same beneficence is extended. But there is a condition that must be met before our sins are absolved. In order for Yom Kippur to atone, we must participate in the mitzvos of the day with the proper respect and awe which this Holy Day demands. However, a person who disregards the significance of Yom Kippur, who treats Yom Kippur like any other day, will not reap the benefits offered by Hashem and will remain with his transgressions. So too with the death of a tzaddik — only the people who recognize the importance of the tzaddik and accord him his due respect while he is alive can benefit through the atonement that comes at the time of his death. However, those people who are not humbled and respectful in the presence of the tzaddik, who do not appreciate how the tzaddik enhances the life of everyone around him, do not reap any benefit at the time of the tzaddik's demise.

Torah Reading for Shemini Atzeres

We read in *Deuteronomy* (14:22-23):

> *"You shall tithe the entire crop of your planting, the produce of the field, year by year. And you shall eat before Hashem, your G-d, in the place that He will choose to rest His Name there."*

Rashi's comments point out that failing to fulfill our duty to tithe may well bring about the failure of our crops. If we do His will, He does our will.

> The Talmud (Taanis 9a) teaches that we may not test Hashem, except in one instance: We may test Hashem in our performance of the mitzvah of tithing. Hashem guarantees that we will be blessed with an abundance of crops and material wealth if we strictly adhere to the laws of tithing our produce and income. However, if we perform a mitzvah in order to receive material reward in this world, won't this diminish our reward in the world to come? Rav Avraham Shmuel Binyamin Schreiber (1815-1879, the K'sav Sofer) explains that indeed we should not tithe in hopes of becoming wealthy per se. Rather we should tithe in hope of amassing wealth from which we can give even larger tithes. If this is our intention, then we shall merit the blessing of wealth without losing any of our reward in the World to Come.

Parashas Vezos Haberachah

The opening verses of the concluding *Sedrah*, read on *Simchas Torah*, are:

> "And this is the blessing with which Moses, the man of G-d, blessed the Children of Israel before his death. He said: 'Hashem came from Sinai, and He shone forth to them from Seir; He appeared from Mount Paran, and He came with some of the myriads of the holy; from His right hand he presented a fire of law to them. He also showed love to peoples; all their holy ones are in Your hands, and they were brought in at Your feet. He would bear Your utterances" (Deuteronomy 33:1-3).

> Rashi comments: "**And this is the blessing ... before his death:** Immediately before his death, for if not now, when [borrowed from Pirkei Avos 1:14].

Commenting on the other passages, Rashi explains that Moshe commenced the blessings with the praise of Hashem, then ventured to mention Israel's needs, then Israel's merit, thereby pressing the plea that they were worthy of His blessing. Then Moshe talked of that enchanting, though overwhelming, phenomenon — the Revelation at Sinai — when Hashem went out to welcome Israel as a groom would go out to greet his bride. Then Moshe talked of the tradition that Hashem offered the Torah first to the Esavites and afterwards to the Yishmaelites, both of whom spurned the offer as not in consonance with their national leanings of bloodthirstiness and lewdness respectively, but Israel accepted it with alacrity: "We will do and we shall obey" (*Shemos* 24:7). Hashem then came with only a part of the myriads of the holy angels, withholding an otherwise most impressive array of angels. The fiery law was written before Him with black fire upon white fire. Also, it was given to Israel out of the fire. "He also showed love to peoples" refers to His love for the tribes of Israel, every one of whom is called a people. "The holy ones are in your hands": These are the souls of the righteous who abide with Him because they bore upon themselves the yoke of Torah.

The Book of *Deuteronomy* opens with the demonstrative pronoun, "these": "These are the words that Moshe spoke to all Israel" (*Devarim* 1:1), and concludes, as does the entire *Toras Moshe*, with a demonstrative pronoun, "this": "And this is the blessing with which Moses, the man of G-d, blessed the Children of Israel." Moshe Rabbeinu is at his life's end. On this day he became 120 years old and was turning over the leadership of Israel to his faithful disciple, Yehoshua. Like our father Yaakov, two hundred thirty-three years earlier, he gave a blessing before he returned to his Maker. And the form of his blessing was modeled after Yaakov's. Just as he opened the repetition of the Torah with an emphatic direction to obey the Torah, so was he equally emphatic at the end in bestowing his blessings upon Israel, turning to Hashem with a plea that Israel deserved His beneficence.

> As mentioned above, the berachos (blessings) of Moshe Rabbeinu before he died resemble those of Yaakov Avinu. Both were careful to bless the shevatim (tribes) according to their specific traits and qualities. Ramban begins the Sedrah with the words of the Midrash (Bereishis Rabbah 100:13) on the verse "And this is what their father spoke to them and he blessed them" (Bereishis 49:28). Yaakov told his children that in the future a man will similarly bless them and will begin where he left off. Therefore, our Sedrah begins with the pasuk "And this is the blessing ...," beginning where Yaakov Avinu left off: "And this is what their father spoke." Yaakov told them that these blessings

would take effect after their descendants received the Torah that says (Devarim 4:44): "This is the Torah ...." The word "this" indicates the ultimate blessing, the Torah, which is our covenant with Hashem, as it says (Yeshayahu 59:21): "This is the covenant." Rabbi Chaim Ibn Attar (1696-1743), in the Or HaChaim, adds that Moshe Rabbeinu's blessing is a continuation of Yaakov Avinu's blessing, since the pasuk (verse) begins: "And this is the blessing with which Moshe, the man of G-d, blessed the Children of Israel before his death." The word "and" indicates a continuation, in this case a continuation of the blessings of Yaakov.

SELECTED WRITINGS

- SHABBOS
- THE FESTIVALS
- MISCELLANY

SHABBOS

WORK AND LEISURE

NISAN 5703 / APRIL 1943

> *"Six days you shall do your work, and on the seventh day you shall rest" (Exodus 23:12).*

IT WOULD SEEM THAT FOR THE PURPOSE OF SABBATH OBSERVANCE IT should be of but little moment whether one subsist by work, whether he eat his bread by the sweat of his brow, or whether he be a person of leisure and live by, say, clipping coupons. The Bible, however, in numerous passages touching upon the subject of the Sabbath, like the one cited above, emphasizes both work on weekdays, on the one hand, and observance of the Sabbath day on the other.

The logical inference to be drawn from this circumstance is that the sanctity ascribed by the Bible to the Sabbath is not to be construed as an element separating this day from the other affairs of life. The idea which seems to underlie this twofold emphasis is that just as work is intended to serve a certain practical purpose and is pursued by a definite process of activity intended to accomplish that purpose, so must the day of rest be conceived as calculated to achieve a specific end, and the means employed therefore must be such as are sanctioned in all one's practical endeavors.

Extremes Shunned

In the light of these considerations, we may conclude that in this matter of Sabbath observance, extremes must be shunned at all costs. To illustrate: There was in the days of antiquity a Jewish sect which enjoined upon its followers an observance of the day so strict as to desist from all activity whatever, including that of movement. A person was supposed to remain in the same position throughout the Sabbath as he did when he entered it. Conversely, certain contemporary writers have advocated converting the day of rest into a sort of chautauqua, a mass affair, participated in by the whole community with games, singing, and similar diversions. It seems that neither system represents the true office of the seventh day.

Answer to a Prayer

What, then, is the proper attitude toward the Sabbath? George Meredith, the extremely versatile and gifted English novelist, in his *The Ordeal of Richard Feverel,* has this pregnant sentence: "Who rises from prayer a better man, his prayer is answered." A comparable idea may be applied to the Sabbath and thus phrased, "Whose observance of the day renders him, because of such observance, a better, more fit man for the serious tasks of life, his observance is right."

Wheat and Chaff

Tested by the foregoing criterion, it should not be difficult to separate the wheat from the chaff, as it were, in this matter. Can it be said that if one chase all over the map on his day of rest in search for pleasure and recreation that he thereby becomes a better man? Obviously not. Such observance is, indeed, an excellent prelude to the blue Monday to follow, from which circumstance this picturesque characterization of the first workday, no doubt, derives its origin.

Is it a source of mental stimulation or moral elevation to lounge about *dishabille* on the Sabbath day, or, dressed in old clothes, perform some odd manual tasks around the house? Both of these things may often have their proper place in a well-ordered life. But the point is that such pursuits do not add to a man's spiritual stature. There are those, of course, who have entirely dispensed with the institution of one-day-a-week rest. And this does not refer to the war-workers who are required to do it for reasons of safety of the state. This denial of a fundamental aspect of civilized living, to say nothing of religious observance, is — regretfully — more prominent perhaps among the descendants of those who had first given the Sabbath to the world than among any other racial stock.

Sabbath Balance Wheel

The proper observance of the day of rest is fulfilled only when a person thereby effects a complete severance from the cares and hustles of his weekday routine. The Sabbath is the balance wheel which serves to regulate the values of our unending efforts and endeavors. It gives us a chance to acquire a perspective upon the things we are about other than that afforded in the midst of pressing duties and ceaseless quests for material gain. However, this may be achieved only when the line of demarcation between work and desisting therefrom is clearly drawn as prescribed by ancient precepts and traditions of our Orthodox faith.

January 1944

> "G-d completed on the seventh day His work which He had done, and He abstained on the seventh day from all his work which he had done" (Genesis 2:2).

THE ANOMALY WHICH THE FOREGOING EXCERPT INCORPORATES IS derived from the seeming contradiction in that the reference states that G-d had both finished His work on the Sabbath and then rested on the same day. Rashi brilliantly clarifies this point in his monumental commentaries on the Bible and Talmud, stating (among other things) that the act of introducing the day of rest is the work referred to in the passage above. This was the concluding and crowning achievement in all the acts of Creation related in the account of the preceding six days set forth in the first chapter of the Bible.

Of course work is a broad term, and it does not necessarily imply physical exertion. In point of fact, the really important work of the world does not consist alone or primarily of manual effort. The story of Creation illustrates this point. For therein we read not of tasks the performance of which require complex procedures but of pronouncements which, merely from our view, are extraordinary in their simplicity: "Let there be light," "let there be an expansion in the midst of the waters," "let the waters under the heavens be gathered together," and similar statements which bring about the desired results.

Furthermore, apparently the notion that work entails hardship and exertion was introduced later. It came in the form of "the penalty of Adam" of Shakespeare's Duke Senior — in other words, as a consequence of "by the sweat of your brow shall you eat bread" (*Genesis* 3:19), the sentence imposed on Adam for permitting himself to be tempted by Eve to eat of the forbidden fruit.

Therefore, it was not originally the natural state of man to be engrossed in pursuits constituting a drain upon his physical energy. On the contrary, judging from the first intimation in the Bible as to the character of creative work and the further statement that so-called "productive" human efforts are in effect an atonement for our sins, we see that what is commonly termed the struggle for existence is *not* to be viewed as our inescapable fate.

A question: In view of the preceding is whether a redemption from the state to which we have been condemned is possible. We find the answer is contained here — in the thought and implicit in the passage cited above.

We are not asserting here that men may be able to dispense with work and create that which they need by the simple expedient of wishing for it. Nor are we implying that even were we to believe that such a fairyland condition had existed during the infancy of the race, it would even be possible to retrieve that ideal situation!

But that which is advanced here is a conception of work that raises our employment, of whatever nature, from that of being a mere laborer to that of becoming an artist. In other words, our adjustment to the lot of drudgery to which a Higher Power has committed us need not entail resignation to an insurmountable barrier but should spur us on to rise above that difficulty and to integrate the distasteful tasks forced upon us by life's inexorable demands into our efforts to achieve creative productivity.

If we do not permit our exacting labors to overwhelm us but on the contrary make them serve the purpose of a higher end in which those labors play a necessary, although not predominant, role, then to that extent we effect our own liberation from the state of being condemned to a life at hard, meaningless work.

How is this goal attained? There must be a period of stock-taking, as it were. Every now and then, we should be able to pause in our activity and review our goals and the means employed to achieve them. That is not to say that we can effectively interrupt the train of ideas, thoughts, and preoccupations which normally fill our minds just because we happen to desist from actual manual effort. But we can hold off the pressing tasks to enable us, in a manner of speaking, to get back to ourselves, to our inmost urges, aspirations, plans, and ambitions — which because of the grinding persistency of those tasks we all but forget!

This, then, is the purpose of the Sabbath rest: to get a little better acquainted with our innerselves. Accordingly, the repose of the Sabbath day is, like the Almighty's work of creation, not a separation from such work, but the conclusion thereof and that which imports meaning thereunto.

Nisan 5704 / April 1944

> *"And you shall remember that you were a slave in the land of Egypt, and Hashem, your G-d, took you out from there with a strong hand and an outstretched arm; therefore, Hashem, your G-d, has commanded you to keep the Sabbath day"* (Deuteronomy 5:15).

It is extremely doubtful if the time will ever come where the cleavage between those who give orders and those who obey them will be obliterated. Some people are born with an ability for directing enterprises, while others have to be content with being guided by the former. This does not in the least detract from the principles of true democracy, which, we hope, will ultimately prevail everywhere in the world. The equality implicit in such society is one of opportunity rather than of authority.

But leadership in a genuine democratic polity must be based not on ability alone: it must be predicated upon the conception that he truly leads others who in the process enhances in those who follow a sense of their own worth as human beings. In other words, such leadership must accept the religious idea of the importance of human relations. The brotherhood of man which religion advocates means just what the term "brother" implies: such a concern for our fellows as to wish them to share with us everything we have, even to the point of making them our betters!

That is why Moses, in reviewing for the Israelites the Fourth Commandment about keeping the Sabbath (cited at the head of this article), incorporates an additional point — namely, that the Jews should remember that they have been slaves in the land of Egypt and that because they had been delivered by the L-rd from their servitude, they must therefore observe the Sabbath.

One might ask what the former state of bondage has to do with the desirability of setting aside one day a week for rest. It may perhaps hint at the idea that since the Israelites had tasted of the bitter fruit of drudgery under a cruel master, they ought to appreciate more keenly the institution of occasional rest. But perhaps the thought goes beyond that. For the Sabbath day is often spoken of in the Bible as a day of rest unto the L-rd. Now, of course, G-d has no need of a day of rest. If, nevertheless, our observance of the Sabbath constitutes an act that is pleasing unto Him, it can be only because in doing so we add to our spiritual stature and thereby justify our claim to have been created in His image.

Now, that claim belongs to all of the human race, and to all classes of people (the Nazis excepted, of course!). The white and the black, the rich and the poor, the able and the backward — we are all made according to the same pattern. And when the Almighty desires a certain institution to add to man's spiritual estate, it applies to all of us, just as a father should want to see all his offspring do well. The offense of involuntary servitude consists not just in making a person do drudgery at the behest of a hated master, but more importantly in the fact that the victim's essential manhood is insulted, and thereby an affront has been committed against his Maker.

Accordingly, the reminder of Egyptian bondage is connected with the observance of the Sabbath, for we are thereby supposed to recall the true offense of Pharaoh in that he had humbled the divine in them. *But by keeping the Sabbath, Jews thereby restore to themselves their true dignity as human beings.*

Tishrei 5705 / September 1944

"Hashem spoke to Moshe on Mount Sinai, saying: Speak to the Children of Israel and say to them: When you come into the land that I give you, the land shall observe a Sabbath rest for Hashem" (Leviticus 25:1-2).

PERHAPS NOWHERE IN THE WORLD IS THE HEBREW SABBATH neglected by the Hebrews as much as it is in these United States, and nowhere is there as little genuine excuse for such neglect as exists here!

This is not an attempt to take issue with those who are opposed out of principle (so to speak) to the traditional observance of the Sabbath. The Reform Jews have come to believe that the Sabbath, as it has been kept for nearly thirty centuries, is merely a relic of the age of barbarism. The radical-minded are biased against this institution as they are against everything else proceeding from religious sources. With these two categories, then, there can be no quarrel. They are entitled to their ideas.

But the preponderant majority of American Jews belong to the class which has great respect for religion in general — and Jewish observances in particular. And yet these Jews are wholly remiss in the matter of maintaining the sanctity of the Sabbath, a principal, if not *the* principal, prop of our faith. And what is the reason advanced by them for this dereliction? The constant refrain is, "This is America, you know," which is supposed to be a complete answer to all the compelling motives and considerations underlying their lack of Sabbath observance.

That is to say, the Almighty has, with His especial loving kindness for American Jews, placed them in a good land, a land of plenty, a land that is indeed flowing with milk and honey. And because there is so much money (spelled with an *m* in place of the *h*) to be gathered in, we simply cannot find the time to obey God's laws, lest in doing so we might miss out on some of the good things of life. For such is the essence of the claim that American business practices make it impossible to keep the Sabbath.

What, pray, would these people say if, had they lived on farms, in addition to keeping the Sabbath they were also required, like the ancient Jews, to observe every seventh year, when it was forbidden to till the soil — in accordance with the injunction cited above relating to the Sabbatical year? One can surmise what the answer would be. But that should be nothing new, for it is anticipated in the Bible, and there it is effectively refuted, as we shall now see.

In the same chapter from which the foregoing passage is culled, we read, "And if you will say, 'What shall we eat in the seventh year? Behold we may not sow, nor gather in our crop.' I will ordain My blessing for you in the sixth year, and it will yield a crop sufficient for the three years. And you will sow in the eighth year, but you will eat from the old crop; until the ninth year, until the arrival of its crop, you will eat the old store. And the land shall not be sold in perpetuity, for the land is Mine; for you are strangers and settlers with Me" (*Vayikra* 25:20:23).

For those timid souls who are fearful that by refraining from employment on the Sabbath they might miss out on some shekels, a like reassurance might be given to them that the good L-rd Who daily cares for their wants and needs will not forsake them even if they keep their businesses closed on Saturdays. For just as all the earth is G-d's, so too is material well-being a gift from Him: "For it is He Who gives you power to acquire wealth" (*Devarim* 8:18). And surely He can send his blessing during the six days of toil to make up for the shortage occasioned by keeping the seventh day.

Viewing the transiency of the values relating to our wealth and prosperity, it is enough to realize how utterly without foundation is the claim that the pressure of business makes it well-nigh impossible to keep the Sabbath — not only because recent years have demonstrated that Jewish property may sometimes go to enrich the coffers of our sworn enemies, but also in light of the fact that economic cycles can make our acquisitions, even under the best of circumstances, an uncertain quantity. Why not keep the Sabbath then? And if Sabbath observance reduces one's bank account somewhat, so there will be that much less to lose!

Kislev 5705 / December 1944

"The Children of Israel shall observe the Sabbath, to make the Sabbath an eternal covenant for their generations" (Exodus 31:16).

A CERTAIN CLOTHIER DISTRIBUTES WITH EACH SALE PRINTED INSTRUCTIONS on how to care for the clothes. For example, the garment should be brushed off on being removed from its bag, and no suit should be worn continuously for too long a time.

Coming from an expert, this may doubtless be considered sound advice; no one need inquire into the scientific reasons that make it so. But if a little brushing off and a period of complete rest are good for an inanimate piece of cloth, may it not be concluded that such may at least be equally serviceable to a human being?

There is within us a constant interaction between the urge to be doing something at all times and the tendency to take it easy. Generally speaking, the average healthy person leans toward the side of industry rather than that of inactivity, so much so that he can never remain at rest for any extended time.

Even the periods of relaxation, while they may be helpful because of the change (which is comparable to the brushing off of a garment), do not induce the restoration of one's faculties to their original and efficient condition. Because of our natural restlessness, the change which ordinary relaxation brings about is — to continue in the metaphor of the suit — not a complete change of garments but merely a different way of wearing the same one, as though it were gone over with a whisk broom.

In the passage cited above, the Bible speaks of the Sabbath as something which is to be kept and *observed;* that is, it is not a matter which may be permitted to take its own course so that all one has to do is merely to desist from work. But the terms employed are those used in connection with pursuits wherein a definite and an affirmative attitude is called for.

The Hebrew term employed literally means not *keep* and *observe,* but *watch* and *do,* which are not expressions to leave things be, but rather which imply some plan, organization, and action. The underlying concept is that the Sabbath-day rest should not be a time for lounging around or for being on the go for pleasure and fun without stopping to think whether the course being pursued is conducive to our carrying out the function of restoring our wasted physique and our human dignity. After all, the restoration of both of these is necessary for good living.

The traditional observance of the Sabbath is marvelously calculated to achieve this objective. The primary rule of refraining absolutely from the slightest menial task is a guarantee that there will be complete rest, rest even from normally recreational activities which sometimes turn out to be more tiring and exacting than work itself!

Then in place of preoccupation with the things that are of the warp and woof of our daily existence, we are bidden by the same tradition to close the door, as it were, and enter the world of the mind and spirit, to dwell upon values which transcend the mere quest for worldly goods. The pattern for this behavior has been established in the customary attendance of services at the synagogue, the reading of the Biblical portion assigned for the week, and the study of Talmud and the commentaries.

The "doing" of the Sabbath after this fashion brings about that complete change of outfit — and possibly outlook — which, like the effect of following our clothier's instruction for the care of a garment, renders us less readily susceptible to the ravages of wear.

"Every man shall revere his mother and his father, and you shall observe My Sabbaths: I am Hashem, your G-d" (Leviticus 19:3).

NORMALLY, NOBODY EVER GIVES PRECEDENCE TO FEAR OF HIS MOTHER over that of his father. In point of fact, no child ever fears his mother; he certainly fears neither father nor mother upon his reaching a man's estate. And it is of a man that the above quotation speaks. The explanation of this seeming discrepancy lies in the fact that Sabbath-observance is coupled with the fear of mother and father.

Love and Fear of Mother

WHILE IT IS TRUE THAT A PERSON AS A GENERAL RULE DOES NOT REGARD his parents with fear, there in an exception to this — after their death. It is remarkable to observe the loyalty with which those bereaved of a parent will flock to the synagogue for the purpose of reciting the *Kaddish*, the prayer for a departed soul. What driving force exerts so singular a compulsion upon one who probably in the past visited the house of worship on but rare occasions and to whom the observance of the ritual incident to mourning is not only strange but most likely also uncomfortable and unpalatable? This self-imposed obligation proceeds from a sense of fear as to what might happen to the soul of a dear departed one, which fear is proportionate to the love which the survivor had for the deceased during the latter's lifetime. Hence, because a mother excites greater affection in a child's breast than does a father, she is the more feared in death — which is added proof that such is the sense with which the Torah speaks in the precept under consideration.

Fear of Parents and the Violation of the Sabbath

It is this writer's view that this injunction, in its first part, is merely declaratory — a statement of fact. But because of the difficulty of rendering Hebrew into idiomatic English, it appears as a directive instead. In order to convey its proper meaning, however, one should translate it as follows: "A man may well fear his mother and father, etc." Thus read, in light of the foregoing explanation, the appending of "and My Sabbaths shall you keep" makes excellent sense. For it is not uncommon to see a mourner who, having attended Sabbath-morning services, will, on leaving the portals of the synagogue, light up a cigarette, step into a big automobile, and go about his secular business, thereby ignoring every attribute which makes the Sabbath a holy day. When this happens, the whole concept which underlies the prayer for the dead is vitiated.

For what is the meaning behind this ritual? Why do people indulge in its performance? In his book *Jews on Approval*, Maurice Samuel gives a revealing characterization, touched up with his own inimitable humor.

What do the words mean? The "worshipers" do not know.

Why say them? The answers ran:

"Say, it don't do me no harm, and maybe it does the old man some good."

"A feller's got to have some religion, ain't he?" And some more along this line.

The Prayer for the Soul of a Deceased Person

The true office of *Kaddish*, which means "sanctification" and is nothing more nor less than a glorification of G-d's Name and a supplication for peace for Israel, is understood when viewed as the climactic act of conduct devoted to complying with the precepts of our faith. Whatever bliss and satisfaction in G-d's hereafter which a parent who has passed on may derive from any act of his or her offspring (and this is the sole basis for this custom of praying for the dead) can proceed only from a surviving child's conduct, which in its entirety should bring credit to the memory of a departed parent. The mere mumbo-jumbo recitation of the *Kaddish* in the face of a behavior divorced from every regard for the injunctions and prohibitions of Judaism becomes a hollow mockery.

Would You Honor a Parent's Memory? Keep the Sabbath!

Sabbath observance is one of the principal pillars of our religion. It is for this reason that the Torah (as we saw in the quotation at the beginning) says in effect: it is all good and well for a man to show his fear for his mother and his father after they have gone to their reward, to perform a rite on their behalf which they are unable to do for themselves. *But all this has meaning only when it is coupled with a devotion to that which Judaism holds vital and dear.* Consequently, the emphasis is placed on "and my Sabbaths shall ye keep" in virtually the same breath that the fear of parents is enjoined. For it is only by the carrying out of his obligations to Judaism that a Jew truly *does* honor to the memory of him or her for whose soul he may recite the prayer of sanctification.

The Festivals

Nisan 5703 (April 1943)

"You shall observe the Festival of Matzos"
(Exodus 23:15).

Among other names, the Passover holiday is called the Feast of Matzohs (unleavened bread). This epithet derives its origin from the fact that when the Israelites left Egypt, they had been in so great a hurry that as they were preparing bread, there was no time to permit the dough to rise. As the Torah relates, "And they baked of the dough which they had brought forth out of Egypt, unleavened cakes, for it was not leavened, because they were thrust out of Egypt and could not tarry, neither had they prepared any provisions for themselves" (*Exodus* 12:39).

In the story which relates the events of our deliverance, matzohs are also called the "Bread of Affliction." It is significant that so joyous a holiday as Passover, when both nature and historical background conspire to make it a glorious event in the Jewish calendar, should be "marred" by confining a principal food, bread, to a saltless, tasteless, and hard-to-digest cracker. This does not detract from the remarkable aptitude of Jewish housewives, who have learned to create the most exquisite delicacies from so unpromising a material as matzoh.

But it is a characteristic of all traditional Jewish gala affairs to intermix with it some discomfort, some sad reminder, some element of abnegation and deprivation. We never quite let ourselves go the complete measure of merited joy. We never quite drink the cup of happiness to its fullness. And so when, for example, a man and a woman standing under the marriage canopy plight one another their eternal troth, they are reminded of the loss of a parent, if such be the case, by the chanting of the memorial prayer. And before the betrothal is consummated, the bridegroom shatters a glass in token of lamentation over the destruction of Jerusalem. The holiday of Succos entails the spending of mealtimes in a booth of temporary construction with weeds for a roof, which scarcely keeps out the inclement weather usually obtaining at that time of year. The Jewish New Year has none of the fanfare with which such an event is ushered in by other nations. Instead, we are required to devote a great portion of the day to prayer and repentance for sins, thereby initiating a period — the Ten Days of Penitence — culminating in Yom Kippur, the most solemn fast day of the year. Examples such as these are plentiful.

Is it because the Jews are naturally a people of "crepehangers" that our ritual of celebration is so replete with unpleasantness? Far from it. The fact is that there is not a people on earth who can draw more solace and satisfaction in a most unpromising situation than we can. If one wished to be cynical, he could even point to the inordinately large proportion of night-club habitues that the Jews supply, to say nothing of the mainstay of the playing-cards business which we constitute.

This accenting of discomfort and sadness at such times, when the opposite would seem to be the order of the day, has a distinct office in our religious observances. Its purpose is to deflate an artificially inflated ego, to prevent us from being carried away by the transient and fleeting aspects of our existence, to enable us to retain a sense of soberness though partaking of the intoxicants of joy — in a word, to keep us close to the fundamentals of life.

This corrective, as it were, functions with respect to our situations as individuals, but it has an even more apt application to our position as Jews. For we should be hard put to find another people who, partly through the force of historic circumstances and partly owing to a strange mixture of national attachments and national escapism, is as hopelessly out of alignment as we are in regard to our essential character on the one hand, and, on the other, our appearance to a hostile world.

We are Jews. Yet the most prominent attitude displayed by the preponderant majority of our people in our intercourse with others is that our Jewishness resides somewhere in the suburbs of our being and that we resemble our non-Jewish fellows like the proverbial two peas in a pod. The tragedy of this situation lies in the fact that what we are attempting amounts to fooling ourselves, for the gentile seldom fails to apprise our position correctly.

This phenomenon is not without its influence upon our present national calamity. Whether or not this thought has occurred to intelligent non-Jews, at least we ought to ask ourselves this question: What seems to be out of joint in the times through which we are now passing that a band of outlaws could venture to pronounce and endeavor to carry out our death sentence while the rest of the world is either bogged down in indifference to our cruel fate or engaged in adding fuel to our oppression? Why should we be so universally wronged by our fellow beings — and this at a period of great scientific strides and when the better part of mankind is in arms against the last stronghold of barbarism — Germany and her Axis partners?

Certainly, no sane person credits any of the accusations against us. We neither deal as a corporate entity with the outside world (so that it is not possible to ascribe the acts of any single person in our midst to the whole people), nor have we any schemes or plans — good, bad, or indifferent — touching the rest of mankind. All that we want is to be left alone, wherever we are. But that cannot be, it would seem. And why? Is it because individual Jews manage to climb the ladder of worldly success to an appreciable degree? What would it benefit the non-Jews if not a solitary Jew were found among the opulent or powerful?

Supposing that a Moses were to arise tomorrow to lead his people, all of them, out of the Diaspora and into the Promised Land — would the situation of the gentiles materially change? If it did, then it should definitely be for the worse. Look at Germany. There the Jews have been completely eliminated as a factor in the national polity. Has that country and its people improved its lot? Aside from the present Nazi madness resulting in incalculable damage to Germany, there was not, there is not, and there never will be a shred of evidence to point out that the Germans as a people have had their condition improved by what was taken away from the Jews. It is, of course, well known that the Nazi campaign against the Jews of Germany was calculated, and shrewdly so, to be a stepping stone toward capturing power. It is equally true that anti-Semitism anywhere can have only one objective and one unfailing result, and that is to confuse the public mind as to who in fact entertains designs inimical to the public good and to further the interest of the self-seeking demagogue. For that reason, it is quite clear that none should gain from spreading Jew-hatred, save those who spread it. And their gain is, as has been shown by events abroad, decidedly the loss of the people as the whole.

All these considerations, it would seem, are quite elementary and should be known to most thinking people. It is not for nothing, for example, that the leaders of the Soviets — and whatever one thinks of them one must credit them with extraordinary political astuteness — have made anti-Semitism an offense against the state. Because it is nothing more nor less than just that! It should, nevertheless, be queried, in all frankness and all sincerity, why we Jews should worry if the gentiles are unwilling to put their own house in order, as it were, by tolerating Jew-hatred — and thus cutting off their noses to spite their faces. The answer to this is that in truth and in fact we neither should nor can we affect the non-Jewish attitude toward us by anything we do or fail to do. But insofar as we Jews fail to keep our own house in order, to that extent are we vulnerable to our enemies' darts. And that our own house desperately needs putting in order is too clear for all to see!

We should understand first that whatever fate holds in store for us as regards what the gentiles will or might do to us, with us, or for us, we shall be at a distinct disadvantage if we evade and overlook the fundamentals of our position. These basic factors are that we are **Jews**, that we are **different** and that we **do not belong.** This writer senses the hue and cry which the timid in our midst will at once raise in perusing the foregoing proposition. Why, this is nothing less (so they will complain) than an attempt to supply ammunition to our enemies! So be it. If to set down the truth helps our enemies, then since we cannot change our enemies, our course must be to reexamine ourselves and not attempt to modify that which is unchangeable — the truth.

Secondly, we must realize that we have failed miserably in an objective, realistic, and adequate appraisal of our tragic situation. We have all but become numb with grief at the spectacle of large sections of European Jewry being mercilessly maltreated and threatened with extinction. But it is a noteworthy fact that the reaction of the great majority of American Jews is far from satisfactory. It is characterized by an ostrichlike psychology — seeking to bury our heads in the sand of the chores of our daily existence.

We must register with a sense of disgust and utter dismay that perhaps never before (hereabouts, anyway) have Jews been so intent on business-promotion and on barter and trade as they appear to be now — at a time when half our people lie prostrate and in imminent danger of extermination. What will the historian of the future have to say on this score? How will he reconstruct the events of this period from an examination of the files of the current Jewish press? Suppose that he will look at a copy of the most influential Yiddish daily in the world: Will he see mirrored in it the shattering grief which should be ours at this critical moment? Will he not be amazed to find in such a newspaper evidence mostly of the business-as-usual tempo of American Jewish life? Will he not be wondering what perverted sense of Jewish journalism could prompt the management of such a publication, at a time when innocent Jewish blood flows like water, to relegate to a corner of *the back page* a report of a meeting, held in New York, appealing to the government of the United States to help save defenseless Jewish women and children who are still alive — all the while in the same issue displaying in a large box, with the utmost prominence on *the front page,* the intriguing announcement that the reader should not fail to commence reading next Saturday — on this sacred day, of all days! — two new serials: to wit "The Shade of His Sweetheart" and "The Evil Doubt"?

Take another instance. It has been proposed that the Jew of America voluntarily don the yellow badge, the same badge which the Jews of Europe are being forced to wear by their Nazi masters as a token of bondage and humiliation — and that this voluntary act be done as an expression of our solidarity with and concern for our persecuted brethren, for all the world to see. The inspiration for this movement came from reading the report that noble-hearted non-Jews in France, Holland, Belgium, Greece, and Denmark have, in defiance of Nazi might, adopted this very badge for themselves, testifying to their sense of profound sympathy with their fellow citizens of Jewish extraction.

How did Jews here react to this proposal? Well, some have said that it would be a pretty good thing to wear the badge here also — for the gentiles! In other words, this whole tragic situation touches us but little. But if the gentiles, however, choose to express their disgust with the dastardly crime committed against human beings who happen to be Jews and indicate this by wearing the insignia of Jewish shame and slavery — why then, we American Jews shall have no objection thereto!

Others have questioned what good this movement would do. Indeed, what good! What good did it do in the days of Queen Esther, when the evil Haman sought to pogromize the Jews of Persia, that Mordecai, upon learning of this design, put on sackcloth and ashes, the traditional signs of Jewish mourning, and in this attire appeared in the very palace of the king and queen? But Mordecai was less concerned about the figure he would cut in this strange attire before his highly placed non-

Jewish friends in the palace and was much more concerned about saving Jewish lives. And who will deny the effect of this very self-humiliating procedure of Mordecai and his fellows all over Persia — that it started a chain of causation which ultimately helped to confound Haman and his schemes? But American Jews are no fools. You have got to show them with mathematical certainty the exact probability of success before they will attempt any such display calling attention to the grievously tragic condition of their people.

Still others have said that the carrying out of this idea would interfere with business. Why advertise the fact that one is a Jew? It is bad enough as it is, they argue, to be discovered as one. Is not anti-Semitism rampant in this country today? Have not the Nazi agents here, in an effort to undermine American democracy, planted the virulent germs of their own brand of Jew-baiting? Why then should we parade our Jewishness before the general public? Perhaps the gentile in his dealing with us might otherwise chance to forget our race. The wearing of the yellow badge, however, would draw attention to that fact, and it might result in inconvenience, discomfort, loss of patronage, and so on.

All of these thoughts proceed from a terrible error into which Jewry here has fallen: That is, the Nazis are responsible for all our woes, and we in America are immune to the fate which has overtaken our people abroad. The particular concurrence of circumstances which have rendered our people the worst victims of the Nazi tyranny is not accidental but the direct outgrowth of our homelessness. The German mind has been prepared for years for the eventuality of attempting to attain worldwide conquest. The advent of the Nazis channeled this barbaric urge and gave it tangible expression. But they needed a trial balloon to test how far the world's conscience could be shocked by deeds of dastardliness without arousing the opposition of decent folk everywhere who alone could become the nemesis of German designs. For once, that conscience has been lulled to sleep; there should be no telling of the lengths of appeasement to which these decent people will not go. A victim was necessary for this experiment: that victim was the Jew. It was not difficult to arouse antipathy toward him, and he was defenseless. No condition could be more ideal for the Nazi beast than this situation. And it was our terrible misfortune that the bulk of our people sojourned in the very path of the German Drang Nach Osten, Pressure toward the East.

But how does this affect us in America? Have we — those of us who hail from Poland, Rumania, Hungary, Russia, and Lithuania — not been placed out of reach of these maddened hordes from Germany and her satellites by an Omniscient Providence? We must then be especially endowed with unusual merit to have been saved by the Almighty and be constituted as the virtual remnant of Israel. What merit, pray, is ours? That we carry the torch of our Torah with the utmost devotion and self-sacrifice? The answer to that can be safely left to our own indolent Jewish conscience. Have we created in America a community which has burdened itself with the responsibility of seeing to it that the masses of our people abroad, driven from pillar to post for already hundreds of years, are being repatriated to the land for which the Jewish heart has been yearning for nearly two thousand years? Let our investment in Palestine for the past twenty years or so, under the operation of the Mandate — an investment which is probably but a small fraction of the money which Jews have exchanged in pinochle games during that same period — testify as to that!

What is our merit? The answer is that we have none. We have merely been given the opportunity — placed on probation, as it were, by the G-d of our Fathers — to apply ourselves at this critical juncture in our history with might and main, forgetful of all our private and personal affairs, to the rescue of our people. "For if," to quote Mordecai's words to Queen Esther, "thou indeed maintainest silence at this time, enlargement and deliverance will arise to the Jews from another place, but thou and thy father's house will perish." Let not this writer be the one to give this quotation any further elucidation.

Which brings us to another objection in the matter of wearing the yellow badge. That is, that we Jews of America are giving of our money, which is about all we can do under the circumstances. Well, granted that with a powerful stretch of our imagination and with the utmost of charitableness, it is conceivable that the giving of money might suffice. But do we contribute to give, in light of the mammoth Jewish needs, anywhere nearly commensurate with our ability to give? Let us not fool ourselves. American Jews are supplied in a fairly ample degree with worldly goods. Our share in the national competence of the American people is larger, but certainly no smaller, than that of the next group. If the 600,000 Jews of Germany were conservatively reputed to have been worth a billion dollars, which incidentally has gone to enrich the coffers of the Nazis, how much property is owned by 4.5 million American Jews, by all odds the richest Jewish community that ever existed? Furthermore, on the basis of a $90 billion annual income by the whole of the American people, our per capita share of it should be at least $3 billion dollars. Now what is the annual budget of the United Jewish Appeal for all causes, including the Joint Distribution Committee, the United Palestine Appeal, and the National Refugee Service, for the whole country? At most, it is a paltry $25 million — or less than three quarters of one percent of our annual income. Talk about giving money! This is not even the leavings from our well-stocked cupboards and pantries, at a time when literally millions of our people subsist on G-d only knows what!

Yes, the present is an excellent time for the Jews of America to indulge in self-scrutiny and self-criticism. This is urged not merely because being honest with ourselves will greatly help our own souls. It is urged also because of a firm conviction that we shall find thereby infinitely more grace in the eyes of our non-Jewish fellows than we should by trying to run away from ourselves. For fortunately, our fellow Americans of other racial antecedents are an unusually great-hearted lot. Most of them believe in fair play. They admire courage and frankness and detest cowardice and fraud. They detest above all anyone seeking to horn in under a false front. Give them the plain, unsophisticated, and unadulterated Jewish person, and they might scoff at and ridicule him, but they will not let him down. They will throw a mantle of protection about him, notwithstanding all his idiosyncrasies and peculiarities. For that is the essence of America's redeeming quality of true sportsmanship.

This Passover holiday, then, with its matzohs, "this Bread of Affliction," its *haroseth*, its bitter herbs — all of which are supposed to symbolize the dire distress of our forebears as slaves of the Egyptian Pharoah — are also reminders to us of this generation to stick close to the fundamentals of Jewish life. These lowly components of the holiday serve to mar somewhat the pleasurable aspects of the festivities, but in doing so they cause us to become aware of the constant intermingling of joy and sorrow in human experience. They point to the fallacy of the belief of him, who riding the high tide, cannot envisage the possibility of adversity. They cause us to strip our ego of the baggage of transient and temporary advantages which we accumulate in our quest after the seemingly good things in life. They challenge us into unremitting attention to the often overlooked and neglected things about us which, in the long run, may be just the ones that really matter. These plain substances join with the other, more inspiring and stimulating components of Passover to make one harmonious whole and are thus to us, of this generation especially, the finger of stern duty pointing with unmistakable clarity to the path ahead, a path of divesting our minds of a belief in false messiahs, of removing from our innermost thinking the hardened crust of lackadaisicalness in dealing with vital Jewish interests, of retaining a sense of proportion in the appraisal of values, and of being able to differentiate between those things that are temporary and those that are eternal, and finally, of turning toward the Source of our being in humble supplication for wisdom to travel our path worthily and courageously.

Kislev 5703 June 1943

> *"And you shall observe the Festival of Shavuos for Hashem, your G-d; to the extent of what your hand can offer ..." (Deuteronomy 16:10).*

THE PENTECOST HOLIDAY, CALLED SHAVUOS IN HEBREW, LITERALLY means "weeks." This term derives its origin from the fact that the Torah enjoins us to count from day to day for a period of forty-nine days, or seven weeks, commencing with the second day of Passover. The fiftieth day in the counting is the beginning of Pentecost.

This procedure, of course, was not designated for the purpose of enabling us to gauge the exact time when the holiday falls. With no other feast is such a system employed, and a calendar is always, or nearly always, available for that purpose. This counting, however, is deemed to be a matter of no small importance in our religious observance. And it has accordingly received considerable stress from Talmudic commentators.

Traditionally, Shavuos also commemorates the time when the Torah was handed down to the Israelites through Moses on Mount Sinai, an event whose far-reaching significance can scarcely be overestimated. It would therefore seem that the arithmetic of the counting, a prelude to the observance of that extraordinary event, has some bearing on the Torah itself.

SCIENCE AND THE HUMANITIES

THE SCIENCE OF MATHEMATICS, OF WHICH ARITHMETIC IS A PART, IS AN exact, if not **the** exact, science. On the other hand, the Torah is popularly supposed to be the most "inexact" of all the sources from which we derive useful knowledge. The so-called fundamentalist will shut his eyes to that in the Torah which he is unable to explain and will, with an unyielding obstinacy, reiterate his faith in the infallibility of Sacred Writ. The doubter and skeptic will just shrug his shoulders at the inexplicable in the Torah, concede it perhaps certain evident excellencies, and then go about his way with an air of superior obliviousness, leaving the whole matter to the keeping of the clerics, the research addicts, or the disputatious.

Now, how may the Holy Book be properly appraised? In endeavoring to evaluate it, it should be stated as a fundamental proposition that the Torah was given not for angels but for men. It does not, consequently, recapitulate such facts as are within the common knowledge and property of humankind. It is intended merely to complement the experience which we are already supposed to possess by virtue of being men.

The writer recalls in this connection a problem in algebra which in his now dim, distant university days he was called upon to solve. It appeared that X, or the unknown, representing persons, was brought down through the intricacies of the algebraic equations to a number that had a fraction in it. It was obvious, therefore, that the solution was wrong, for an answer that contained a fraction of a person could not possibly be conceived as the correct one. But, as the wise professor later pointed out to the class, the compiler of the textbook had purposely so formulated the problem that in attempting to solve it, one could easily be misled into arriving at that unlikely answer, and the wide-awake student was expected to supply by means of his common sense the missing factor, whereupon the solution appeared quite simple.

MAHEMATICS OF LIFE

SIMILARLY, IT IS PROBABLE THAT THE GREAT COMPILER IN OFFERING US the Torah as the text for the Mathematics of Life had deemed it wise to leave a number of things unsaid or to say them in a manner so incomprehensible as to leave us flabbergasted. Nevertheless, all that is needed in this problem, comparable to the one made so clear in the classroom, is just a bit of common sense, the supplying of facts which we glean from our own daily experiences.

Let us set forth one or two examples. In the Book of *Genesis*, where the work of creation is set out in considerable detail, there appear a number of paragraphs recounting the specific acts of Creation, and each account concludes with the phrase: "And G-d saw that it was good." On the sixth day when G-d made man, the statement contains a variation: "And G-d saw everything that He had made, and behold it was very good" (*Genesis* 2:31).

WORK OF CREATION MUST BE PERFECT

ON REFLECTION, THESE STATEMENTS IN THE TORAH APPEAR, ON reflection to be extraordinary in the extreme. If we ascribe, as we assuredly do, omnipotence and omniscience to the Creator, then how can anything to which He sets His hand be aught but good, but perfection? Furthermore, "He beholdeth the end of everything before it is begun," as is stated in the noble measure of Maimonides. How unlike G-d, therefore, it would seem, to have it related that on viewing His handiwork He found it good, for it could hardly be otherwise! Any such affirmative declaration would seem to be superfluous.

The Festivals / 201

There is another significant passage, besides, which must be considered in connection therewith. Further on in the same book we read: "And it repented Hashem that He had made man on the earth" (*Bereishis* 6:6). Here is indeed a strange situation. G-d has made man, following which He pronounces upon Creation "and behold, it was very good" — notwithstanding that, however, the job turned out poorly after all! For "the wickedness of man was great on the earth, and every product of the thoughts of his heart was only evil continually" (*Bereishis* 6:5).

Torah — A Human Document

THE EXPLANATION OF THE FOREGOING LIES PRECISELY IN THE FACT that the Torah, although Divinely revealed, is a human document speaking through the universal human tongue. And just as the things set forth therein are intended for guidance to men, so too do the experiences of which it is an account dovetail with our own experiences. When a person performs a certain task — be it in whatever branch of human endeavor — if the work be more or less successfully consummated, it is natural for such person to stand aside, as it were, and view his achievement with an inner sense of satisfaction. It does not follow that the product will always turn out to be perfection itself. The great likelihood is that it may be considerably improved upon as time goes by. It is even possible that the original estimate of its excellencies may, on later appraisal, turn out to have been grossly exaggerated. All this is, nevertheless, a part of the creative process. We build, test, apply, and constantly improve.

Creative Process

WHAT IS THE CREATIVE PROCESS? GENERALLY, IT IS THAT WHICH differentiates us from the lower animals. For strictly speaking, the physical resemblance between a human being and a creature of the lower order is very striking. It is commonly assumed that we differ from animals in that we possess the capacity to think, or, more accurately, in that we have imagination. The reactions of an animal are entirely instinctive. They proceed either from characteristics which are native to the species or from the exercise of the faculty of memory following repeated occurrences of a certain phenomenon. Man, however, is able to project his mind into a new or future situation and anticipate his course of action thereby.

How does he attain creativeness? The process as such is quite inexplicable. But the fact, nevertheless, is that we know from an inner experience when it is that we are engaged in that process. We have also an additional criterion, which is the tendency to view our tentative achievements with a sense of serene satisfaction in having done something worthwhile, which prompts the thought, whether expressed or not, "behold, it is very good."

It is then and then only that man draws away from his animal self and draws close to spirituality — to G-d. Thus the sole element which differentiates us from other creatures may be our ability to submerge our physical characteristics in a striving to reach out after the Divine in life. It is this sense that the Torah employs when it states: "And G-d created man in His image; in the image of G-d He created him; male and female He created them" (*Bereishis* 1:27). For in no other sense can man possibly be conceived as bearing any resemblance to his Creator, except as that which relates to a spiritual level. And by the same token, when man descends from that level, immersed solely in attending to his physical urges, then he pursues the opposite path: i.e., he draws away from his Maker and becomes at one with other animals whose general constitution he shares.

Freedom of Choice

It will thus be seen that one does not have to profess any religious faith to be a religious person, for to be such means to deport oneself, consciously or otherwise, as a being made in His image. This is not to say that nonreligiousness or irreligiousness is to be encouraged. Quite the contrary: the difference between belief in a Divine order of things and the lack of such a belief is the difference between a positive and a negative attitude toward life. It is, furthermore, the difference between a person who does good because it enhances his own human worth and one who refrains from doing evil because it may entail disagreeable consequences. In addition, man is endowed with the power of choice by reason of the fact that he shares with his Maker the property of being creative, in consequence of which he is his own master in the matter of applying that ability in life and to that extent in stamping his course with a fidelity to his G-dlike nature — or resigning, in effect, his high spiritual estate, thereby incurring all the risks that accompany baser conduct.

People are often heard to say, in extenuation of their or others' dereliction, that human frailties are not our responsibility, since we have thus been endowed by the Creator. This leaves entirely out of consideration the fact that we have equally been endowed with the power of rising above these frailties and that the exercise of that power is within the province of our own choosing. In that realm Hashem leaves us severely alone, each to his own respective devices.

Returning then to the beginning of this part of the discussion, it will be observed how the Biblical reference to the Almighty's viewing His work of Creation and pronouncing it good — far from presenting an attitude irreconcilable with the nature of Divinity — expounds in fact the morally invigorating doctrine of human dignity and potentialities, thereby making it possible for us to rise above our animal nature by investing us with the power of choice, which is at the basis of the concept of a free will, a concept which Judaism stands for. To interpret Scripture in such a manner requires its constant involvement in our everyday human experiences.

THE SACRIFICE OF ISAAC

LET US TAKE ANOTHER EXAMPLE, THE SACRIFICE OF ISAAC. HERE IS AN episode of the most intense dramatic interest — Abraham, at the bidding of G-d, prepared to bring his only son as a sacrifice. Nothing, it would seem, could be more repulsive to a father than to submit thereto, and, in point of fact, nothing is more repulsive to Judaism than human sacrifices. For the Torah specifically enjoins: "Whatsoever man of the children of Israel, or of the stranger that sojourn in Israel, that giveth any of his seed unto Molech shall surely be put to death" (*Vayikra* 20:2). It is no answer to say that Abraham was prevented from carrying out this rite at the very moment of its proposed consummation and that the whole proceeding was but a trial to test his faithfulness to the Almighty. The very suggestion of such an act would appear wholly alien to the spirit of the Torah.

But this singular tale, noteworthy as an illustration of the perfect faith in G-d, is such not by reason alone of a willingness to offer the most exacting sacrifice that a human being can be possibly asked to make, but primarily because Abraham, the man who knew G-d so well as has been the portion of very few people, knew that, notwithstanding appearances to the contrary, he would not be required to carry out this act. And therein lay the Patriarch's greatness — in a word, moral courage — courage not of the reckless, thoughtless sort, but rather of the caliber which, implemented by a profound faith in a beneficent Providence, cheerfully shoulders a most hazardous risk for the sake of a worthy cause, strongly confident that things will turn out well.

The Meaning of True Courage

This should not be confused with the pseudocourage of the person whom Kipling thus characterizes:
"If you can make a heap of all your winnings,
And risk it all in one turn of pitch and toss,
And lose and start again at your beginnings
And never breathe a word about your loss."

This is not the Jewish conception of courage. There seems to be little reason for throwing all one has willy-nilly upon the wheel of fortune, hoping for the best but prepared for the worst — unless it be done for a noble objective — and even then, when one calculates his chances of success, he sees that the venture bears promise. This is most probable when one approaches a dangerous task with a sense of dedicating his effort to G-d and with implicit faith in Him. In such a frame of mind, one does not anticipate loss or failure, and he proceeds to steel himself to meet the possibility of defeat but contrarily, he concomitantly builds up his moral fiber to an expectation of prevailing in whatever he is about, notwithstanding the great odds against its success.

Torah Given for Men, Not Angels

We thus see the story of the sacrifice of Isaac projected against the background of what we know of our father Abraham and the religion which he founded. In consideration, furthermore, of the quality of true courage as exemplified by the noble leaders of mankind throughout the ages, this story assumes a significance which has a definite bearing on our practical conduct in a workaday world in which we are required to make decisions, to act, to take risks. This brings us back to the proposition with which we started — that the Torah was given for men and not for angels, and that its sole objective is to teach us how properly to evaluate our normal human experiences and how best to integrate them with the signposts and guides set up in the Book of Life.

This being the case, the Torah cannot legitimately be viewed as a document whose applicability resides in the sphere of theology, mythology, or morality in the abstract with but incidental reference to the burning issues of the day. Quite the opposite: it is a means of charting our course on the broad highway of life in a manner so as to serve our most vital interests with the utmost probability of success, not in the superficial but in the intrinsic connotation of that term.

LITMUS TEST

OURS IS THE TASK OF ACQUIRING AN INTIMATE ACQUAINTANCE WITH THE contents of the Torah in order to be able to read it correctly. This is achieved by approaching the matter contained therein with a friend who seeks enlightenment and who trusts the Torah as a means par excellence toward reaching that end. The inexplicable or seemingly self-contradictory elements in it are then resolved with the aid of the common experience of mankind, just as a litmus test in the chemical laboratory determines the presence of acids, or the transposition of the factors in an algebraic equation helps to isolate the elusive unknown.

May this holiday of Shavuos, which concludes the seven weeks of counting and commemorates the giving of the Torah, bring with it a new realization of the supreme worth of the Sacred Book in our lives as individuals and as a people.

Nisan 5704/April 1944

"Seven days shalt you eat unleavened bread"
(Exodus 34:18).

PASSOVER IS A HOLIDAY OF "FIRSTS." IT IS CELEBRATED IN THE FIRST month of the Jewish calendar, Nisan. Though technically the month of Tishrei, when Rosh Hashanah (the New Year) falls, occupies that position, the Torah calls Tishrei the seventh month, while of Nisan it says, "This month shall be unto you the chief of months; the first shall it be unto you of the year" (*Shemos* 12:2). Passover is also the first in the order and importance of our three principal holidays, the other two being Shavuos and Succos.

THE PRIMACY OF PASSOVER

FURTHERMORE, PASSOVER COMMEMORATES OUR BEGINNING AS AN organized people. For theretofore, our ancestors had been but a horde of helpless slaves. It was Moshe's task not only to wring concessions out of Pharaoh, but — what was equally if indeed not more important — he also had to weld the Children of Israel into a disciplined and cohesive group. This he succeeded in doing by the only test which then, even as now, determines the right of a nation to self-sufficiency, that of a willingness and a capacity to fight for that right. For the Jews had, shortly after their liberation, met and conquered (not without Divine intercession) two formidable enemies, the redoubtable Pharaoh and Amalek.

Passover, the symbol par excellence of our deliverance from Egyptian slavery, is by the same token the principal reference to the practices of our faith, just as the Exodus is the event with which most of those practices and pronouncements are tied up. Commencing with the First Commandment, "I am the Lord Thy G-d, Who has brought thee out of the land of Egypt" (*Shemos* 20:2), to "A stranger thou shalt not vex . . . for strangers ye were in the land of Egypt" (*Shemos* 22:20), to "And thou shalt remember that thou hast been a servant in the land of Egypt and that the Lord Thy G-d brought thee out from there with a mighty hand and by an outstretched arm; therefore hath the Lord thy G-d commanded thee to observe the Sabbath" (*Devarim* 5:15), and through a great number other declarations and directions, this act of emancipation is the center around which is woven our religious and ethical system. Consequently, the same primacy in its sphere must also be accorded to the holiday which celebrates that event. Examples of such characterizations are plentiful.

THE EATING OF MATZOS

AS TO THE OBSERVANCE OF PASSOVER ITSELF, IT IS MARKED BY ONE main distinguishing attribute, that of the eating of matzohs, or unleavened bread, for the entire seven-day period. The Torah is quite clear about the great importance which attaches to this ritual, for it says, "Seven days shall you eat unleavened bread, but on the first day you shall have put away leaven from your houses; for whosoever eats leavened bread, that soul should be cut off from Israel" (*Shemos* 12:15). It should be added, parenthetically, that Passover is celebrated for eight days in the Diaspora.

To many this will sound like magnifying a mere detail into a matter of undue importance. It is quite proper, the argument might go, that the observance of Passover should also include the eating of matzohs as a reminder of what our forebears ate when in haste they departed from Egypt. But to subsist on that food in place of leavened bread for more than a week is, it will be said, beyond any reasonable necessity for the effectiveness or impressiveness of the symbol. There are those, notably certain members of the Reform persuasion and others of nonreligious or irreligious tendencies who nonetheless appreciate the ennobling significance of Passover, who in deference to the tradition will eat token pieces of matzoh during the holiday meals, along with the customary food served all year round.

The difficulty in this situation is, as usual, not with the infallible authority, the Torah, from which this instruction is derived, but with those who are unwilling or unable to comprehend the profound implications of the injunction against leavened foods. As has been pointed out, Passover is a holiday which occupies a position of primacy in Judaism and is at the basis of our religion and culture. What directly ensues from this holiday is more than just an occasion for reminiscing about the wonders wrought by the Almighty for our forefathers, which certainly is an important function; Pesach also marks a time for rededication to the service of G-d and our people. But beyond that, it is a practical instrument for the achievement of that rededication, which means nothing more nor less than our becoming better human beings.

The Earmarks of Wholesome Human Beings

What are the earmarks of a wholesome human being? Perhaps Shakespeare came nearest when he said, in *Hamlet:*

> *This above all: to thine own self be true,*
> *And it must follow as the night the day,*
> *Thou canst not then be false to any man*

But secular notions like this one are seldom adequate unless supplemented from religious sources — that is, from the Torah. We must therefore add to the Bard of Avon's characterization

King Solomon's admonition: "The fear of Hashem is to hate evil, overbearing, arrogance, and the evil way" (*Mishlei* 8:13). This concept and fidelity to oneself are a matchless combination.

Finiteness and Infinity

Now what are the supporting considerations for such a standard of behavior? The human mind is finite; that is to say, its comprehension is limited. This concept of finiteness implies both an end as well as a definite beginning, since the opposite of that concept, infinity, implies neither beginning nor end. Most people will readily grant that one cannot know everything, that ultimately all our speculations must terminate or remain suspended because of our inability to be omniscient. There are those who at the commencement of their thought processes will start with that which to them is considered the known and insist that they can be guided only by that criterion; therefore, they rely on their own knowledge. In other words, they fail to see that their beginnings are as susceptible of erroneous analyses as their conclusions are lacking in finality.

Faith in G-d

To illustrate: take the matter of faith in G-d. The same people, who will readily admit that beyond a certain point in their thinking they must of necessity feel thwarted and therefore rely on a Higher Power, will sometimes argue that they cannot conceive of such a Higher Power, because His origin and work are not explainable on the basis of what they choose to call their available knowledge. But is it not fair to argue that finiteness cannot judge infinity if it is bound by the ultimates of our probing, the beginning and the end? And if we must take refuge in G-d by reason of our inability to see too far ahead, must we not also concede that the same Authority leaves off at the point where we first begin to understand? What we need, therefore, in our mental equipment is certain Articles of Reference, to use a term from the field of government, with which to check our performance. One must be able to say to himself: This is where I begin; along this path do I proceed, and thus far only may I go. Applied practically, this approach must begin with faith in a Benevolent Providence, to fear Whom is the same as "to hate evil, overbearing, arrogance, and the evil way," as King Solomon counseled. Then one must be true to himself, which, together with an implicit faith in G-d, is but another phase of remaining true to Him. For we can know G-d best as He is manifest in our own innermost being. In the exigencies which each of us experiences in his daily affairs, he will find — call it what you will — the small, still voice, conscience, inner logic, hunch, sixth sense — but there is something there, vital and impelling, which tells us what is right. And that something is the Divine in us with which we have been endowed by the Almighty.

Act in the Living Present

Lastly, a person must act. It is not enough to know what is right, proper, and serviceable, for "not learning but doing is the chief thing" (*Pirkei Avos* 1:17). Acting with dispatch, even if erroneous, is better than to fail to make up one's mind for fear of being wrong. Furthermore, one who approaches his task, whatever it may be, with faith in the Almighty, and consequently with self-assurance, need seldom fear that such a task, within certain reasonable limitations, might miscarry.

Setting the Form of Conduct

RETURNING NOW TO THE MATTER DEALT WITH EARLIER IN THIS ARTICLE: The scrupulous observance of the eating of unleavened bread for the full eight days of Passover, far from being an undue overemphasis on a mere detail, in fact constitutes a direction for setting a highly useful example by which one may learn to conduct himself in a thoroughly wholesome manner. In view of its position as the epoch-making introduction to our national culture, Passover is a vital element in the formulation and development of guides and signposts for proper living. And as in every other sphere of human activity, the making of a good start is of great importance.

Thus the adherence to the injunction touching upon the eating of unleavened bread makes it necessary for a person to choose a course which, although entailing some difficulty in its being carried out, focuses upon the salutary idea of self-control. And to be able to curb one's appetite is the very essence of self-discipline. Thence, the further acquisition of a sense of the duties and obligations which each of us owes the Almighty follows as a matter of logical course.

Tying in With a Standard

LET A PERSON TRAIN HIMSELF TO GUIDE HIS CONDUCT ALONG LINES conforming to a standard set up outside his corporeal desires. He thus not only develops strength of character, but by tying in his actions with such standards he actually raises his potential for accomplishment because he is able to harness powers other than his own limited ones to the tasks at hand. And with faith in Providence, fidelity to oneself, and fearlessness in execution, he will discover the result to be a gratifying one. Let this lesson of Passover enable us to **live** successfully, in the intrinsic rather than in the superficial meaning of the word.

Tishrei 5705/September 1944

Memorial proclaimed with the blast of the horn (Leviticus 23:24).

ACCORDING TO THE CALENDAR RECKONING OF THE TORAH, ROSH Hashanah, the Hebrew New Year, takes place not, as might have been expected, on the first day of the year, but rather on the first day of the seventh month, *Tishrei — Nisan* being considered the first month of the year.

Seven is a charmed number in Hebrew religious lore: "Six days shall you labor and do all your work. But the seventh day is the Sabbath to Hashem, your G-d" (Exodus 20:9,10).

"And you shall count for yourself seven sabbaths of years, seven years seven times; and the days of the seven sabbaths of years shall be for you forty-nine years" (Leviticus 25:8). "And you shall hallow the fiftieth year, and proclaim liberty throughout the land for all its inhabitants; it shall be a jubilee to you; and you shall return every man to his possession, and you shall return every man to his family" (Leviticus 25:10).

"Six years shall you sow your field, and six years shall you prune your vineyard and gather the fruit. But in the seventh year, there shall be a Sabbath of rest for the land, a Sabbath for Hashem; your field shall you not sow, and your vineyard shall you not prune" (Leviticus 25:3-4).

> "And the glory of Hashem abode upon Mt. Sinai and the cloud covered it six days; and He called to Moses on the seventh day from the midst of the cloud" (Exodus 24:16).
>
> "And you shall count for yourselves from the morrow after the day of rest, from the day that you brought the Omer of the waving; seven weeks shall there be complete" (Leviticus 23:15) "And you shalt observe the Feast of Weeks (Pentecost) even of the first fruits of the wheat harvest" (Exodus 34:22).
>
> "Seven days shall you eat unleavened bread, as I have commanded you, in the time of the month of Aviv" (Exodus 34:18). "You shall keep the Feast of Tabernacles seven days, after you have gathered in from your threshing-floor and from your winepress" (Deuteronomy 16:13).
>
> "... for in six days Heaven made the heavens and the earth, and on the seventh day He ceased from work and rested" (Exodus 31:17). "At the end of every seventh year you shall make a release. And this is the manner of the release: every creditor shall release that which he has lent to his neighbor" (Deuteronomy 15:1-2).

The foregoing is not intended to present an exhaustive collection of passages, but those cited fairly establish the proposition that the number seven receives uncommon stress in the Torah.

And so it is quite appropriate that there should also be stated in the Torah: "In the seventh month, on the first day of the month, there shall be a solemn rest unto you, a memorial proclaimed with the blast of the horn, a holy convocation" (*Vayikra* 23:24), from which passage, as will be noted, the phrase appearing at the head of this article has been culled.

The Torah made the first day of each month an occasion for additional offerings. But the New Moon of the seventh month was established as a festival of special solemnity, which later came to be known as Rosh Hashanah, or New Year's Day. And this day, unlike the custom of other nations (when revelry is in order), was to be an occasion of the most profound religious and spiritual

The Festivals / 215

significance for the Hebrew nation — a day of searching in the annals of one's memory; a day of self-scrutiny; a day of establishing a balance between the urge for acquisition and aggrandizement and the still, small voice of conscience; a day of seeking G-d's intercession so that He remember us in His dispensation of goodness in light of His mercifulness, and not according to our meager deserts.

As previously intimated, human wisdom has no inkling of the reason for the extraordinary significance attached by the Torah to the number seven. That this is not at all a case of hocus-pocus goes without saying; that there is an immutable law of life underlying this phenomenon must be the judgment of all who learn the Torah, the infallible source of the knowledge of life that it is.

There can be no doubt G-d's creation of the world in six days and His resting on the seventh, as related in the Book of *Bereishis*, is the origin of this primacy which attaches to the number seven. As likely as not, there is a cycle in human life and action which, stemming as it does from the Source of all life, must, in emulation of that Source, accommodate its conduct within the framework which had been set in the beginning, when "G-d created the heaven and the earth" (*Bereishis* 1:1).

And so man must rest on the seventh day, an institution which has been calculated to maintain the ideal, proper balance between labor and rest. It will be remembered that there had been religious rebels who, seeking to strip the Torah of its authoritarian influence, wanted to change the day of rest to one day in ten, as at the time of the French revolution, or, more recently, to one day in five, as during the Russian revolution, but apparently without notable success, for the attempted change did not prevail.

The same is true concerning the regulations contained in the precepts relating to the Sabbatical year, when all the land was to lie fallow. During the Jubilee year, the fiftieth after the elapse of seven Sabbatical years, the Hebrew slaves were emancipated, and all property reverted to its original owners. These laws constituted a system of jurisprudence, the observance and enforcement of which were calculated to assure a state of social justice.

> ...For during the Sabbatical year, the produce soil was not harvested but devoted to G-d by being left for everyone, including the poor. This year, furthermore, was to be set aside for teaching the people the laws and statutes promulgated by Moses. The Jubilee guaranteed to everyone a fair start by restoring that to him which through the exigencies of the struggle for existence his predecessor had been forced to relinquish. Consequently, there had been, in effect, a redivision of the land every fifty years, a provision the salutariness of which, from the standpoint of the enjoyment by all of a fair and equal share of the common wealth, cannot be overemphasized.

These and other rules enjoined upon the Israelites and set up with due regard to their synchronization with the count of seven must have some element in them which, upon the proper keeping of those rules, brings some definite moral and spiritual benefit for the individual as well as for society — whether it be in the matter of affording to each an equilibrium of his physical and mental powers, or as regards the assuring to all of equality of opportunity in life, or regarding any other aspect of our existence wherein our endowments of freedom of choice and capacity for rising above our animal instincts play a role. And thus too, the first day of the seventh month, Rosh Hashanah, must fit in with the general cycle of sevens and that which is implicit as well as explicit therein.

As has been intimated, the Hebrew New Year is primarily an occasion for moral bookkeeping, for ascertaining balances, for closing accounts, for determining statements of assets and liabilities, but (above all) for trying to keep out of the moral red, by having our deficiencies eradicated by our Heavenly Father on condition of our repentance and our promises to conform henceforth with His will, and thus we may commence the new year with a new start in life.

May this conception of Rosh Hashanah be our guiding principle in these days of world-shaking events, when the props have all but been knocked out from under the collective life of the Hebrew nation, and may each one of us in the year ahead do his full share to bring salvation to Israel, tried as never before in the crucible of affliction.

> *"A Day of Blowing the Horn, a Holy Convocation"* (cf. Leviticus 23:24).

Rosh Hashanah, the Hebrew New Year, has a number of designations, perhaps the most picturesque of which is a Day of Blowing the Horn, for the synagogue services thereon are interspersed with the blowing of the shofar, or ram's horn. Some commentators consider this rite of greater importance than the prayers themselves.

Tradition has assigned various explanations as to why we blow the shofar. Some commentators claim that it symbolizes the renewal of our covenant with G-d made with the patriarch, Avraham Avinu, following his attempted sacrifice of Yitzchak. As is well known, this story describes the supreme faith in Hashem which Avraham possessed, so much so that he did not shrink from what appeared to be a Divine command to sacrifice his only son, after which the order was recalled by its Author. Thereupon, the Almighty made a promise to Avraham to multiply his children as "the stars in the heavens and the sand on the shores of the sea" (*Bereishis* 22:17). Then finding a ram, Avraham sacrificed it in place of Yitzchak. Therefore, the sounding of the ram's horn is in the nature of a subtle supplication to G-d for beneficence in the year to come for the seed of him whose religious faith was so demonstrably perfect; it is a plea to make good the promise to Avraham. It seems to be imploring the Creator that we have long, too long, been considered no better than sand and dust to be ruthlessly stepped on and driven away as if rootless. Accordingly, will not He, Whom our common ancestor had served so devotedly and wholeheartedly, bring to realization also the other portion of that promise to render us at last a fixed abode like the stars of the skies?

This interpretation of the function of the shofar emphasizes perhaps more than anything else the collective nature of the ritual of Hebrew worship. A Jew's prayer for himself, though not necessarily by himself, is only a superficial act of communing with his Maker. A Jew truly partakes of Divine service only when therein he resorts to an expression of his deep concern for the whole of the House of Israel. Thus the preponderant majority of the prayers, both daily and those of the High Holy Days, are couched in the plural. We seek not, each alone and singly, to secure the favorable intercession of the Power on High; instead, we plead for succor and assistance as members of a group inextricably tied together by a common history and tradition, and just as dependent upon one another in present-day affairs as we were in the past.

This centripetal Jewish force is of incalculable significance to our existence as a people. It alone unquestionably accounts for the miracle of our survival as such. And it is this community-mindedness which contains the answer to the vexing problems which now more than ever agitate Jewry.

In recent times, there have been, so to speak, dissenters within Jewish ranks. They have promulgated doctrines which seek to undermine our religious beliefs and observance. If they have even conceded the existence of a "Jewish collectivity," they have nebulously interpreted it as a so-called "mission," but not in terms of our authoritative Torah. And that which makes this position particularly vulnerable is the fact that those advancing these concepts have neither the scholarship nor the saintliness with which those who elaborated upon religious matters have been imbued in the past.

To illustrate this point, we can refer to a story set in the old Russia of the Czars, one of whom had issued a ukase mandating the collecting of great objects of art from his vast domain. When this task was accomplished, an exhibition was staged. Those in charge, certain that everything had been flawlessly arranged, offered a prize to anyone who could find the slightest imperfection at the exhibition.

The Festivals / 219

Men of international reputation as connoisseurs of art called and scrutinized the splendid collection; however, they had nothing but praise for it. Then there happened along a *moujik,* a peasant. He pointed to a painting showing a tiny bird perched on a stalk of corn. "This," quote he, "is bad. A stalk of corn supporting a bird should be slightly bent. This one is straight." The judges were amazed and awarded him the prize.

Encouraged, the *moujik* tried his luck once more. He wandered into the Jewish section of the exhibition, the judges following at a respectable distance. He stopped in front of a painting of a venerable Hebrew at prayer. "Ho, ho!" commented the *moujik,* "There is something wrong here, too. When he prays, a Jew sways back and forth, but the one here is motionless." This time the judges sighed with relief. Addressing the lowly critic, one of them said, "Farmer, you may know birds and corn and things like that, but no *moujik* can possibly know how a devout Jew prays."

On what spiritual meat do our Jewish "experts" feed that gives them the colossal temerity to lecture the rest of Jewry on their conduct both as members of an ancient people and as citizens of modern commonwealths? Where do these gentry, who have traded (largely out of convenience) a noble birthright for a mess of pottage and whose professed principles are but a rationalization of that trading, get the impudence to ascribe to our people whatever quality that their caprice dictates?

There has recently been organized in this country a self-styled American Council for Judaism. Under this preposterously misleading name, a group of a hundred or so of these self-appointed mentors — both clerics and laymen who command considerable influence largely owing to their inherited wealth and social position, and not at all because they possess any substantial degree of scholarship or saintliness (as we mentioned above) — have sought (through the vast publicity that their opulence has purchased) to undermine the attempt at repatriating the remnants of our poor despised nation to Palestine, there to be rehabilitated and integrated into a new community as a "publicly recognized and legally secured" Jewish state.

Every now and then, the men of this Council break into print with broadsides against Jewish national aspirations. Mr. Lessing J. Rosenwald, of mail-order-house fame and fortune, had some months ago as his "pulpit" for expounding his brand of Judaism the columns of *Life Magazine*. There, with that tedious rehashing which has come to grate on our nerves and drive us almost to distraction, he unearthed, dusted up, and trotted out with Rip-Van-Winklish naivete all the old arguments which are the stock-in-trade of the assimilationists.

Yes, he admits, the postwar situation will present a serious problem for our people. But, he cautions us, the attempt to create a Jewish commonwealth in Palestine along racial and national lines is both a bad thing and entirely obsolete. Furthermore, he assures us that Jews have long since discarded any such outmoded notions. We might well be astonished at the remarkable scope of one person's perception of what it is that moves the hearts and minds of our people — especially in light of that individual's notable lack of commitment to the venerable tenets of our holy faith. There are those, however, whose pulses beat in rhythm with those of their Jewish brethren, who could assure Mr. Rosenwald and his Council that the masses of our people are fired up by the prospect of a revival of our national and racial distinctiveness in a homeland of our own, as nothing else in our long and harrowing dispersion has been able.

Judaism, he further insists, is merely a religion. But supposing, Mr. Rosenwald, that a man born a Jew decides to embrace Christianity or Mohammedanism: Does he thereby shed his racial inheritance? The answer to this question has been written by the Nazis in the innocent blood of thousands of our martyred brethren.

Mr. Rosenwald further — and rightly — decries the Axis attacks against the Jews, which have been motivated by preposterous theories of racial and nationalistic separateness. Therefore, he concludes that we, as victims of the Axis onslaught, should not lend ourselves to the same practice by sponsoring a separate and self-governing Jewish state in Palestine. To demonstrate the unfairness and utter untenability of this comparison, one need only push the same argument further and say that by the same token Poland, Denmark, Norway, Czechoslovakia, and other states robbed of their sovereignty should henceforth desist from any further struggle to reestablish their statehoods, because to do so would betoken the same nationalistic and racial separateness to which the Jews also aspire. The fact that we have been despoiled of our independence two thousand years may be a source of profound wonderment in that we are still here to claim our motherland, but it is not an argument in favor of our having to relinquish the inherent right of every people to its own national existence in a land of its own. To suggest that this aspiration falls into the same pattern as the brutal and brutalizing Nazi ideology is to be guilty of a gross calumny against the Jewish people, as well as other peoples who seek to develop their innate character and gifts in a peaceful, congenial atmosphere.

The Orthodox beliefs and practices, particularly as they reach their climax in the High Holy Days services, are calculated to reaffirm our faith that Israel is still one people. The shofar's blast is the clarion call to all the children of Abraham, Isaac, and Jacob to rally around the symbol of our dedication to the service of Him to Whom Father Abraham fearlessly offered the greatest sacrifice that any man can be called upon to make — yet through Whose beneficence Abraham emerged triumphant in the end. May the sounding of the horn at this critical stage of our tortuous history unite us as children of a common Father and impel us to the same self-sacrificing and heroic devotion for the glory of the G-d of Israel and the salvation of His suffering people.

MISCELLANY
PEARLS FROM PIRKEI AVOS

According to the commentators, *Pirkei Avos* opens with "Moses received the Torah from Sinai" to underscore that the guidance and ethics which follow proceed from Sinai, where the Torah was given.

According to Rabbi Simon the Just, the world exists on three things: the Torah, serving our Heavenly Father, and practicing charity. This threefold emphasis according to the commentators means that "but for Torah" the world might not have been created at all. Serving Him in the days of yore when Temple service was accomplished through animal sacrifices implied the determination to rid our nature of the animal in us and embrace the spiritual part, in which respect we are created in His image. Nowadays, we substitute prayers for sacrifices; practice of charity is noble, but nobler yet is to lend people in want the material means so that they can support themselves with dignity. The Bonds of Israel campaign is an example.

The conclusion of the first chapter has a comparable statement by another Simon, Rabban Simon the son of Gamliel: "The world exists on three things: truth, justice, and peace." All three are desperately needed in this day and age. The first two are inseparable: If there is no truth there is no justice and vice versa. Rashi elsewhere comments that a judge who dispenses true justice rises to the stature of being a partner with our Heavenly Father. The problem of peace is so much a part of our daily anguish and agony that it may be said that there have been few generations like ours in the history of mankind who have appreciated this elusive commodity as much as we do. That is why our Sages say that the word *shalom* in Hebrew is inscribed on the Throne of the Author of our being.

OF MITES AND MEN

July 4, 1971

I WAS WATCHING AT MY DESK A MINIATURE INSECT, PROBABLY AN eighth-of-an-inch long, racing over the length of the blotter. I tried to place an obstacle in its way so that the creature might quickly change its course. I tried several other maneuvers to test its reaction; it instinctively made adjustments to allow it to reach whatever goal it sought. I pondered whence this fragile bit of life — which could be crushed by the tapping of a penholder over it — derived its energy, and what purpose did its conduct serve? What must be the extraordinary constitution of this mite to carry on and sustain itself in whatever span of time was allotted to it? Who is the Supreme Intelligence that fashioned this minute being and endowed it with what seems to be a determined clinging to consciousness? Who indeed has fashioned everything about us, from the blade of grass to the mighty planets that inhabit space?

I thought further: Supposing that this little insect were capable of some reasoning — although it surely could not bring me within the focus of its limited vision — it could muse, "Is there someone that has anything to do with my direction?" It might even consider the impediments which suddenly appeared in its path as not particularly meaningful, just as part of a vast, unfeeling system which it did not understand. To assure itself of this belief, the insect might further ponder the invisibility and seeming lack of any guiding force. Another insect, however, might come along and say to the first one that although you have perceived no supervising agency, yet you cannot explain away the cumulative effect of movements which must have an intelligible source. Still, the doubting Thomas insect remains unconvinced.

The disproportion between the Supreme Intelligence and ourselves, human insect, is infinitely greater than the disparity between the little insect I saw on my desk blotter and a human being, and the evidence of His guiding Hand in our affairs and environment is so overwhelming that whoever fails to see it does so only because of the insectlike vision with which he is afflicted. Consider for a moment the great miracles about us. Think of your child: Do you wonder how his conception and birth were brought about? Sufficient superlatives in our language simply do not exist to describe our wonderment at this amazing process of inception, development, and fruition. Furthermore, we may even be justified in inquiring as to which is the greater miracle — the creation of the embryo and the birth of the human being, or his growth from a helpless infant to a self-sufficient adult. His heart begins to beat while he is still a fetus in the womb and does not stop until his last breath. It is a pump that moves one hundred thousand times daily in a closed-circuit system. There is nothing chaotic about it, for there is harmonious orderliness in the entire universe of which we are but a part. How can anyone with a modicum of common sense hold forth that this impressive manifestation is anything else than the product of the Supreme Author, Who devised, organized, and created it down to its smallest detail to function with flawless accuracy? One may as well say that our massive downtown building came into existence without the builder's architectural planning and precise attention to the minutest detail, as to question the validity of belief in the Great Architect.

Every phase of our lives bears witness of this. In his fourth message to the nation, the president [Richard M. Nixon —

editor's note] touched upon the fact that on the threshold of the second centennial of our independence, we have risen from the original thirteen colonies which loosely united its then three million inhabitants to the world's mightiest, most forward-looking nation, sheltering within its hospitable shores representatives of all branches of the human race, living together in amity and pride in our common American heritage. Despite the setbacks that we have experienced, we, her children, will not fail America, just as she has not failed us. Here the Author of our being has given mankind a second chance, and by and large we have made good on it. Anyone who does not see the hand of Divine Providence in this nation's growth is as incapable of perception as was the insect on the blotter which was thoroughly unaware of my movements. The founding fathers of this nation never wavered in their faith in our Heavenly Father, and they derived their inspiration from Holy Writ, which was a source of inspiration both to them and to their posterity. Our answer to vexing and perplexing problems of today will be solved most effectively with the same faith and the same resilience. Robert Louis Stevenson wrote of the Torah:

> *Written in the East, these characters live forever in the West; written in one province, they pervade the world; penned in rude terms, they are prized more and more as civilization advances; product of antiquity, they come home to the business and bosoms of men, women, and children in modern days.*

As a scion of my patriarchal ancestors, Abraham, Isaac, and Jacob — and compatriot of the Israelis who have written a glorious chapter in Jewish and human history — I aver that the miracle of the rebirth of my nationality in the ancient patrimony is the work of Him Whose Name these my ancestors first made known to the world, and in Whose Name the Hebrew Prophets have foretold this great return. It was only because He stood by their side when in 1948, at the proclamation of the State, that a handful of 650,000 men, women, and children stood up against a sea of Arabs and held their own. Nineteen years later, when the misguided kinsmen of ours — the Arabs, who are of the same Semitic stock as we — sought to overwhelm the fledgling State with the most sophisticated weaponry, He again said to the intrepid Israelis: "Fear him not, for I have delivered him into your hand" just as 3,500 years ago He said to Moses, who stood up to our enemies then.

THE KIPPAH

The Editor July 27, 1972
The Jewish News
17515 Nine Mile Road
Southfield, Mich. 48075

Sir:

In your issue of July 21, Mrs. K. details her tribulations over her yeshiva boys wearing yarmulkes and the taunts of other Jewish children toward them. This, unfortunately, is a part of the evil of the *Galuth*. In Israel, it has been reported that the yeshiva youths there — wearing yarmulkes, of course — are considered as the moral elite of the community's rising generation, a factor in the alleviation of any deviational tendencies on the part of the youth in Israel.

Locally, it has been shown that Jewish children who attend yeshivas and day schools are not subject to the ominous derelictions which have invaded the traditionally wholesome Jewish youth, some of whom have become obsessed with the permissiveness which is so evident in the larger community of America. To the extent that the wearing of a yarmulke is a mark of self-discipline and a sense of responsibility, it is to be encouraged, notwithstanding the jeers of the know-nothings. And this may well apply to children as well as to adults.

This writer knows of an instance in which a religious Jewish teacher was named to a post in a Detroit high school; reporting to work wearing his yarmulke, he was cautioned by the principal that it would not be permitted.

The young man removed his yarmulke, put on his hat and coat, and turned to go out, with the remark that if he could not be loyal to his faith while at his post he would not want to work there. "Wait!" said the principal, or words to that effect, "If your faith means so much to you, then you are just the man we want to inculcate morality in our young people." He is still at this post and still wearing the yarmulke.

It is reliably reported that in such a populous Jewish area as New York, Jewish attorneys appear in court with their yarmulkes covering their heads and are not abashed to do so. It is further reliably reported that the yarmulke helps to win cases, for judge and jury are impressed with him who does not fear criticism in obeying the dictates of his faith; judge and jury know that the word of this type of a lawyer may be relied on, and this makes a difference in the trial of a contested case.

In sum, the wearing of a yarmulke is not something bizarre to be taunted about; it is a badge of honor, a mark of respect and self-respect, and above all an acknowledgment of the acceptance of the yoke of Heaven. If there are those who look with disdain upon this, well, let them; who cares? Mrs. K. need not care, for the future will tell who will amount to something — her children or those who tried to burn their yarmulkes. I think the answer is clear: neither her children nor their parents will ever regret wearing a yarmulke.

M. M. Merzon

Regarding: Jewish Law on wearing a head covering 8/3/74

To: Hon. James Montante
Circuit Judge
1507 City-County Bldg.
Detroit, Mich. 48226

My dear Judge:

Following your gracious inquiry concerning the Jewish Orthodox requirement that a person of that persuasion should be permitted to appear with a head covering, this requirement is cited herewith. Incidentally, I am deeply grateful to you for the opportunity to present supporting authorities, and for your own uniform courtesy in allowing me in your court to adhere to this obligation. Invariably, all the judges before whom I have occasion to appear are very understanding in this matter.

Citing from the *Code of Jewish Law,* by Rabbi Solomon Ganzfried (1804-1886), published by the Hebrew Publishing Company, 77 Delancey, New York, N. Y., from Volume I, Chapter II, Section 6: "A man must not walk four cubits nor utter a single word of holiness with uncovered head. Also the little ones must be accustomed to have their heads covered in order that the fear of Heaven may be upon them. As we find with the case of Rabbi Nachman b. Isaac, to whose mother the astrologers said (when he was young), 'Your son is destined to be a thief.' He would not allow his mother to cover his head, so she said to him, 'Cover your head so that the fear of Heaven may be upon you' (and he grew up to become a great rabbi)."

Essentially, Your Honor, courts of law are in Jewish lore places of sanctity (*Psalms* 37:28 and *Psalms* 82:1). Whoever administers justice performs a Divine task (*Deuteronomy* 1:17). The mark of respect that a Jew is required to have in all matters pertaining to holiness extends to and embraces courts of justice, where the head covering is thus indicated.

Very respectfully yours,
M. Manuel Merzon

YORDIM

"Readers' Forum" *The Jewish News* 5/16/80

Some American Jews will castigate Israelis who choose to leave their country in search of economically more comfortable areas, particularly the U.S. One of the *yordim*, a *sabra*, a veteran of the wars that Israel has had to fight, who settled in our midst some years back and became a successful builder, explained it this way: None should question the esprit de corps of those who find it expedient to emigrate from their country, nor should they wonder about their pure and genuine devotion to their land and nation, but how much more could they have taken?

When I suggested to him that it was fortunate that the overwhelming majority of Israelis remain at their posts or else where would Israel and, for that matter, Jewry be, he nodded assent. I asked further as to whether there were many who shared his point of view, and his simple answer was yes. He agreed that this was Zionism in reverse.

Then my friend asked me this devastating question, conceding that I appeared to be, as all Jews are, deeply concerned about Israel: Why am I not there? The lanes are wide open.

Whatever my answer was is unimportant. However, I would recommend to my fellow American Jews to mull over that thought as they feel disposed, perhaps somewhat justifiably, to criticize these *yordim*.

M. Manuel Merzon

7/4/80

Several weeks back "Readers' Forum" had a piece of mine dealing with emigres from Israel, under the caption of "In Defense of the *Yordim.*" Some of my friends took exception to my attitude. The fact is that while the letter may have been in defense of those who choose to leave Israel, to go to more attractive economic areas, it was not in defense of *yerida,* the act of leaving the country. There is a difference between the two. It may be said that all of us Jews, even those in the Diaspora, who are able to settle in Israel and fail to do so are similarly to be charged with *yeridah.*

When we assemble in our synagogues on Yom Kippur and declare at the conclusion of the fast enthusiastically *"L'shanah haba'ah birushalayim:* Next year in Jerusalem," we are expressing a hope that now may be fulfilled, if we but will it. And if we fail therein, then we too may not escape the criticism attached to *yeridah.*

M. Manuel Merzon

The Ten Commandments

The Editor, *The Jewish News*
8th Fl. 17515 W. 9 Mile Road
Southfield, Mich. 48075

Sir:

The Ten Commandments, your frontispiece of the Shavuos issue, in the revised Jewish Publication Society's translation, was most apropos, though the novel rendition detracts from their sublimity. However, the objective of the revisers to make the text consistent with modern usage and idiom *is* a mistake. A book of such Supreme Authority were best translated literally.

Language styles change. The American Declaration of Independence, a work of enduring value for all time, penned by Thomas Jefferson, would not pass present-day literary standards. In considering the Torah our concern is with inner truth and object-lesson, and the translation in question in many instances gives only a pallid rendition of those objectives. Who would deny the power of the imagery of "Thy rod and Thy staff they comfort me" — and the so-called improvement, of the revisers is wholly irrelevant.

I refer specifically to the substitution of "impassioned" for "jealous" in the Second Commandment; Webster tells us that "impassioned" means characterized by passion or zeal, showing warmth and feeling, like an impassioned oration. What a tepid substitute! No less a literateur than H. G. Wells, cited by Rabbi Hertz under this section, speaks of "jealous" as conveying the terrible truth that trifling with the stern unity of things will not be tolerated. Another so-called correction: In the same Commandment, His opprobrium of those who "hate" Him has been changed to "reject." We members of the generation who have experienced afflictions suffered by our people at the hands of the haters can better understand the original meaning. Another emendation: The Fourth Commandment, in which we are bid to remember (and keep) the Sabbath unto Him has been revised to read "of," rather than "unto." The first speaks of homage to the Author of all, while the second has only a possessive meaning.

Very truly yours,
M. Manuel Merzon

JEWISH YOUTH IN AMERICA

The Editor
The Jewish News
17151 W 9 Mile
Southfield, Mich. 48075

October 1, 1973

Sir:

Your Rosh Hashanah editorial message, touching upon the perplexing American Jewish scene today yet sounding a note of reassuring hope, was a balm to jaded traditional nerves. Yet we must not be lulled by the exultation of those who view what they characterize as the entering of American Jewry into the mainstream of American society as an unmixed blessing.

We cannot but be extremely wary of the phenomena in the Jewish community which are most disturbing: the plague of intermarriage which threatens to atrophy our spiritual content; the cult of superstardom which has snared many of our senseless youths, whose woeful neglect of religious training has made them an easy mark to abandon the sumptuous table of our religious heritage and snatch crumbs from others' tables. Apropos this, our Welfare Federation is going to spend nine million dollars on a new Jewish Center, but the yeshiva day schools in our community go begging. The hitching by some of their wagon to this lackluster star means only that they will experience reflection for their efforts, and to boot, they will end up siding with our Arab enemies. The new left in our midst are ready to betray Israel and to receive a traitor's welcome in that same Arab camp. And drug addiction which is generally found among adolescents also victimizes Jewish youth, to the terrible chagrin and bewilderment of their families.

These and other unfortunate manifestations on the American Jewish scene are cause for gratitude to the *Jewish News* for your reassurance that there is still hope.

APPENDIX

- THE KEYS OF AN HONEST LAWYER
- BIOGRAPHY
- EULOGY FOR BERTHA MERZON
- GLOSSARY

THE KEYS OF AN HONEST LAWYER

AN APPRECIATION OF M. MANUEL MERZON

by Michael Hohauser
President, Oakland County Bar Association

EACH YEAR THE INCOMING PRESIDENT OF OUR BAR ASSOCIATION chooses a theme or topic for his or her Presidential year. Larry Ternan, one of the most professional of men, has chosen professionalism as this year's theme.

There will be numerous committee activities in support of this theme over the year including articles in LACHES, the creation of an Inn of the Court, and seminars. It is a theme which I know we all support.

There are many elements to being a professional. Integrity, intellect, and ethics come immediately to mind. At times the qualities of professionalism and those of being an advocate seem to conflict. Being an advocate, however, does not require taking positions which are merely arguable. Unfortunately, there are some in the profession who do not agree. Every day, one hears positions taken which are "merely arguable," but upon deeper investigation have no merit. This is not to say that it is less than professional to argue a position based upon a reasonable interpretation of facts or documentary evidence. It is, however, to say that too often attorneys encourage litigation by supporting merely arguable positions. I remember one attorney who did not accept such a point of view, who would not take a position that was "merely arguable," but adhered to the highest intellectual and ethical standards. That attorney was Rabbi Manuel Merzon, who many of you may remember. Allow me to share a memory I have of Manny Merzon.

It was 1974; I was as green as the new corn. A friend's father-in-law had an uncle who passed away. The uncle left a Last Will and Testament. The uncle, who passed away in his 80's and never married, left a substantial estate in his will. The will named two nephews. Had the deceased's two nephews both survived, they would have shared his estate equally. The will was drafted in such a way that it was clear to any reasonable reader that the survivor of the two nephews would inherit. However, one could argue that the uncle intended that the children of a deceased nephew would stand in their father's place. It was quite clear on the face of the instrument that that was not what the language said. But it was arguable.

As a young lawyer, I did not know what to expect. The language was clear to me, but I also saw the potential argument. The children of the deceased nephew hired Manuel Merzon as their attorney. Mr. Merzon and I made an appointment to meet in my office. I remember to this day sitting at my little desk with this older attorney seated across from me. We had the will in front of us. There was conversation, both general and specific. Ultimately, Attorney Merzon said, "One could argue that this will was intended to mean that the children of the nephew who passed away should inherit with your client. But I can see by reading it that it is only an arguable position. We might use it and get some compromise from your client. But that would not be right. I will advise my clients that this is not a proper position to take. By the way, here are your client's uncle's keys."

One day soon after that conversation I appeared at one of the old Detroit Bank and Trust branches in Detroit with a representative of the Michigan Department of the Treasury and two of Merzon's clients. In those days, the Treasury came with you to see what was in safety deposit boxes. I had never attended one of these box openings before and did not know what to expect. When the I box was opened, there were hundreds of thousands of dollars, all in different kinds of envelopes, wallets, bands, all in $20 bills. Mr. Merzon's clients watched the gentleman from the Treasury count it.

In spite of the temptation of that money, which I am certain they could have used as much as my client, and in spite of the arguability of a position as a result of which they might have received a compromise settlement, these fine people took the advice of their attorney who was, as it is clear to me today, more than a mere attorney. There was never a contest. There was never a claim. All the money went to my client. I received one of my first fees.

From that day, in the winter of 1974 to this day, the winter of 1996, I have kept the keys given me by Manny in my desk. Every time I open my desk drawer for a pen or a paper clip, I see those keys. There have been hundreds of times in twenty-one years of practice that I have held those keys in my hand and pondered their meaning and the meaning of that wonderful professional, Manny Merzon. Each of my children and my nephews knows this story and understands what these keys mean to me. Anyone who wishes is invited to stop by and look in my desk drawer. The keys are still there. They will be there until I have a child or a nephew to whom I may pass them on.

It is my pleasure to participate with Larry and all of the other members of the Oakland County Bar Association in this great theme which I think will do more than just transcend the year to come, but will become the theme by which our profession rises or falls as the millennium approaches: professionalism. There are many definitions of the term, but I have a concrete reminder of the real meaning — the keys given me by a principled attorney.

Perhaps the first lesson to be drawn from this anecdote lies not in the decision made by an attorney to suggest that which he concluded was the moral course to his clients as opposed to the arguable one. For me, the most significant point is that the clients accepted their attorney's advice. I am sure that those people were informed of the other course open to them. But such was the moral authority of the advocate in that case that money did not prevail over principle. For me that is the ultimate goal of the professional: to act with intellectual and moral integrity, expressing wisdom which transcends the merely adversarial. The keys in my desk are a constant reminder that it can be done.

THE MERZONS

Observations: "Be glad in Hashem and rejoice, O righteous, and shout for joy all who are upright of heart" (Psalms 32:11). Normal human action proceeds from one or more of three approaches: impulsiveness, intuitiveness, and reason. Impulsiveness, a purely emotional reaction, is seldom a proper guide and should be shunned. Intuitiveness, or intuition, is sometimes known as a sixth sense. Its soundness depends on whether resort to it is accompanied by being "upright of heart," as culled from the psalm cited above. Reason alone, or combined with either of the others, is the crowning endowment of humankind and should thus be enthroned as the guide for action ... "for in the likeness of G-d made He [man]" (Genesis 5: 1).

M. Merzon

MANUEL MERZON WAS BORN ON SEPTEMBER 14, 1898 IN a small province in White Russia known as Mogilov. Taibel, Manuel's mother, was born in the city of Shiletz, the daughter of Yenta and Moshe Orechkin. The family name Orechkin, meaning "related to soil," aptly describes their occupation as farmers in a small Jewish village. Taibel, married at age 23, was a deeply religious woman, greatly devoted to the welfare and growth of her children. Manuel's father, Menachem Mendel, son of an accomplished *chazan,* Tzvi Merzon, was born in Smolyon in 1856. The name Merzon, meaning "more sons," emanated from an earlier ancestor who chose the name after celebrating the birth of a long-awaited first son with the hope that he would be granted more sons! Manuel analogized this to the birth of our Biblical ancestor Joseph, who had been named by his mother Rachel; she had entertained a similar hope that additional sons would be born to her.

Manuel's early years were happy ones. The youngest of seven children, he had two older brothers and four sisters. His parents concentrated on rearing a son steeped in Torah and tradition. By the time he was 13, he had already completed the study of two tractates of Talmud and was a mature, budding scholar. The Merzon home was a happy and hospitable environment where, although poor in material goods, each child felt he had all he wanted.

Manuel's bar mitzvah, observed at his home in Mogilov, was a high point in the lives of the Merzon family. His parents had great hopes for their young son and enrolled him in a private gymnasium (university) to begin studying for a career in medicine. A senior medical student was hired to tutor Manuel for his entrance exam; however, midway through his preparation, family pressures brought his medical career to a premature halt. Taibel, Manuel's mother, was suffering from cancer. She took leave of the family to travel to Warsaw to consult with a specialist. This was a difficult and worrisome time for the family, fears increasing as her absence grew longer. Shortly after Taibel returned home, her condition began to deteriorate quickly with no medical cure available, culminating in her tragic passing on the 11th of Adar, 1911.

Remembering the evening of her death in vivid detail, Manuel described his father waking the children in the middle of the night to break the tragic news. "It was a terrible night forever etched in my memory. The funeral was held the next morning. The coffin was carried on our shoulders; we wept tragically as she was laid to her final rest."

The abrupt and heartbreaking passing of his mother forever changed the course of Manuel's journey to adulthood. He abandoned his plans to become a doctor and instead, aided by his cousin Laizer Gardner, began an apprenticeship in a local fur shop. Manuel's work in the fur shop had an unfortunate side effect. He found himself medically adverse to the materials he was handling, precluding him from using the skill he had learned for future employment, another fateful twist in his journey to adulthood.

His older brother, Yonah, took leave of his family shortly after his mother's passing to attempt a career in America. He was a brave and determined young man eight years Manuel's senior. His ultimate goal was to begin life anew, with the hope of eventually bringing his entire family to America. Although he intended to train as a barber, his mother had frowned upon this choice and had suggested instead a career in photography.

Upon his arrival in America, Yonah, a handsome and debonair young man, took up residence with the Markowitzes, cousins living in Brooklyn, New York. He found employment at White Studios on Broadway as a photograph retoucher only weeks after coming to America. The relatives were so astonished that he could earn $15 a week that at first they didn't believe it to be true. Yonah was very skilled at what he did and soon was living quite comfortably.

After a few of years in New York, Yonah sent passage money for Shmuel, the second-oldest Merzon son, to come to America. Shmuel, however, opted not to make the journey, thus allowing the third son, Manuel, to come in his stead. Shmuel eventually began a family in Russia, who were later tragically wiped out by the Nazis during World War II. Manuel lamented his poor brother's fate, many times, shedding tears of anguish over Shmuel's choice not to come to America. The hand of the Almighty placed Manuel in the position of the liberated son so that he could escape the harsh and tragic fate awaiting the rest of his Russian family.

In 1914, Manuel began his journey across the sea, profoundly changing the course of his life. The goodbyes at the port were heartbreaking, although Manuel was hopeful of a reunion at a later date. This reunion never came to pass and was a source of consternation to Manuel for the rest of his life. The fact that Manuel was accompanied on the trip by his elder cousin Mary made the trip less lonely and more bearable. The days went by quickly, the voyage filled Manuel with great anticipation of what would await him in America.

As a 16 year-old lad, dressed in a brown-belted jacket and high-waisted trousers and sporting a brown cane, Moshe Manuel Merzon made his maiden entry onto U.S. soil. His father sent him to find a haven far from the tyranny of Czar Nicholas II, to begin a new life in freedom's welcome grip. Manuel's port of entry was Baltimore, Maryland, where he arrived via Bremen, Germany on July 29th, 1914, on a vessel called *The Rhein*. He was a slight five foot two inches tall and weighed 125 pounds.

In his private writings, Manuel described his first and very telling memory of America: "As we were going through customs, my eye caught the front page of a newspaper displaying the picture of the Czar. In that week, World War I broke out, which was the beginning of the cycle of events disastrous for all humanity, and especially for my people, the Jewish people, the repercussions and consequences of which we are still suffering."

These thoughts and the outbreak of World War I became increasingly more troubling for him in future years, when he realized that he would never again see any of his beloved family whom he had left in Russia. Throughout his life the suffering of his family at the hands of the Czar and later at the hands of Hitler engendered a passionate desire to avenge Jewish blood.

AMERICA

Observations: The two principal intangible characteristics with which man is gifted are a mind that understands and freedom of will. It is no exaggeration to say that most men use only a fraction of their mental capacities in their normal activities and that they are often playthings for forces over which they appear to have no control. Without minimizing the effects of 'fate' and what men are pleased to call 'luck' or 'breaks,' a person's course could be materially improved if in all endeavors, relying upon Him Who is in heaven, he applies his best thoughts with determination and relish.

M. Merzon

Upon arrival in America, Manuel and Mary were greeted by the Feiken family of Baltimore, Maryland, cousins of Manuel's father. The Feikens were special and kind-hearted people who treated Manuel and Mary with love and affection. The families remained in close contact throughout their lives. Manuel was endlessly grateful for their help. Cousin Mary eventually settled in New York, where she married Sam Nissenman and where she lived until her demise in 1981.

Manuel's first year in America was exciting, yet very difficult. He missed his family in Russia greatly; his thoughts were never far from the home he had left in Mogilov. Each day in America, however, was a new adventure as he began his assimilation into American culture.

Manuel felt at home with the Feikens, a modestly situated, middle-class family consisting of a husband and wife, five young children, and the elderly parents of Mr. Feiken. The latter and his two young sons had come to the United States directly from Moscow following the banishment of Jews from that city by edict of Czar Alexander III, father of Nicholas II, the last Czar. The home itself was a three-story structure; the third floor consisted of bedrooms, one of which was given to Manuel. The second floor was the dining, living, and kitchen area. The first floor had a workshop where the family operated a small business.

Before leaving Russia, Manuel had concluded his primary-school education in a government-sponsored school exclusively for Jewish children. His mode of dress signified a certain degree of behavior and maturity. The brown cane, although a status symbol of sorts in Russia, was discarded by his American relatives for fear that the local neighbors would think that Manuel was a cripple!

A Feiken family consultation resulted in the decision that Manuel was already sufficiently educated and, therefore, should begin to learn a trade. He would become an apprentice in the family shop, earning $6 a month plus room and board. Any other necessity was to be provided by his brother Yonah.

Shortly after he began his Baltimore apprenticeship, he was invited to Windsor, Ontario, Canada, to visit the Gordner family, relatives of Taibel Merzon (Manuel's mother). After a short stay, it was agreed in consultation with the Feikens that Manuel should remain and enter the local public high school rather than continue to work in Baltimore. There they hoped his English would improve, thus allowing for a possible post-high-school education.

The Gordner family, originally from Celetz, Russia, consisted of four brothers — Shlomo, Chaim Yitzchok, Laizer and Moshe — all very devoted to each other. They welcomed Manuel into their family and guided him throughout his residence in Windsor. They treated him with great kindness and helped him in his climb up the ladder of success. Manuel was immensely indebted to them for their special friendship and kindly aid, never failing to remind his children and grandchildren of how grateful they must be to people who have helped them.

Manuel's first years in school were a foreshadowing of his accomplishments throughout his life. He graduated with high honors and was awarded special prizes for writing and oratory. His academic achievement in Windsor transformed him from a Russian-speaking immigrant into a rather sophisticated young North

American. After a very successful high-school career, Manuel was admitted in October 1919 to study at the University of Michigan.

In August 1918, in an effort to map out his future, Manuel composed a private outline entitled "My Life's Program." At 21, he had developed a unique and mature approach to life which would guide him throughout the rest of his days. He wrote that his objectives must be to "work for the promulgation of every policy that tends to exterminate injustice, maintain righteousness, and bring happiness to people everywhere."

These objectives and his life's program truly became the road map of his entire life.

My Life Program

8/19/18

I HAVE OUTLINED AND DETERMINED THIS PROGRAM AS A RESULT OF MY present views and the conditions prevailing at this particular time. It is subject to change if I shall see fit to do so in the future.

I. My Object
   To assume a commanding generally useful and important position in life.

A. Material Standing
   To be perfectly secure and have abundantly to cover all necessary as well as secondary requirements.

B. Intellectual Standing
   To be fully equipped with an intelligent education and a creditable knowledge above that which is considered ordinary.

C. Political Standing
   To work for the promulgation of every policy that tends to exterminate injustice to maintain and augment righteousness, love, and happiness among people everywhere.

D. Social Standing

   Avoid enmity even at some cost. Acquire an ability to be sociable. Make friends, but be choosy in associating. Maintain a friendly disposition to all who care to have it and refrain from abusing it.

E. Moral Standing

   Try to be clean not only in action but in spirit as well. Be frank and truthful but tactful at the same time. Avoid usage of profane language. While not trying to be a saint I must not acquire any degenerating habit.

F. Physical Standing

   Cleanliness is the first law of hygiene. I must therefore always observe it. Eat in time, secure sufficient sleep. As far as possible, take care systematically of every organ of the body.

   Important pivotal elements of life and conduct:

1. Obligations to family
2. Helpfulness with relatives
3. Esteem to friends
4. Work and occupation
5. Being just and courteous to all

His years at the University in Ann Arbor were bittersweet times. The tuition and board were very expensive, and Manuel struggled to keep his head above water. He took odd jobs as a dishwasher in order to pay his obligations. Many times in the future, he told his children and grandchildren that he frowned on any thought by anyone in his family of attending a secular university away from home. He felt that the moral standards at such places put a person in peril. He felt that his religious observances were challenged in the Ann Arbor college environment and thus regretted his days there greatly.

Midway through his college career, Manuel settled on pursuing a law degree. At that time, the rules permitted one to enter law school without a college degree; however, the advice he was given was to complete his college degree first and then enter law school. He commented, "Later in life I realized that I should have forgone the extra years achieving a Bachelor of Arts. Each year of my studies was both expensive and taxing." In 1923, Manuel began law school at the Detroit College of Law, where he graduated with distinction in the top part of his class.

Manuel was admitted to the Michigan bar in 1926 and shortly thereafter began working with a general-practice firm — Finkelstein, Lovejoy, and Chilson on the seventeenth floor of the Buhl Building in downtown Detroit.

In June 1927, Manuel left the Finkelstein firm and opened his own office at 258 Erskine Street in Detroit. He concentrated primarily on trial work, spending a good deal of time on appellate practice. In 1935, Manuel began to move his practice away from trial work to real estate, taxation, and business transactions. In February 1942, he began to devote less time to the law practice to concentrate on a bimonthly religious publication known as *The Detroit Jewish Review*. As editor and business manager, he wrote all the articles and spent considerable time soliciting advertisements to pay for the publication. His primary intent was to publicize the plight of his Jewish brethren in Poland, Germany, and Russia, and to raise the consciousness of the American public to the atrocities being wrought against his people.

MANUEL AND BERTHA

Observations: Few married men realize the debt of gratitude that a man owes to his wife for properly fulfilling her function in their wedded life. Altogether aside from the expected delight that woman brings to man, and in normal family life that she gives birth to their children which is their crowning achievement together, she provides a shield to her husband against the usual harassment and buffets he faces daily in the outside world, where mutual consideration in interaction between people is conspicuous often by its absence. It is on returning home, where the balming goodness with which a beneficent Providence has endowed the woman is had, that his emotional equilibrium is restored. Traditional observance of the Jewish Sabbath and holidays is a most valuable agency in conserving domestic felicity. It may be further added that those of our people who are remiss in this observance do not know what they are missing in family happiness and the good life.

M. Merzon

IN THE SUMMER OF 1928, BERTHA RUBINSTEIN, A YOUNG SCHOOLTEACHER from Aurora, Illinois, came to Detroit to visit her cousin, Ida Sendrafisky, and family. One Sunday, Bertha was invited to a picnic and was introduced to Manuel. Bertha recalled that Manuel's first words to her were: "Where have you been all my life?" This statement initiated a romance which lasted nearly sixty years! As Bertha was about to leave the gathering, Manuel inquired as to where he could reach her. She answered curtly, "In the phone book."

After that he made it his business to find her and phoned to ask for a date. Bertha was quite impressed with him. "He had a fine education and an upstanding profession and was of good Jewish stock."

Manuel and Bertha's courtship lasted nearly three years. Finally, Bertha remembers, a marriage proposal was forthcoming. "He talked at great length and I listened patiently and he said to me, 'I do not want you to feel that you are treating me as a fine deal, but to recognize that I am a person of merit who wants to marry you.'" Bertha postponed her answer until she returned home and told her parents.

Manuel was extremely proud of Bertha's *yichus*. Knowing that she hailed from a rabbinical and highly religious family, he wrote a letter and a short Torah thought to her family. Upon reading Manuel's exegesis on *Megillas Esther* and the Purim story, her father, Rabbi Rubinstein, passed a favorable judgment on the match. Afterwards, Bertha wired Manuel by Western Union that her answer was "yes."

Sometime later he traveled to Chicago, and she came by train from Aurora to meet him. They both went to Zaide Rubinstein's home and a *tanaim* was performed (with a handkerchief for a *suddar*), a formal sign of engagement. Manuel bought her a wristwatch as an engagement present. The engagement was inordinately long because of the difficult economic conditions prevailing at the time. Manuel wrote to Bertha every day and sent her mail by special delivery on legal holidays and Sundays, thereby reporting on his activities and sharing his thoughts and feelings with her.

Finally, the wedding took place on Sunday afternoon, June 21, 1931, at the Young Men's Hebrew Association Synagogue on Temple Avenue. The officiating Rabbi was Zaide Chaim Tzvi Rubinstein. A large family dinner was served at Bertha's Fox Street home in Aurora. Bertha wore a pink taffeta dress, a large veil, and silk gloves without fingers. Rebbetzin Rubinstein made all the food, and three large tables were set in the Rubinsteins' home. After the wedding, they remained at the Stevens Hotel on Michigan Avenue in Chicago, and they spent a short honeymoon traveling by boat to Boblo Island for two days of rest and recreation.

The Rubinsteins

Rabbi Chaim Tzvi Rubinstein, Bertha Merzon's paternal grandfather, was born in the city of Slonim in 1872, the son of Rabbi Osher Rubinstein. Slonim became part of Russia in 1795 and was not restored to Poland until after World War I. In 1939, because of the Nazi-Soviet pact, Slonim came under Soviet rule. It is now part of the independent state of Belarus.

Chaim Tzvi was educated in the Slonim and Volozhin yeshivas under the tutelage of Rav Chaim Brisker. He received *semichah*,

Biography / 253

rabbinical ordination, at the age of 17 from his teachers Rav Chaim and Rav Naphtali Z.Y. Berlin (the Netziv). He later received *semichah* from Rav Shmuel Salant in Jerusalem. At the age of 19 he married Chaya Sara, the daughter of Rav Osher Hakohen, niece of Reb Tzadok Hakohen of Lublin. After their wedding, they moved to Palestine, where he served as Rosh Mesivta of Yeshivas Etz Chaim for five years and then became the head of Yeshivas Sha'arei Torah in Yaffo for the next thirteen years. (The name Yeshiva Sha'arei Torah was reapplied by Rabbi Chaim Tzvi Rubinstein's grandson, Rabbi Berel Wein, in Monsey, New York, in 1978 to his yeshiva. Rabbi Wein, a great scholar and prolific writer, has become one of the great Jewish personalities of the twentieth century.)

Rabbi Chaim Tzvi had four sons and three daughters. His oldest son, Naphtali Hersch, was born and raised in Palestine. After his bar mitzvah, Rav Chaim Zvi sent him (accompanied by an adult) to a yeshiva in Hungary. At 18 he returned home to Yaffo, Palestine.

The *gabbai* (secretary) of Rav Chaim Tzvi's yeshiva was Reb Simcha Bunim Novovolsky, Bertha's maternal grandfather. Simcha Bunim was born in Bialostok, Russia, and was married to Sorah Leah Osenholtz. In Russia Reb Simcha Bunim owned a dairy that produced various kinds of cheeses which were shipped to cities in Russia. He was active in the *Chovevai Zion* (Lovers of Zion) society; thus in 1890, when the Czar passed an edict that all Jews had to relocate to the urban areas, Simcha Bunim sold his property and immigrated to Palestine with his family. In Yaffo, where he lived, he opened a haberdashery, selling women's and men's clothes and yard goods. He purchased the products in Beirut, where he himself selected the merchandise. He had three daughters and three sons. Simcha Bunim's daughter, Faige Malka, was 20 when Naphtali, Rabbi Chaim Zvi's son, returned home to Yaffo. The pair was matched, and Naphtali married Faige Malka. Naphtali and Faiga Rubinstein had one son in Palestine, Moshe Michel. Afterwards, the young couple and their son moved to Hungary. There they had four daughters — Bluma (Bertha Merzon), Aidel, Rochel, and Dena.

In 1912, at the age of 40, Rav Chaim Tzvi Rubinstein immigrated with his family to the United States and was accepted as rabbi of Congregation Bikur Cholim of Chicago. Later he became the *rav* of B'nai Reuven Sha'arei Tefila. In 1915, he established a *yeshiva ketana* in his home, and his wife took on the responsibility of supplying the food and lodging for the students. The *yeshiva ketana* blossomed into the Bais Medrash L'Torah Yeshiva which is flourishing today in Skokie, Illinois.

Upon settling in Chicago, he wrote to his son Naphtali (Bertha's father) to join him and the rest of the family in America. Naphtali went alone to America to secure a position that would adequately provide for his family. Before he left Hungary, he sent his wife, who was pregnant at the time, and his five children back to Palestine to be with her family. Naphtali received a post in Spring Valley, Illinois, as rabbi, cantor, teacher, and *shochet* (ritual slaughter). Six months after his appointment to that position, he sent for his family. The three-week journey across the ocean proved to be a terrible trip for his young wife. In Spring Valley another son was born, Isadore. Upon their arrival, their neighbor, a Jewish woman, gave the children English names. Bluma was named Bertha (in Palestine she had been dubbed Shoshana in kindergarten), Aidel became Ida, Rochel became Rose, and Dena became Diane.

Naphtali Rubinstein held subsequent positions in Chicago, in Indiana, and finally in Aurora, Illinois. He sang in a beautiful tenor voice and learned to give sermons and speeches in English. At 55 he had a stroke from which he never completely recovered. As a result, Naphtali Rubenstein moved to Detroit to be with his daughter and son-in-law, Bertha and Manuel Merzon. He passed away in Detroit, the first of Teves, December 7, 1942. His father, Rav Chaim Zvi Rubinstein, passed away eleven months later, on the eighth day of Cheshvan, November 5, 1943.

This is a Grievous Mourning
(Genesis 50:11)

We join with American Jewry in mourning the passing of the late Rabbi Chaim Zvi Rubinstein of Chicago, who departed this life on Friday, November 5, 1943.

On the back cover of this issue will be found the eulogy for this sterling son of Israel. We wish to state here that words are inadequate to accord the memory of the deceased his full due. Much has been said by the distinguished rabbinical and lay leaders of Chicago and other cities in the country about the irreversible loss which Jewry here has sustained in this death. We can only add an intimate reference.

It was our great fortune to have entered the family of Rabbi Rubinstein some years ago through marriage to his granddaughter, Bertha, the child of the late Rabbi Naphtali Hersch Rubinstein, of blessed memory, who was a son of the elder rabbi and whose untimely death preceded that of his father by eleven months.

We have been brought back through this relationship from the stranger pastures to which we had previously wandered — more accurately, strayed — when we had drifted from the path which our own parents, of blessed memory, had so laboriously blazed for us; we had thus been returned to the fold of observance and loyalty to tradition through contact with the family of this patriarch whom we now mourn, and whose debt we shall never be able to discharge, save as we might try to emulate his character.

It is difficult to put one's finger on the trait in him which had been his most outstanding virtue. As we have stated, others have undoubtedly done justice to his memory much better than we can hope to achieve. If it be adding but one single thought to what has been so well and earnestly said by greater men, we wish to register here this: that falsehood,

> deceitfulness, and insincerity would disappear under the benign scrutiny of the late Rabbi Rubinstein as completely as the snow which is melted by a sudden burst of glorious, warm sunshine. We bow our head in grief over the grave of him whom we have been honored to call grandfather.
>
> M. Manuel Merzon

THE EARLY DAYS

Observation: One of America's popular games is to keep up with the Joneses, to reach them, and possibly to overtake them. Mr. Jones, however, is an elusive and — if the term may be used — a split personality. No sooner is he reached than he assumes a divisiveness of a dozen or more Joneses, each one on a higher rung than the previous one. And the aspirant well-nigh despairs of ever being able to keep up with him. The remedy for the perplexed is to bear this in mind: "Who is rich? He who rejoices with his portion" (Pirkei Avot 4: 1).
M. Merzon, from "Choson Torah" Oct. 28, '83.

MANUEL AND BERTHA HAD TWO CHILDREN. MELVIN WAS BORN ON March 27, 1932, and Bonnie on June 8, 1935.

During the early days of their marriage, Manuel earned a meager income and often had difficulty paying the rent. The family moved frequently because of their inability to maintain a steady income. Several times Bertha and the children went to stay with her parents in Aurora, Illinois, who had a home on 637 Fox Street. When her parents moved to Kenosha, Wisconsin, after

Biography / 257

Reb Naphtali suffered his stroke, Bertha and the children, Mel and Bonnie, went to stay with them. Manuel rented a room in Detroit for himself. Bertha recalled, "I cannot remember how many times we moved. We moved so many times. How did I ever manage? I used to do all the packing myself. Dad was wonderful in helping to raise our two dear children, but all the planning and worrying about our homes and offices fell on my shoulders."

Manuel's law practice was quite slow: business was hard and finding clients proved difficult.

After a few years of business successes, they decided to move up. They made a down payment on a very attractive single home on Griggs and Curtis in Detroit. They moved the office to Curtis and Wyoming near the Beth Yehudah Shul, where Manuel attended services every morning and evening. Bertha gave him breakfast to take along to eat in the office.

THE WAR'S REFUGEES

Observation: Those who are given to following the path of least resistance, theirs is "an evil lot." Their behavior is responsible for the permissiveness which plagues our society. However, to try too hard may also be unproductive. Sometimes, instead of reaching an objective, one finds himself further away. All normal people are endowed by their Creator with native gifts. Consistent with "check and double check" and the use of sound judgment, those gifts should be allowed free play, for "... it is not thy duty to complete the work, but neither art thou free to desist from it" (Pirkei Avot 2:20).

M. Merzon from "Choson Torah," Oct. 21, '83

WHEN THE REFUGEES ARRIVED FROM EUROPE IN DETROIT AROUND 1949, they came to Manuel's practice because he could speak Yiddish (or Jewish, as it was called then), English, Russian, and German — and, more important, he was very sympathetic to their plight.

His clientele consisted of refugees mostly, "Wiederguttmachung." The West German Government decided to reimburse the Jews for the time they had spent in concentration camps at the rate of $1 per day. The Polish Jews had been incarcerated for four to five years under the despicable Nazis; the Hungarian Jews, for only one year. Those whose health was damaged are still receiving monthly pensions from Germany. Once a year these individuals are required to sign an official certificate to show that they are still alive, for when they pass away, their pension ceases. Bertha legalized these certificates.

When the refugees first arrived, Manuel took their information in Yiddish. Then he dictated to a German secretary whom he hired exclusively for this work. When Bertha saw that Manuel spent too much time on these cases, at the price of neglecting other legal work, she took over the German reparations' work and continued it for the next thirty years.

Through these efforts, Manuel and Bertha became the trusted and cherished advisors of hundreds of refugees who relied upon their counsel and generosity.

During these years, Manuel attempted to pierce the veil of the Iron Curtain to learn of the fate of the family he left behind. The loss of contact with Russia and his family caused him great heartache. He wrote hundreds of letters to officials in both Russia and America to locate family who may have survived the ravages of World War II in Eastern Europe. A month did not go by without a letter sent to the Red Cross, the State Department, or the Russian Embassy imploring officials for the news of his family. He kept up a steady stream of correspondence and gifts to his Russian nieces and nephews whom he had located, and eventually these actions became the catalyst for their arrival in Detroit two years after his passing to settle and become part of the extended Merzon family in Detroit.

Shortly after Manuel's passing, his sister Rachel's children, Yosef and Bella, immigrated to Detroit, where they were finally reunited with the extended family. Yosef, an award-winning optical engineer, and his son, Leib, actually ended up working side by side.

Manuel felt that the hand of G-d which brought him to America required of him a high degree of service to his people and the Almighty. He never took lightly the Heavenly intervention in his escape from the tragic fate which befell his family, and he therefore carried with him a desire to sanctify their eternal memory through charitable and communal acts of kindness.

Parenthetically: he observed so many *yahrzeits* for lost relatives that he was a cause of consternation to shul *gabbais* in the synagogues he attended. When one well-meaning synagogue officer complained, he explained to the man, ever so patiently, that he was remembering relatives who left no one else to represent them in this world.

As the Beth Yehudah Synagogue on Wyoming and Curtis began to decline, Manuel and Bertha made a decision to relocate their home and office to Oak Park, Michigan, so as to be near the Young Israel of Oak Park. They purchased a home on West Hampton, and they subsequently moved to Oak Park in 1969 and hired a handyman to convert the porch into an office.

Manuel was an articulate, highly skilled attorney who concentrated his primary practice on serving the new Jewish immigrants who came to Detroit as refugees from the Nazi onslaught during World War II. So many individuals depended on him that his days and nights were filled with a steady stream of supplicants seeking his attention. His passion for helping the less fortunate translated into a strong desire to protect and uplift the hundreds of immigrant families who reached his doorstep.

He was involved with nearly every Orthodox communal cause, doing legal work at no charge for hundreds of individuals and tens of organizations. He organized synagogues, schools, cemeteries, and charitable funds. He did not differentiate between political or religious affiliations. He provided the very first offices for Lubavitch, helped create the local Satmar and Stolin organizations, was secretary and treasurer of the Yeshiva Beth

Yehudah, and was instrumental in the local development of the Zionist and Jabotinsky societies.

He devoted a great deal of time to his study of the Torah. He had weekly learning sessions with Rabbi Leon Skorski, of blessed memory, and he attended the *shiur* of the Rosh Yeshiva, Rav Bakst, every Monday night for over thirty-five years. A *Mishnayos,* a *Chumash,* and a *Tehillim* were always within easy reach. His learning began at 5:30 a.m. and continued until his eyes closed at nearly 1 a.m. each night.

He helped encourage his "clients" to construct and maintain a Jewish foundation in their lives. He worked hard to convince as many as possible to put their children in Jewish day schools, to use religious burial societies, to avoid disagreements among family members, and to stand fast on moral and ethical issues. He was instrumental in the charitable gifts that helped encourage a number of communal projects, including the Korman Machon L'Torah Building and the home, shul, and *mikvah* which constituted the site of the K'hal Chasidim Synagogue, led by Rabbi Deutch, of blessed memory.

For most of his adult life, Manuel spent the last two hours of his day (11 p.m. to 1 a.m.) in deep, introspective silent prayer. His *Krias Shema* was a long, well-developed personal prayer to Hashem which encompassed many areas of concern which he felt needed to be communicated to Hashem *Yisbarach.* In a dark room, he paced endlessly amid the sound of quiet yet constant prayer. What was the content of these sessions? He divulged that he had composed a number of personal prayers which expressed his hopes for his family and his people. Even in his waning days at home, he never abandoned this task.

Until the very end, his life fostered Jewish unity and family harmony. Manuel Merzon never faltered in his devotion to his family and to his people. He also never ceased serving the Almighty; his piety grew every day of his life, as did the intensity of the prayers and supplications he uttered for the welfare of Klal Yisroel. He continually protested against evil while stressing the need for furthering Jewish continuity.

Even at the conclusion of his life, Manuel Merzon remained regal, holy, and compassionate. Although the last few weeks of his life were spent in a care facility — where, incidentally, he left an indelible impression on all who met him — his final act in this world was to don his *tefillin* and utter prayers to the One Above. No sooner had he concluded these prayers and had lain down on his bed, he was taken from this world in a breath — what our Sages call *neshikah,* a Divine kiss, the death of the righteous! He was laid to rest in the Beth Shmuel cemetery, over which he had ministered without a fee for more than forty years.

In short, Manuel Merzon's life was extraordinary not on account of his accumulation of wealth or property — but rather because of his steadfast devotion to the Torah he studied and obeyed.

EULOGY FOR BERTHA MERZON

THURSDAY, MAY 3, 2001

OUR BOBI IN PARTNERSHIP WITH OUR ZAIDY, OF BLESSED MEMORY, mastered in a most unusual way the opportunity to spend their lives providing shade and comfort to so many around them.

As the daughter and granddaughter of the Rubinstein *Rabbanim*, Bobi grew up in a home where riches and wealth were measured in deeds and mitzvos, not in belongings and fancy accouterments. Her desires and pursuits were structured to be in concert with the Torah values she was raised with. She was grateful for each of G-d's blessings and never, never wasted any of the resources with which she was blessed. Looking back on her magnificent and accomplished life, I marvel at all she was able to do.

She raised two beautiful and dedicated children, Bonnie and Melvin. She was the backbone, the strength, the chauffeur, the nourishment, and the inspiration for her holy and remarkable husband, Moshe Ben Menachem Mendel. Their lives were intertwined and inseparable from the *sh'eiris hapleitah* — the remnant who escaped from the dastardly clutches of Hitler, *yemach shmo* (may his name be blotted out).

Each of these souls became their responsibility, their charge, their friends to influence and nurture — and in many cases to support and uplift. Time and effort were commodities used to excess to do the right thing at almost any cost. The best and most accurate description of Bobi was one of a regal and holy woman who never pursued any course unless it was absolutely appropriate and collectively beneficial to her family and her community. She was the ultimate *ezer kinegdo,* helpmate, to her devoted husband. Her every action was calculated to fine-tune his accomplishments and his goals.

My sister Julie told me last night that it was Bobi's and Zaidy's example of communal service that drove their next generation's desires for involvement in good causes. It was Bobi's Shabbos table and the warmth and comfort of their home that nurtured the Torah observance of generations to follow her. It was the modest and remarkably generous pocketbook that illustrated to her subsequent generations that money was to be used to better the lives of those around us, not (G-d forbid) to lead us in directions not encouraged by our holy teachings and traditions.

How pleasant was her shade and her fruits! Somehow when Bobi cooked or made a dish, it had the look, fragrance, and taste that combined the world of yesterday with the scent of the World to Come. The *Shabbosim* that we spent with Bobi and Zaidy were without a doubt the foundation for everything we replicate in our homes today. The *zemiros* (table songs), the food, the spirit, the camaraderie that we enjoy now are all derived from the moments we spent in their home. She was sweetness personified — always so pleasant, so sweet, so disarming, so approachable, so gifted — such an unusual and wonderful person.

In 1985, we gave Bobi an empty book of remembrances for her to fill out for us. She wrote to us that her mother taught her to be frugal, charitable, educated, and devoted to family; to be polite and clean. She wrote us about the day on which Zaidy proposed. She said, "He talked to me at length and I listened patiently. He gave me a simple gold ring, which I have worn for fifty-three years."

Her deepest values, she told us, were devotion to parents, husband, children, grandchildren, and great-grandchildren. She was most proud of how her husband, our Zaidy, managed to go to school to find a job when he could hardly speak English, to get through high school with honors, to attend the University of Michigan (washing dishes in order to pay for his meals), and to earn a degree to go to law school completely by himself. She spoke of the many fine friends he had made along the way and the great accomplishments of his life.

She was grateful that she married Zaidy and that they overcame many hardships in nearly sixty years of marriage. She was very proud of the achievements of her children, and she was convinced that her great-grandchildren would follow in similar paths. She was proud that my sister Lissie received a college degree and that she became such a splendid and exemplary mother.

She was proud to have helped both people in need and in need of help, not always money-wise but through acts of kindness, helpfulness, and attentiveness — thereby allowing them to confide in her in their times of need. She cannot recall the names of all these people because she said that they would fill many, many pages, but she was grateful to G-d that He had given her the opportunity to be of service to people throughout the world.

Today, our dear Bobi you are buried in the cemetery that you and Zaidy guarded and protected for over forty years without any personal benefit — strictly for those who came before you and for those who would come after you. I know in my heart that your life, your exemplary accomplishments, and all your special acts of kindness will undoubtedly lift you to the Almighty's promised and cherished domain. As we bid a most sad farewell to a wonderful sister, mother, grandmother, and great-grandmother, we pray that you and Zaidy will be *malitzei yosher*, steadfast ambassadors, for our family, for our community of Detroit, and for the people of our world — and that as you monitor our progress, we hope and pray that you will be satisfied that all the generation planted from you will live up to the high ideals that you have set for us.

Gary Torgow

10th of Iyar, 5761

GLOSSARY

ALL ENTRIES ARE HEBREW UNLESS OTHERWISE NOTED.

Adar — twelfth month of the Jewish lunar calendar
Aharon — Moshe's older brother, Aaron
Ahavas Yisrael — love for a fellow Jew
Akeidah — the binding, see Akeidas Yitzchak
Akeidas Yitzchak — the binding of Isaac
Akeres Habayis — the mainstay of the home, the wife
Aleph-Dalet — the first two letters of a Name of G-d
Amora — one of the Rabbis of the Talmudic Era
Avinu — our father
Avraham — Abraham
Bamidbar — the fourth book of the Pentateuch, *Numbers*
Bava Basra — a tractate of the Talmud
Beis Din — Rabbinical court which decides Torah law
Beis HaMikdash — Holy Temple in Jerusalem
Bais Medrash — a Torah study hall
ben — son (of)
ben Torah — a student of the Torah, imbued with its spirit
berachah (pl. **berachos**) — blessing
Bereishis — the first book of the Pentateuch, *Genesis*
Bikur Cholim — visiting the ill
Bikurim — the first fruits to ripen that were brought as an offering to G-d in the Beis Hamikdash
B'nei Yisrael — the children of Israel

Degalim — division of B'nei Yisrael into distinct camps each with its own distinctive ensign
derech eretz — proper conduct
Devarim — the fifth book of the Pentateuch, *Deuteronomy*
Eretz Yisrael — the Land of Israel
galus — exile, the Diaspora
Gehinnom — hell
Gemara — Talmud
goyim — gentiles
Haggadah — the story of the exodus of the Jews from Egypt, read at the Passover seder table
halachah — Torah law
Hallel — Praise of G-d from *Psalms*, Chapters 113-118, recited on Holidays
Hashem — (lit. "The Name") G-d
hasra'ah — warning administered by witnesses to a crime, thereby informing the perpetrator of the severity and consequences of his intended action
ibn — Arabic for son
Iyar — the second month of the Jewish lunar calendar
Iyov — Job
Kisei Hakavod — the Throne of Glory
Klal Yisrael — The Congregation of Israel
Ma'asim Tovim — good deeds
Matan Torah — giving the Torah from G-d to B'nei Yisrael at Mt. Sinai
Medinas Yisrael — the country of Israel
meilitz yosher — a steadfast advocate
menchlichkeit — Yiddish for decency
Menorah — candelabra
metzora — a person afflicted with a disease of the skin caused by sin, often mistranslated as "leper"
midah k'neged midah — when G-d administers a punishment reflecting the crime
Midrash — anthology of Bible commentaries from the Talmudic period

Mishkan — the Tabernacle
Mishnah — the Oral Law as taught by the great Sages between the years 100 B.C.E and 200 C.E.
mitzvah (pl. **mitzvos**) — a Torah commandment
Nisan — the first month of the Jewish lunar calendar
olah-offering — a burnt-offering, one of the animal sacrifices brought in the Temple in Jerusalem
pasuk — verse
Pesach — Passover
Pirkei Avos — (Ethics of our Fathers) a book of the Talmud
Rabbeinu — our teacher
Ramban — Nachmonides, 1194-1270; also denotes his commentary on the Torah
rasha — wicked person
Rashi — Rabbi Shlomo ben Yitzchak, 1040-1105; his commentary on the Torah was the first-known Hebrew book to be printed in Rome, in 1470 and to this day is the basic text of every Jewish child and adult throughout the world.
Ribbono Shel Olam — Master of the Universe
Sanhedrin — Supreme Rabbinic Court in the times of the Holy Temple
Sedrah (pl **Sedrahs**) — weekly Torah portion
Shabbos — Sabbath
shalom bayis — a house where peace and contentment reign
Shavuos — Pentecost
Shechinah — Divine Presence
shekel — Biblical coin
shemittah — Sabbatical year, during which the Torah requires that the land in Eretz Yisrael be left fallow
Shemos — second book of the Pentateuch, *Exodus*
She'ol — a level of Hell; the underworld
Shevat — eleventh month of the Jewish lunar calendar
shevatim — tribes of Israel; Jacob's sons who were the forebears of the tribes
shtetl — Yiddish for small town

Simchas Torah — holiday upon which we celebrate the completion of the Torah
Succah — temporary dwelling covered by leaves, bamboo, tree boughs, and the like; Jews are commanded to dwell within the *succos* for the entire seven-day period of Succos
Succos — Feast of Tabernacles
Talmud — the embodiment of the Oral Torah comprised of the Mishnah and Gemara; the Talmud comprises both the Jerusalem Talmud and the Babylonian Talmud (which was completed later)
Talmud Yerushalmi — Jerusalem Talmud
Tanna — one of the Rabbis of the Mishnaic Era
Targum Onkelos — commentary of the Bible authored by the convert Onkelos
teshuvah — repentance
Tikun Olam — the perfection of the world
Torah — Bible; the G-d-given Law
Toras Emes — the Law of Truth; true insight into the words of the Torah; the absolute truth embodied in the Torah
Toras Moshe — the Law transmitted via Moshe
Toras Yisrael — the Law of Israel
Tosafos — the twelfth-century Franco-German commentaries on the Talmud
tzaddik — righteous person
tzara'as — a disease of the skin caused by sin, often mistranslated as "leprosy"
tzidkanios — righteous women
Vayikra — the third book of the Pentateuch, *Leviticus*
Yaakov — Jacob
yahrzeit — Yiddish for "anniversary of a death"
Yehudah — Judah
yeridah — emigration from Israel; any descent
Yeshivos Gedolos — Torah academies
Yeshivos Ketanos — Torah elementary schools
yetzer hara — evil inclination

Yibum — the marriage of a childless widow to her brother-in-law
yichus — genealogy; pedigree
Yiddishkeit — Yiddish for Judaism
Yisbarach — may He be blessed
Yitzchak — Isaac
Yud-Hei — the first two letters of G-d's ineffable Name
yordim — people who leave Israel
Yosef — Joseph
z'chus — merit